41514

HQ
1106
- W6527
1993

DATE DUE

CRIAW/ICREF
Canadian Research Institute for the Advancement of Women
Institut canadien de recherches sur les femmes

WOMEN AND SOCIAL LOCATION

Our Lives, Our Research

NOS VIES,

NOS RECHERCHES

Reflet de notre société

**Edited by/Sous la direction de
Marilyn Assheton-Smith & Barbara Spronk**

gynergy
books

Editor: Käthe Roth

Cover Art: Stained glass entitled *Daughters, Dream, and in Dreaming, Take Back the Night* from the Illuminated Series by Deborah J. Fleming

Printed and bound in Canada by: Les Ateliers Graphiques Marc Veilleux Inc.

gynergy books gratefully acknowledges the generous support of the Canada Council.

Published by:
gynergy books
P.O. Box 2023
Charlottetown, P.E.I.
Canada C1A 7N7

Distributed by: General Publishing

CANADIAN CATALOGUING IN PUBLICATION DATA

Main entry under title:

Women and social location = Nos vies, nos recherches

Selected proceedings from the 15th annual conference of the Canadian Research Institute for the Advancement of Women held in Edmonton, Alberta, in 1991.
Text in English and French.
Includes bibliographical references.
ISBN 0-921881-27-4

1. Women — Canada — Congresses. 2. Feminism — Canada — Congresses. I. Assheton-Smith, Marilyn I. II. Spronk, Barbara Jane, 1947- III. Canadian Research Institue for the Advancement of Women. Conference (15th : 1991 : Edmonton, Alta.) IV. Title: Nos vies, nos recherches.

HQ1106.W66 1993   305.4'0971   C93-098648-2E

DONNÉES DE CATALOGAGE AVANT PUBLICATION (CANADA)

Vedette principale au titre:

Women and social location = Nos vies, nos recherches

Comptes rendus partiels de la 15e conférence annuelle de l'Institut canadien de recherches sur les femmes, tenue à Edmonton, Alberta, en 1991.
Textes en anglais et en français.
Comprend des références bibliographiques.
ISBN 0-921881-27-4

1. Femmes — Canada — Congrès. 2. Féminisme — Canada — Congrès. I. Asseton-Smith, Marilyn I. II. Spronk, Barbara Jane, 1947- III. Institut canadien de recherches sur les femmes. Conférence (15e : 1991 : Edmonton, Alb.) IV. Titre : Nos vies, nos recherches.

HQ1106.W66 1993   305.4'0971   C93-098648-2F

Acknowledgments

We asked for gold leaf, but the publishers said, No, it's too expensive, and anyway, it rubs off. Nothing but such extravagance seems appropriate as a way to recognize the work that the women in the back room have devoted to making this book happen. Early on in the process, Kelly Murphy and Carole Bishop, both graduate students in the Department of Educational Foundations at the University of Alberta, organized our paper clutter and helped us feel that we really could do this. As the book emerged from the papers, Linda Schulz and Christine Nesdoly, also graduate students in the department, accomplished an amazing amount of correspondence, editing and computer "stuff" that enabled us to work with clean copies, allowed our authors the benefit of reviewing what we had done to their work and kept us on schedule. Brigitte Paradis, a free-lance researcher working out of the Misener/Margetts Women's Research Centre, whom we had the good fortune to co-opt, was Linda and Christine's Francophone counterpart. Without her, the book could not have been *bilingue* and we would have missed many good laughs, in both languages. All of these women accomplished these tasks while writing theses, comprehensive exams and project reports and looking after babies and partners — one more entry in that Big Book of Life on the line that says, Even though we don't seem to be able to have it all, we still seem to be able to do it all.

Finally, we owe a huge debt to Linda Clippingdale and her staff at CRIAW/ICREF, who assisted with translations and were there with moral support when we needed it. All this labour makes our contributions as editors look paltry by comparison, and we hope that you, our readers, will give these women praise and assign us any blame.

Remerciements

Nous avions demandé un livre doré sur tranches, mais les éditrices nous ont répondu que les frais seraient exorbitants et que de toute façon, la dorure disparaîtrait à l'usage. Pourtant rien de moins ne saurait reconnaître la contribution que les femmes qui ont travaillé dans les coulisses ont consacré à la réalisation de cet ouvrage. Dès le début, Kelly Murphy et Carole Bishop, toutes deux diplômées du département des fondations éducatives de l'Université de l'Alberta, ont mis de l'ordre dans le fouillis de nos papiers et nous ont convaincues que nous pouvions effectivement venir à bout de la noble tâche que nous entreprenions. Quand le livre a commencé à prendre forme, Linda Schulz et Christine Nesdoly, elles aussi diplômées du même département, ont entrepris la rédaction d'une quantité considérable de lettres, la mise au point des textes et le « pitonnage » sur ordinateur, ce qui nous a permis de travailler avec des copies propres, de donner à nos auteures la possibilité de revoir ce que nous avions fait de la matière qu'elles nous avaient livrée et de respecter nos échéances. Brigitte Paradis, chercheuse indépendante au Misener/Margetts Women's Research Centre, que nous avons eu le privilège de recruter a été l'homologue francophone de Linda et Christine. Sans elle, le livre n'aurait pas été bilingue et nous n'aurions pas ri avec autant de coeur ... dans les deux langues officielles ! Et ces femmes sont venues à bout de tout ce boulot tout en terminant des thèses, en passant des examens, en rédigeant des rapports de projets et, bien sûr, en prenant soins de bébé et de partenaire. Encore une fois le « grand livre de la vie » aura eu raison de dire : nous ne semblons pas capables de tout avoir, mais nous semblons bien capables de tout faire !

Enfin, nous avons une dette énorme envers Linda Clippingdale et son personnel de l'ICREF qui ont contribué à la traduction des travaux et nous ont donné l'appui moral dont nous avions besoin. Notre travail d'édition semble bien peu important si on le compare à cette précieuse collaboration. C'est pourquoi nous espérons que vous, notre public lecteur, attribuerez à ces femmes les félicitations qu'elles méritent et que vous nous réserverez vos reproches.

Contents

CONTENTS

Preface

In October of 1990, a group of Edmonton women met at the Misener/Margetts Women's Research Centre on the campus of the University of Alberta to begin planning CRIAW'S fifteenth annual conference. Our theme, "Global vision globale/Local action locale," was a timely one, given the dramatic events of that year. The defeat of the Sandinistas in Nicaragua, the freeing of Nelson Mandela, the reunification of Germany, the failure of the Meech Lake Accord, the Iraqi invasion of Kuwait, the resignation of Margaret Thatcher — each evoked powerful emotions, ranging from despair to elation, in women who, like us CRIAW conference planners, were committed to social and political transformation, on personal, local, national and global levels. We thought to ourselves: Think of the energy that could be generated and focussed by a gathering of hundreds of Canadian women, all intent on making connections between the personal, local and global issues that confront women in their daily lives; think of what could be accomplished.

Thinking was fun. Doing was tough. Collectively, we worked out our own vision/action dialectic, squeezing out of too-crowded schedules the hours needed for meetings, phone calls, faxes, drafts, revisions and proposals. Anxieties grew and shifted as the weeks flipped by and the conference took shape. Were we meeting all the needs? Would there be enough money? Would there be enough papers? Would anyone come?

In the end, we may not have met all the needs, but the more than 350 women who joined us the weekend of November 8–10, 1991, in the Edmonton Westin Hotel appeared to have a very good time, and in both official languages. There wasn't enough money, but we made it stretch. There were more than enough papers, however. In fact, there were so many promising abstracts that we were hard pressed to find enough space to accommodate all the presenters.

As for what was accomplished, the conference, like all CRIAW conferences, enabled the women who attended to affirm old connections and make new ones, to define existing positions more accurately and take risks with less firmly established ideas, trusting that their efforts might meet with challenges but never with denial or rejection. As a way of providing a more lasting record of some of those connections and ideas, two of the conference organizers have assembled this selection of the conference papers. To guide our selection, we have relied on a number of criteria. Of necessity, our first consideration was readiness for publication. Of more than one hundred presenters, fewer than two-thirds had papers that they were able to send us for consideration. From these submissions, we based our choices on two principles: resonance with the conference theme, and advancement of the work of relating vision, action and location. We looked for authors who located themselves in the work, who drew reflections, so that we could highlight the rich ties women are making between vision and action, the personal and the political, the local and the global. As a way of advancing that work of making connections, we looked for papers that add to and enrich our understanding of some domain of women's existence, that reflect in a scholarly way on what exists but seek to transform rather than justify.

Applying these criteria still left us with more papers than time and the budget would allow us to publish. We have included as an appendix to this volume a list of all the presenters at the conference, to give you, the reader, some idea of the riches from which we had to draw. This volume is our way of paying tribute to all our participants. With your visions, your actions, your words and your commitment, you created our conference, and we thank you.

Marilyn Assheton-Smith
Barbara Spronk

▨ Préface

En octobre 1990, un groupe de femmes d'Edmonton s'est réuni au Misener/Margetts Women's Research Centre sur le campus de l'Université de l'Alberta pour planifier le quinzième colloque annuel de l'ICREF. Notre thème « Global vision globale/Local action local », traduisait bien l'actualité, compte tenu des événements dramatiques survenus cette année-là. La défaite des Sandinistes au Nicaragua, la libération de Nelson Mandela, la réunification de l'Allemagne, l'échec de l'Accord du lac Meech, l'invasion iraquienne du Koweit, la démission de Margaret Thatcher, des événements tous chargés d'émotions fortes allant du désespoir à l'allégresse qu'ont ressenties des femmes qui, comme nous qui préparions le colloque de l'ICREF, étaient déterminées à faire intervenir la réforme sociale et politique tant sur le plan personnel qu'à l'échelle locale, nationale et mondiale. Imaginez l'énergie que pouvaient dégager une centaine de Canadiennes réunies, toutes aussi déterminées les unes que les autres à créer un lien entre les problèmes auxquels elles se heurtent dans la vie de tous les jours, sur les plans personnel, local et mondial ! Voyez ce que peut accomplir autant de détermination !

La réflexion nécessaire à une telle entreprise a été une véritable source de plaisir. Passer à l'action a été plus difficile. Ensemble, nous avons peu à peu donné un sens précis à notre dialogue, utilisant au maximum les horaires trop serrés dont nous disposions pour nos réunions, nos appels téléphoniques, l'envoi par télécopieur de documents, la rédaction et la révision de nos textes et de nos propositions. Nos appréhensions croissaient et changeaient au fil des semaines et le colloque a finalement pris forme. Répondait-il aux besoins ? Y avait-il suffisamment d'argent ? Y aurait-il suffisamment d'exposés ? Y aurait-il quelqu'un au rendez-vous ?

En fin de compte, nous n'avons peut-être pas répondu à tous les besoins, mais les quelque 350 femmes qui se sont jointes à nous du 8 au 10 novembre 1991 à l'hôtel Westin d'Edmonton ont semblé très bien s'amuser ... dans les deux langues officielles. L'argent se faisait rare, mais nous l'avons étiré. Il y a eu finalement des exposés en nombre plus que suffisant, à tel point que nous avons eu de la difficulté à accommoder toutes les présentatrices et leurs très intéressantes thèses.

Quant au résultat, le colloque d'Edmonton, comme tous les autres colloques de l'ICREF, a permis aux femmes qui y assistaient de renouer avec d'anciennes connaissances et d'en faire de nouvelles, de définir avec plus de précision certaines positions reconnues, d'avancer à tout risque des idées moins bien acceptées, sachant qu'elles se heurteraient à des contestations, mais jamais à des refus ni à des rejets. Pour conserver le souvenir de certains liens qui se sont noués et de certaines des idées qui ont été avancées au colloque, deux organisatrices ont réuni une sélection de documents qui y ont été présentés. Leur choix s'est fondé sur un certain nombre de critères. Les documents déjà prêts à publier ont nécessairement d'abord été retenus. Au nombre de la centaine de documents présentés, moins des deux tiers nous ont été soumis à des fins de publication et nous avons arrêté notre choix en nous fondant sur deux principes : la concordance avec le thème du colloque et la promotion des liens à créer entre notre vision, notre action et notre milieu. Nous avons recherché parmi ces ouvrages ceux qui insistaient sur l'appartenance de leurs auteures à une cause, ceux qui suscitaient la réflexion, ceux qui mettaient en relief les rapports solides que les femmes créent entre l'imaginaire et la réalité de leur vie personnelle, de leur intervention politique à l'échelle tant locale qu'à celle de la planète. Nous avons cherché parmi ces excellents documents, ceux qui nous aident à mieux comprendre certains aspects de notre vie de femme et qui portent un jugement éclairé sur ce qui existe dans le but de transformer plutôt que de justifier.

Malgré tous ces efforts pour finalement arriver à un nombre de documents que nous pouvions raisonnablement publier tout en demeurant dans les limites de notre budget, nous avons dû nous rendre à l'évidence : il en restait encore un trop grand nombre. C'est pourquoi nous avons ajouté en annexe au présent volume une liste des ouvrages présentés au colloque qui vous donne une idée de la richesse de la matière que nous avons dû en extirper. Ainsi, nous rendons hommage à toutes les personnes qui ont bien voulu participer à notre colloque. C'est à leur vision, leur action, leur discours et leur détermination que devons le succès du quinzième colloque de l'ICREF et nous les en remercions.

Marilyn Assheton-Smith
Barbara Spronk

INTRODUCTION

INTRODUCTION

Women & Social Location: Our Lives, Our Research

The title of this book attests to the ongoing commitment of feminists to leading integrated lives, lives that are woven in whole cloth, as we recognize that we cannot separate the personal from the political, daily work from daily lives and, least of all, the creation of knowledge from our political actions and the social relations in which we find ourselves. For us, the "relations of ruling," to use Dorothy Smith's felicitous phrase, are most sharply exemplified in the gender order into which we are born and with which we must struggle.

It is not enough for us to understand the gendered structure of relationships that forms our social and political reality. We seek to change it, and in doing so we often find that we must turn inward and change ourselves, as an integral part of changing "the other." As Ellen Dubois remarks, "Feminist theory reaches out to movements for political change on the one hand, and reaches within, to the inner reality of women's lives, on the other" (1983:x). When we do this, we find that there is no single social location for women, any more than there is for men or children. As we move from the parochial nature of "sisterhood feminism" (Andersen, 1988:4, citing Forman) to a clearly recognized global feminist movement, we must recognize the multiplicity of our locations, the many voices with which we speak and the ways in which we contribute not only to each other's joy and liberation but also to each other's pain and oppression.

Our learning of the complexities of our locations as women, and our active participation in relations of ruling that work against ourselves and other women, may occur in laughter or in tears, as teachers or as students, in community action or in writing a thesis, in reflecting on images in history or literature, in working for and with women, in work we do in other countries or in our own country, or in working directly against the attitudes of men and other women that make our lives especially difficult. All of these types of situations are described and analyzed in the texts presented here.

We have sandwiched the selected papers between a précis of the first keynote of the 1991 CRIAW conference, Claire Bonenfant's description of the constitutional development of Quebec from the viewpoint of women, and Glenda Simms' closing speech, "Sisterhood is Global: Or Is It?" Bonenfant addresses the position of women in Quebec who have chosen the nationalist project, vis-à-vis the constitution of Canada. Detailing problems that arise in a nation-state such as Canada, in which the division of powers is distributed between two levels of government, she argues that women must be involved in building the new society, the sovereign Quebec that seems essential to her and other women. Simms locates the constitutional structure of Canada much differently, speaking rather of a national evolution based on the contrasting improved position of European women coming to this "new land" and a greatly diminished position for the women who preceded them here (as aboriginal women) or who arrived under slavery as Africans in diaspora. Between these two papers, the works of fifteen authors are divided into four sections.

Section 1: Connecting through Images and Myths

In the first section, Diana Relke begins by writing not of women's identity but of Canada's identity and cultural images. These are contrasted with those of the United States and provide the basis for an inferred link between Canadian identity and feminine identity, and of a postmodern diverse and changing self. Relke makes it clear that she locates this work in an English-language literature in Canada, and does not reflect the whole of the multifaceted Canadian consciousness.

The next two papers in this section are quite different. Susan Stone-Blackburn reports briefly on the personal experiences that resulted in her late coming to feminism, then puzzles with us about how to incorporate women's plays into academic classroom teaching and get them onto the stage. She presents us with some tentative answers to two questions: Should feminism support any well-crafted play written by a woman or only those that conform to feminist ideals? And is the phenomenon of women's theatre companies a step forward for women playwrights or an invitation to a ghetto in which work is not noticed or recognized by others?

Renate Krause, in contrast, writes from the position of a married woman with a deep involvement in and commitment to a Christian church, who suddenly found herself reflecting on her reality as a woman as a result of enrolling in a creative-writing class. Transforming Woolf's "room of her own" into a metaphor for her own life, Krause describes the work she does, both externally and internally, to create her own space and fill it with activities and orientations that are "conducive to constructive and healing work."

Section 2: Creating a Life, Pushing Against the Barriers

In this section we have included four items, the first of which is a short poem by Sylvia Vance. Although it is a narrative poem about creating a life, it conveys both the awe and the pain that arise when barriers and circumstances make that creation an event other than what each woman hopes for. It thus symbolizes the longer texts that make up the rest of this section, which describe women's efforts to create their own lives or to be partners with other women struggling to "make a life."

Can others do our marching for us? Karen Blackford picks up on Patricia Marchak's statement about the real difficulty academic feminists face, trying to divide our labour so that "we write the scholarly texts, others do the marching." Blackford "explores territories" that are part of her private life: territories of the mother with disabilities and her relations with her children. She writes not as an academic observer, but as an academic who is also a mother with a disability: Interviews with other women and children plus her own reminiscences provide the data for this work. Selected feminists and social scientists help her "make sense" of these data, but her reflections on her own experiences lend the greatest power to her theorizing.

The next paper in this section, by Danielle Forth, speaks to the experience of being a young woman in the feminist movement. The literature written about such young women by "first-generation" feminists firmly presents them as "other," as people being "talked about" rather than as people participating in the movement. Using the metaphor of diving deep and surfacing, Forth asks older feminists to listen to young women's voices, to not deny their experience. While younger feminists may need to learn networking and organizing for change from older feminists, older feminists need to recognize younger feminists' life experiences as different from their own, and to do so in a non-judgmental way. This paper stands as a sharp reminder to any feminist over thirty that it is not easy to recognize a generation gap, while it is easy to invalidate other women's experience simply because they are in a different social location.

In the final selection in this section, Pauline Fahmy presents us with a description of women workers in Quebec City, based on questionnaire responses. What is it, she asks, that makes women forsake their professions and lack a "career perspective" toward their work? In fascinating detail, she teases out an answer to that question, documenting and explaining her respondents' constant drive to change through "self-improvement," rather than taking action to change the society around them.

Section 3: Teaching, Learning, Researching

The third section of the book brings together papers that focus on teaching, learning and researching as the site of action and learning by the authors. There are four papers in this section, speaking to classroom teaching and thesis writing.

The first paper consists of letters exchanged between two academics about their experience of teaching as it relates to racism in the university classroom. Jaya Chauhan, foreshadowing Simms's paper at the end of this book, identifies herself as a black woman in diaspora trying to teach students to unlearn racism. At times poignantly, at times painfully, she addresses a situation in which she wishes to decentre authority, to refuse to claim superior knowledge based on being the professor. But her students are predominantly white and middle-class, and she finds that they simply do not interpret events as she does, that their experience of police, racism and black-white relations are such that she often finds herself on the defensive with them. She concedes that she is disillusioned by the end of the term. In contrast, Anne-Louise Brookes, who is white, responds with her experience of teaching and the approaches she uses that enable her and her students to shift from the defensive and work together to understand their experience of institutionalized racism.

Elizabeth Epperly writes of the results of using Barrett-Browning's poem *Aurora Leigh* to help students "confront their own ideas on gender, sexuality, art and love." Most importantly, she expects the text to provide the confrontation, rather than herself. This mediating role of text in the teaching process perhaps helps to explain why her teaching experience was less painful than Chauhan's. Even so, she suggests another explanation, based on her own reflective learning associated with writing and presenting the paper: perhaps she is too polite with her students; perhaps she needs to push them harder.

Evangelia Tastsoglou describes her learning as a student rather than a teacher, using her "uncensored voice" to address the experience of dissertation writing as "a silencing and alienating process." Hers is the experience of an immigrant academic woman in North America, a woman who locates herself "at the cross-section of her social class, gender, ethnic origin and life experience in Canada." We can all learn from Evangelia's tale more about the conflicts in our own gendered lives, and about the paths to their resolution.

Conflict and pain also fill Sharda Vaidyanath's piece, which, like Tastsoglou's, recounts the events that led to her writing a dissertation. The content of that work springs from the violence that she and the women central to her life have suffered in the institution of Hindu marriage. Vaidyanath traces these oppressive traditions from their roots in Hindu scripture to their continuing presence in the lives of first-generation Hindu women in Canada. Vaidyanath presents a compelling case against a cultural relativism that ignores women's pain and oppression in counting all traditions as equally worthy of support.

Section 4: Living and Working in Communities

This section includes three papers that address work as employment or wage-labour and community work and research, sometimes under the rubric of community development. Colette St-Hilaire writes of the Phillipines, using her experience there to address questions of social location and identity. It is, first, an elaboration of the discourse of development that draws her attention, a discourse derived largely from international-development agencies such as CIDA, which construct a particular type of person as a woman in their "women in development" projects. Sites of resistance to that discourse exist, but they are constantly under threat. St-Hilaire's final challenge is to the very idea of "universal woman," an idea that contributes to a denial of diversity and an absorption of the other's experience and struggle into our own. She proposes strategies for action based in the multiplicities of our identities rather than in some unity of feminism.

Lynn Bueckert addresses the word "global" in a way that suggests that it may be code for the international exploitation of women, rather than a term synonymous with solidarity and sisterhood. For her the site is office work, the pink-collar ghetto that provides the support work for so much Canadian business. With the advancement of computer and information technology, women in Canada lose employment to women in developing nations. Bueckert details this process of transfer of labour and analyzes its consequences both for the women losing work (in Canada) and for those gaining work but losing in other areas of their life (in other countries). She argues for the building of coalitions among women in the world from that perspective.

Denyse Côté points to the situation of women as invisible workers, and asks if "community development" does not rely on that invisible work, thus exploiting women under the guise of development.

In the final paper in this volume are Glenda Simms's remarks from the last day of the conference. She picked up the title of the conference, naming her paper "Global Vision, Local Action," but we retitled it "Sisterhood is Global: Or Is It?"

References

Andersen, Marguerite. "Women's Thought: the Road of Feminist Research in Canada." In *Feminist Research: Prospect and Retrospect*, 3-10. Edited by Peta Tancred-Sheriff. Montreal: McGill-Queens University Press (CRIAW/ICREF), 1988.

Dubois, Ellen Carol. "Introduction." In *Feminist Theories: Three Centuries of Women Writers*, ix-xiii. Edited by Dale Spender. New York: Pantheon Books, 1983.

Nos vies, nos recherches : reflet de notre société

Nos vies, nos recherches : reflet de notre société, un titre de livre qui atteste de l'engagement continuel des féministes envers des vies intégrées, des vies de femmes pleinement conscientes de leur rôle dans la société, des vies qui ne nous permettent pas de séparer le personnel du politique, le travail quotidien de la vie quotidienne et encore moins l'acquisition des connaissances de nos actions politiques et de nos relations sociales. Nos rapports avec le pouvoir, pour utiliser une expression de Dorothy Smith, sont assurément délimités par notre sexe qui détermine les luttes que nous aurons à mener.

Il ne suffit pas de comprendre la hiérarchie des rapports entre hommes et femmes qui forment le cadre de notre vie et de nos réalités sociales et politiques. Il faut changer cette structure, mais dans cette quête de changement, nous devons souvent nous tourner vers nous-même et accepter de changer si nous voulons changer « l'autre ». Ellen Dubois remarque que la théorie féministe tend vers les mouvements qui œuvrent pour le changement politique d'une part et se tourne vers l'intérieur, vers la réalité intérieure de la vie des femmes, d'autre part (1983:x). Ce faisant, nous constatons qu'il n'y a pas de lieu social simple et unique pour les femmes, pas plus qu'il y en a pour les hommes ou les enfants. À mesure que nous nous éloignons de l'aspect local ou paroissial du féminisme (Andersen, 1988:4, citant Forman) pour nous acheminer vers un féminisme mondial clairement accepté, nous sommes contraintes de reconnaître la multiplicité des lieux et des voix avec lesquelles nous nous exprimons et les façons dont nous contribuons non seulement à la joie et à la libération des unes et des autres, mais aussi à leur peine et à leur oppression.

Notre apprentissage en tant que femmes des complexités de notre société et notre participation aux décisions qui vont à l'encontre de nos idéaux et de ceux d'autres femmes, peuvent se produire au milieu de rires ou de larmes, chez des enseignantes ou des étudiantes, au sein d'une action communautaire ou pendant la rédaction d'une thèse, au cours de réflexions sur l'histoire ou sur la littérature ou de la création d'œuvres originales ou encore au cours de travaux pour et avec des femmes, à l'étranger ou dans notre pays, ou au cours de luttes contre certaines attitudes d'hommes et d'autres femmes qui rendent nos vies particulièrement difficiles. Toutes ces situations sont décrites et analysées dans les textes présentés ici.

Nous avons inséré les textes choisis entre un résumé de la première allocution de notre colloque de 1991, soit la description que Claire Bonenfant a donnée en français de l'évolution du dossier au

Québec vue par les femmes, et l'allocution de fermeture prononcée par Glenda Simms, intitulée « Le féminisme est-il ou n'est-il pas universel ? ». Mme Bonenfant parle des impressions sur la constitution du Canada qu'ont les femmes au Québec qui ont opté pour le nationalisme. Elle explique en détail les problèmes qui surgissent dans une nation comme le Canada où les pouvoirs sont répartis entre deux ordres de gouvernement et soutient que les femmes doivent participer à l'érection d'une nouvelle société, un Québec souverain qui lui semble essentiel à elle et à d'autres femmes. Mme Simms décrit la structure constitutionnelle du Canada de façon bien différente, parlant d'une évolution nationale fondée sur la situation améliorée des Européennes qui arrivent dans ce « nouveau pays » comparativement à la situation inférieure des femmes qui les y ont précédées (à titre d'autochtones) ou qui y sont arrivées à titre d'Africaines esclaves. Entre ces deux textes, les travaux de quinze auteures sont divisés en quatre parties.

Partie 1 : Les images et les mythes : le lien qui nous unit

Dans la première partie, Diana Relke décrit non pas l'identité des femmes, mais celle du Canada et de ses images culturelles. Elle fait la comparaison avec les États-Unis et indique les liens sous-jacents entre l'identité canadienne et l'identité féminine et l'image diversifiée et changeante du soi des temps modernes. Mme Relke dit clairement qu'elle situe son texte dans la littérature anglaise au Canada, qui ne reflète pas toutes les multiples facettes de la conscience canadienne.

Les deux autres textes sont tout à fait différents. Susan Stone-Blackburn rapporte brièvement les expériences personnelles qui l'ont amenée sur le tard au féminisme, puis nous met au défi d'incorporer des pièces de théâtre rédigées par des femmes aux programmes universitaires et d'obtenir qu'elles soient produites sur la scène. Elle tente de répondre à deux questions : le féminisme devrait-il appuyer toute pièce bien structurée écrite par une femme ou seulement les pièces conformes aux idéaux féministes ? Le phénomène des compagnies de théâtre dirigées par des femmes représente-t-il un progrès pour les femmes dramaturges ou une invitation à pénétrer dans un milieu fermé, un ghetto où le travail n'est pas remarqué ni reconnu par d'autres?

Renate Krause, par contraste, écrit du point de vue d'une femme mariée, qui est très engagée et participe activement au travail d'une église chrétienne, qui se prend soudainement à réfléchir sur sa réalité de femme à la suite d'un cours en rédaction créative qu'elle a suivi. Elle compare la « *room of one's own* » de Woolf à sa vie, elle décrit son travail tant à l'externe qu'à l'interne pour créer son propre espace, sa « propre chambre », et pour remplir cette chambre avec des activités et des orientations qui l'amènent à faire du travail constructif.

Partie 2 : Créer une vie, repousser les barrières

Dans cette partie nous avons inclus quatre articles, le premier étant un court poème de Sylvia Vance. Bien qu'il s'agisse d'un poème narratif sur la création d'une vie, il s'en exhale un respect et une souffrance lorsque d'autres barrières et circonstances font de cette création un événement autre que celui que chaque femme espère pour elle-même et pour les autres. Il symbolise ainsi les textes plus longs qui constituent le reste de cette partie qui décrivent les efforts que la femme déploie pour se faire une vie ou être partenaire d'autres femmes dans la lutte pour créer une vie pendant leur passage sur la planète.

D'autres femmes peuvent-elles contester pour nous ? Cette question que se pose Karen Blackford résume son exposé. Elle reprend la déclaration de Patricia Marchak concernant la véritable difficulté à laquelle se heurtent les féministes universitaires qui essaient de diviser notre tâche de façon à ce que nous rédigions les textes et que d'autres contestent à notre place. Mais Mme Blackford veut explorer des « territoires » qui font partie de sa vie privée, des territoires de la mère handicapée et de ses rapports avec ses enfants. Elle écrit donc non pas à titre d'observatrice, mais à titre d'universitaire qui est aussi une mère handicapée. Son ouvrage regroupe des données recueillies au cours d'interviews avec d'autres femmes et des souvenirs personnels. Certaines féministes et spécialistes des sciences sociales lui aident à donner un sens à ces données, mais ce sont ses réflexions sur ses propres expériences qui constituent le véritable pouvoir de sa théorie.

Le texte suivant, de Danielle Forth, raconte l'expérience d'une jeune femme dans le mouvement féministe. Les textes qui concernent les jeunes femmes de ce genre de la première génération de féministes les présentent comme étant « les autres » ou des gens « dont on parle » plutôt que des personnes qui participent avec les femmes plus âgées au même mouvement. En se servant de l'analogie du plongeur qui revient à la surface, Mme Forth demande aux féministes plus âgées d'écouter la voix des jeunes femmes et de ne pas dénigrer leur expérience. Bien que les jeunes féministes puissent avoir besoin d'apprendre comment créer des réseaux et s'organiser pour faire intervenir le changement, les féministes plus âgées feraient bien de reconnaître sans porter de jugement les expériences des plus jeunes comme étant différentes des leurs. Ce texte rappelle à toute féministe âgée de plus de trente ans qu'il n'est pas facile de reconnaître un écart de génération, mais qu'il est facile d'invalider l'expérience d'autres femmes tout simplement parce qu'elles vivent dans un milieu social différent. Pauline Fahmy nous présente une description de travailleuses dans la ville de Québec, fondée sur des réponses obtenues à un questionnaire. Elle demande qu'est-ce qui entraîne les femmes à délaisser leur profession et à ne pas considérer leur travail dans l'optique d'une carrière. Avec beaucoup de détails, elle façonne une réponse à cette question qui explique du même coup la volonté constante de ses répondantes à faire intervenir le changement en s'améliorant personnellement plutôt que d'essayer de changer la société autour d'elle.

Partie 3 : Enseigner, apprendre, rechercher

La troisième partie de ce livre réunit des documents qui traitent de l'enseignement, de l'apprentissage et de la recherche comme étant au cœur de l'action et de l'apprentissage des auteures. Quatre documents sont réunis dans cette partie et vont de l'analyse de l'éducation et de la rédaction de thèses.

Le premier document est constitué de deux lettres échangées entre universitaires concernant leur expérience de l'enseignement sous l'angle du racisme dans une classe à l'université. Jaya Chauhan se présente comme une Noire de la diaspora essayant d'enseigner à ses étudiants et étudiantes à se défaire du racisme. Parfois elle réussit douloureusement à traiter une situation où elle ne voudrait pas faire figure d'autorité, où elle refuse d'admettre qu'elle a des connaissances supérieures parce qu'elle est professeure. Mais ses étudiants et étudiantes sont en majeure partie de race blanche et de la classe moyenne et elle trouve qu'ils n'interprètent tout simplement pas les événements comme elle le fait, que leur expérience de la police, du racisme, des relations entre Noirs et Blancs est telle qu'elle se trouve souvent sur la défensive avec eux. Elle admet qu'elle est désillusionnée à la fin de l'année scolaire. Par contraste, Anne-Louise Brookes, qui écrit en tant que Blanche, répond à la première lettre en relatant son expérience de l'enseignement et les méthodes qu'elle emploie pour lui permettre à elle et à ses étudiants et étudiantes de délaisser l'attitude défensive et de travailler ensemble à comprendre le racisme institutionnalisé.

Elizabeth Epperly raconte comment l'étude du poème *Aurora Leigh*, de Barrett-Browning, a aidé ses étudiants et étudiantes à confronter leurs propres idées sur le sexe, la sexualité, l'art et l'amour. En fait, et c'est ce qui est le plus important, elle s'attend à ce que le texte, plutôt qu'elle-même, suscite cette confrontation et c'est ce rôle médiateur du texte dans l'enseignement qui aide peut-être en partie à expliquer pourquoi son expérience de l'enseignement a été moins douloureuse que celle de Mme Chauhan. Mais elle propose néanmoins une autre explication, fondée sur ses propres réflexions sur l'écriture et la présentation de son texte : peut-être est-elle trop polie avec ses étudiants et étudiantes ; peut-être a-t-elle besoin de les éperonner davantage ?

Evangelia Tastsoglou décrit sa recherche de soi au cours de la rédaction d'une thèse de doctorat. Elle raconte sans ménagement que l'acte d'écrire a été pour elle un processus qui l'a réduite au silence. Sa vie est celle d'une femme universitaire immigrée en Amérique du Nord, une femme qui se situe à la croisée de sa classe sociale, de son sexe, de son origine ethnique et de son expérience de vie au Canada. Elle nous fait souhaiter que notre propre expérience de la rédaction d'une thèse ait été aussi gratifiante, mais son récit nous permet d'en apprendre davantage sur les conflits de nos propres vies de femmes et des chemins qui conduisent à la solution de nos problèmes.

L'exposé de Sharda Vaidyanath exhale aussi le conflit et la douleur. Tout comme Mme Tastsoglou, elle raconte les événements qui l'ont conduite à la rédaction d'une thèse dans laquelle elle décrit la violence qu'elle et les autres femmes dans sa vie ont subie au sein d'un mariage hindou. Mme Vaidyanath retrace ces traditions oppressives jusqu'aux racines des écritures hindoues et à leur persistance dans la vie de la première génération de femmes hindoues au Canada. Mme Vaidyanath présente, à titre de femme hindoue, un argument convaincant contre le relativisme culturel qui fait fi de la douleur et de l'oppression des femmes en tenant pour acquis que toutes les traditions méritent d'être conservées.

Partie 4 : Vivre et travailler dans nos communautés

La partie suivante comprend trois textes. Nous avons combiné des documents qui traitent du travail dans le contexte de l'emploi ou du travail rémunéré, de même que des documents qui traitent du travail et de la recherche communautaire, parfois sous la rubrique d'épanouissement communautaire. Colette St-Hilaire parle des Phillipines, relatant son expérience pour expliquer certaines questions relatives au milieu social et à l'identité. Ces textes sont avant tout une explication du discours sur le développement qui attire son attention, un discours largement axé sur des agences de développement international comme l'ACDI, qui façonne un type particulier de personnes comme la femme qui figure dans leurs projets sur « les femmes et le développement » et une réalité particulière qui entoure ce genre de femmes. Il y a de la résistance à ce genre de discours, mais cette résistance est constamment menacée. Mme St-Hilaire conteste finalement l'idée même de femme universelle que sous-entendent les expressions comme féminisme mondial, une idée qui contribue à nier la diversité et à intégrer l'expérience et les luttes d'autrui aux nôtres. C'est de ce point de vue qu'elle propose des stratégies d'action fondées sur les multiplicités de nos identités plutôt qu'une certaine unité dans le féminisme.

Lynn Bueckert traite du terme « mondial » d'une façon qui laisse entendre qu'il s'agit peut-être d'un code pour l'exploitation internationale des femmes, plutôt que d'un terme synonyme de solidarité et de solidarité féminine. Elle parle du travail de bureau, ce ghetto de cols roses qui assure le soutien d'un si grand nombre d'entreprises canadiennes. Avec les progrès de l'ordinateur et de l'informatique, les femmes au Canada perdent leur emploi au profit de femmes qui travaillent pour un salaire minimum dans les nations en développement du Sud. Mme Bueckert explique en détail ce processus de transfert du travail mais, ce qui est plus important, elle analyse ses conséquences tant pour les femmes qui perdent leur emploi (au Canada) que pour celles qui obtiennent du travail mais perdent d'autres aspects de leur vie (dans d'autres pays). Elle insiste sur la nécessité de créer des coalitions parmi les femmes du monde, à partir de ce point de vue.

Denyse Côté signale la situation des femmes en tant que travailleuses invisibles de la communauté et nous demande si le « développement communautaire » n'est pas fondé sur ce travail invisible qui exploite les femmes sous le vocable du développement.

Le dernier texte qui termine cet ouvrage est l'allocution que Glenda Simms a prononcée le dernier jour du colloque. Elle a repris le titre du colloque, intitulant son texte « Vision mondiale, action locale », mais nous lui avons donné un nouveau titre, « La solidarité féminine est-elle un phénomène mondial? ».

Références

Andersen, Marguerite. « Women's Thought: the Road of Feminist Research in Canada », dans *Feminist Research: Prospect and Retrospect*, réd. Peta Tancred-Sheriff, Montreal, McGill-Queens University Press (CRIAW/ICREF), 1988, p. 3-10.

Dubois, Ellen Carol. « Introduction », dans *Feminist Theories: Three Centuries of Women Writers*, réd. Dale Spender, New York, Pantheon Books, 1983, p. ix-xiii.

L'avenir des femmes dans un Québec en devenir

Claire Bonenfant

L'avenir du Québec est en jeu. La forme politique retenue pour le Québec ainsi que son statut constitutionnel auront des incidences directes sur l'organisation sociale et politique du Québec.

Dans quel genre de pays voulons-nous vivre ? Quel projet de société voulons-nous défendre dans ce pays ? Et pour ce faire, de quels pouvoirs avons-nous besoin ? Ce sont les questions que nous nous sommes posées à la Féderation des femmes du Québec et auxquelles nous avons tenté de répondre dans notre mémoire présenté à la Commission Bélanger-Campeau.

Les femmes sont porteuses d'un projet de société et nous voudrions que ce projet soit incarné dans le Québec de demain. Nous voulons une société non discriminatoire et démocratique qui crée un environnement favorable au plein exercice des libertés civiles et civiques de la population.

La F.F.Q. croit qu'au delà des allégeances politiques de ses membres, elle doit faire un choix par rapport à un projet politique non-partisan, c'est-à-dire sans égard à un parti. Notre voix en est une de citoyennes féministes. Nous avons voulu dire devant cette commission quel projet nous désirons pour le Québec et de quels pouvoirs le Québec a besoin pour réaliser ce projet.

Au-delà du statut constitutionnel du Québec, c'est le projet social et politique qui nous intéresse. Nous croyons que la marge de manœuvre quant à l'inscription de changements importants dans l'organisation sociale et politique du Québec sera proportionnelle au degré d'autonomie que le Québec se donnera.

En ce sens, et bien que nous soyons tout à fait conscientes que l'autonomie politique n'est pas la seule condition à de tels changements, nous croyons que les femmes, comme groupe social, ont intérêt à choisir la plus grande autonomie possible pour le Québec.

L'appartenence du Québec à la Confédération canadienne nous empêche d'élaborer un projet de société qui corresponde à nos besoins particuliers. C'est ce que la F.F.Q. a constaté au fil des ans, en étudiant différents dossiers du point de vue des intérêts des femmes.

L'analyse de nos positions antérieures montre que les limites rencontrées se situent à deux niveaux : premièrement, le partage des compétences entre les deux paliers de gouvernement, et deuxièmement, le caractère distinct de la société québécoise.

Le partage des compétences

Dans le régime fédéral actuel, le partage des compétences entre Ottawa et Québec est source d'incohérence au niveau des politiques et les Québécoises en font souvent les frais. Qu'il s'agisse de juridiction sur le mariage et le divorce, de la réforme des régimes de rente, de la formation professionnelle ou du congé de maternité tributaire de l'assurance-chômage, nos analyses nous amènent à constater que non seulement le partage des compétences entre les deux paliers de gouvernement mais aussi la concurrence que se livrent ceux-ci génèrent des incohérences.

On se retrouve toujours devant des situations aussi aberrantes que celle-ci : au Québec, on se marie sous une loi provinciale, on divorce selon une loi fédérale et on partage ensuite les biens selon une loi du Québec. Ce qui nous amène à conclure que — tant que nous aurons deux gouvernements en compétition — il sera très difficile de définir des orientations cohérentes et de bâtir un projet collectif.

Le caractère distinct

L'expérience de la F.F.Q. avec les groupes de femmes canadiens et québécois, acquise depuis une dizaine d'années, lui a permis de constater que les Québécoises, à l'encontre de leurs consœurs canadiennes, font davantage confiance à leur gouvernement provincial qu'au gouvernement fédéral.

D'ailleurs au Québec, en concentrant nos interventions au niveau provincial, nous avons marqué de réels progrès au chapitre de la condition féminine. Progrès qui ne sont pas étrangers au caractère distinct du Québec. D'un point de vue féministe, nous comprenons l'importance de l'autonomie et de l'identité. De tels enjeux furent et sont encore au cœur de la lutte des femmes. Nous connaissons aussi le prix de l'autonomie mais aussi sa valeur !

À la lumière des considérations que nous venons d'énumérer relatives à un nouveau projet de société, fort de la position prise par ses membres lors de son assemblée générale annuelle, la F.F.Q. pense donc que les intérêts des femmes seraient mieux servis par un Québec autonome et souverain.

Quant à l'aménagement de la souveraineté — ce qu'il nous faut définir collectivement — ce sont non seulement nos liens avec le Canada mais aussi ce que sera ce nouveau pays du Québec ; c'est l'ensemble des nouveaux rapports sociaux qu'il nous faut repenser.

Le projet de constitution devrait comporter, outre la déclaration d'indépendance ou de souveraineté, l'enchâssement de la Charte québécoise des droits et libertés de la personne incluant, entre autres, un chapitre particulier consacré aux droits spécifiques des femmes de même que la reconnaissance des droits ancestraux des premières nations tels que définis dans la Charte canadienne des droits.

L'élaboration du projet de constitution devra être assurée par une assemblé constituante élue au suffrage universel et composé d'un nombre égal de femmes et d'hommes.

Notre mémoire contient des recommandations sur l'organisation du nouvel état du Québec sur les plans politique, juridique, judiciaire et économique de même que sur les liens à établir avec les autres pays et la communauté internationale.

Depuis le dépôt de notre mémoire à la Commission Bélanger-Campeau en décembre 1990, le débat évolue continuellement. Aussi, considérons-nous que ce mémoire n'est qu'une première étape dans la discussion que nous devons poursuivre et ce, dans le but d'actualiser nos positions sur l'avenir du Québec et d'ainsi maintenir la contribution indispensable des femmes à l'élaboration d'un nouveau projet social.

The Future of Women in a Changing Québec[1]

Claire Bonenfant

The future of Québec is at stake. It is clear, however, that whatever the final outcome vis-à-vis the political or constitutional direction for Québec, the impact on social and political structures will be significant.

In what kind of country will we want to live? What kind of "societal project"[2] do we want to advocate? What kind of power would we need to carry out such a project? These are the questions that we have asked ourselves at the Federation of Québec Women (F.F.Q.),[3] and that we have sought to answer in our brief to the Bélanger-Campeau Commission.

Women are an integral part of any societal project, and we would like this project to be enshrined in the Québec of tomorrow. We envisage a society that is nondiscriminatory and democratic, in which civic and civil liberties can be exercised to their fullest.

The F.F.Q. is of the view that whatever the political allegiances of its members, it must support a political project that is not specifically aligned to any party – that is, nonpartisan. Our voice, in this regard, is that of feminist citizens. We have explained to the commission the project we wish for Québec and outlined the powers that Québec would need in order to make this project operational.

Beyond Québec's constitutional status, it is the societal and political projects that interest us. We believe that the room to manoeuvre, insofar as the introduction of important social and political changes for Québec is concerned, will depend to a great extent on the degree of autonomy that Québec is able to garner for itself.

In this sense, and although we are perfectly aware that political autonomy is not the sole condition required for the changes to which we refer, we nonetheless feel that it is in the best interests of women — as a social group — to choose the greatest possible autonomy for Québec.

Because Québec belongs to the Canadian confederation, women are hindered in their attempt to develop a societal project that meets their particular needs. The F.F.Q. has ascertained this over the years, after examining various documents relating to women's issues. An analysis of our previous positions has revealed that the major stumbling blocks have been located at two levels: the division of powers between the federal and the provincial governments, and the distinct character of Québec society.

Division of Power

In the federal structure, the division of power between Ottawa and Québec often leads to inconsistencies at the political level, and Québec women often pay the price for this. Whether it pertains to jurisdiction over marriage and divorce, pension reform, professional or technical training, or maternity leave depending on eligibility for unemployment-insurance benefits, we have concluded that it is not only the division of power between the two levels of government but also their rivalry that leads to these policy inconsistencies.

The following illustrates some of the aberrations to which we refer: In Québec, couples get married under provincial law, divorce under federal law, and the division of their property is carried out under provincial law. As long as we have two governments seemingly in competition with each other, it will be difficult to define clear objectives and to put together a coherent blueprint of the type of society we want.[4]

Distinct Society

The experience of the F.F.Q. with feminist groups in Canada and in Québec over the last decade has led it to conclude that Québec women (as opposed to their Canadian sisters) have more faith in their provincial government than in the federal government.

By concentrating our efforts at the provincial level, we have been able to achieve significant progress with regard to the status of women, progress that is in keeping with the distinct character of Québec. From a feminist point of view, we understand the importance of autonomy and identity. These issues were, and still are, at the core of the feminist struggle. We know the cost of autonomy, but at the same time we recognize its value.

Taking into consideration all the ramifications of a new societal project, and having noted the views expressed by its members at its annual general meeting, the F.F.Q. believes that women's interests would be better served in an autonomous, sovereign Québec. How would this sovereignty be organized? We think that it should be defined collectively and should consider not only how the partnership with Canada would work but also what this new country called Québec will be; in other words, it is all the relationships among the people of its society that should be rethought and defined.[5]

Accordingly, in addition to a declaration of independence or sovereignty, the constitutional plan must include the enshrinement of the Québec Charter of Rights and Liberties of the Person and, among other things, a section specifically concerned with the rights of women as well as one recognizing the ancestral rights of the first nations as defined in the Canadian Charter of Rights. The constitutional plan must be developed by a constituent assembly elected by universal suffrage and composed of an equal number of women and men.

Our brief contains recommendations for the political, economic, legal and judicial organization of the new Québec state, as well as the relationships which should be established with other countries and with the international community. Since we presented our brief to the Bélanger-Campeau Commission, in December, 1990, the debate has continued to evolve. We want our brief to be a first step in a continuing process of defining the F.F.Q.'s position on Québec's political future, and to ensure that women continue to play an important part in the formulation of a new societal project for Québec.

Notes

1. Translation by Brigitte Paradis.
2. "Projet de société" in the original version.
3. Fédération des femmes du Québec is the untranslated name of the organization.
4. "Projet collectif" in the original version.
5. This notion of relationship is referred to as "rapports sociaux" in the original version.

CONNECTING THROUGH IMAGES AND MYTHS

LES IMAGES ET LES MYTHES : LE LIEN QUI NOUS UNIT

The work of envisioning engulfs us in the world of images and stories. Once created, these images take on lives of their own and join us in our work of making connections between who we are, what has shaped and is shaping us and how we in turn are shaping the world around us. In the words of Marsha Rowe (1982:26), "The images of women show the tangible connection between our imagination and the world outside ourselves, and the new images we produce represent the changes we experience and hope for."

The three papers that follow demonstrate the work that images can do, the power they possess, and the amazing variety of domains in which they exercise that power. The authors tackle a number of disparate issues — Canada-U.S. relations, women's plays, the work of composing a life — of which only women's plays would seem at first glance to have anything to do with myth and image.

Not so. Diana Relke, for example, in her paper "The Feminization of Canada," looks to cultural mythology for ways of illuminating for a European audience Canada's relations with its predatory neighbour. First, in the images of Greek myth, Canada in Relke's rendering becomes Persephone to Great Britain's Demeter and America's Dis, thereby transforming the War of 1812 and NORAD, NATO and the free-trade agreements into tales of "abduction, rape and retaliation." Next, Relke turns to Victorian courtship metaphors to illuminate the moves and motives that characterized Canada's relations with the lecherous "Brother Jonathan" in the early post-Confederation period. As the "compliant wife," Canada pays the price for dependence, for example, by becoming deeply implicated in American military policy. Then, in the sixties, the dependent wife begins to rebel against her Southern partner, the macho man/cowboy hero, a rebellion in which Relke sees a convergence of nationalism and feminism, nowhere more evident than in the literary arena.

Susan Stone-Blackburn's paper also deals with struggles in the literary arena, but those among men and women playwrights, producers and directors, rather than those among nations. Male domination of the theatre world prevents the voices and visions of women playwrights from being heard or seen, Stone-Blackburn contends. She documents this argument, and then goes on to explore what the implications might be of freeing the theatre from this domination. Plot lines might be propelled by a pull toward intimacy rather than the drive toward dominance that characterizes male-dominated theatre. A female aesthetic might emphasize process and the complex weavings of the ambiguities of relationships rather than the male fixations of clarity and linearity. Stereotypes of female character and "appropriate behaviour" might go by the boards. Having shared these visions and possibilities with us, Stone-Blackburn then pulls us back to earth by reminding us that the struggles for women's theatre involve struggles between women as well as between women and men, as women of the theatre seek answers to such questions of the moment as: Should any women's plays, or only feminist plays, be produced? Are women's theatre companies a vehicle for feminist visioning, or for ghettoization and marginalization?

Renate Krause's paper deals with yet a third kind of struggle, and the ways in which metaphor and image can be both a woman's enemies and her allies. Krause's struggle is to create a self within an environment of conventional marriage and motherhood whose imposed images of women as "property" and "angel of the house" she had come to feel were alien and hostile. With great gentleness and searing honesty, Krause traces for us the images that she was able to draw from literature to help her penetrate and transform the "closet of her life" into a "room of her own." As this room takes shape, she invites us to join her in it, detailing for us the process by which she gives each furnishing and decoration from her former, forbidding closet a new form and meaning. In the end she discovers that nothing from her old life — marriage, motherhood, religion — need be discarded, because she now possesses her own, inner room in which all these have a new shape, place and value.

All three authors take us on a journey of discovery of the ways in which images — Relke's myths and heros, Stone-Blackburn's women playwrights and Krause's room — help energize the forces necessary for change by enabling us to connect more powerfully with the visions that are our future.

Reference

Rowe, Marsha. "Image." In *Spare Rib Reader*, 25–26. Edited by Marsha Rowe. Middlesex, England: Penguin Books, 1982.

The Persephone Complex: A North American Myth of Identity[1]

Diana M.A. Relke

La plupart des nations ont une tradition mythique stéréotypée fondée sur une figure masculine ; le mythe américain des frontières et du cowboy en est un exemple. Le Canada ne possède pas de tels mythes. Mais il se peut que le mythe de Perséphone et sa répulsion et son attraction cycliques par le dieu des enfers soit une métaphore appropriée pour décrire la place du Canada en Amérique du Nord. En fait, de nombreux aspects de l'histoire et de la littérature canadiennes invoquent Perséphone comme étant particulièrement descriptive du Canada en tant que contrepartie « féminisée » des États-Unis.

Most nations have a cultural myth of identity with a masculine figure as its central stereotype; the American myth of the cowboy on the frontier is an example. Canada has no such myth. But perhaps the myth of Persephone with its cyclical pattern of repulsion from and attraction to the God of Hell, is an appropriate metaphor for Canada's place in North America. Indeed, many aspects of Canadian history and literature invoke Persephone as particularly descriptive of Canada as a "feminized" counterpart to the United States.

One of the things that many white, middle-class Canadian writers and academics have always envied about the United States is its cultural mythology. In Canada, we have nothing that compares with the myth of rugged individualism as embodied in the image of the lonesome cowboy, that strong, silent rider of the American range whose primary relationship is with his horse. This absence of a strong, masculine, national self-image once prompted the poet Earle Birney to complain that Canada is haunted by its lack of ghosts. I disagree. There are plenty of ghosts in Canada. What I would like to do here is invoke a few of them and set them within the context of a cultural myth that has been evolving since at least 1867, the year in which Canada became Canada.

We supposedly pride ourselves on being a multicultural nation, yet when each of those cultural groups looks back on its history, it is confronted with the spectre of its own disempowerment. Aboriginal peoples, Japanese Canadians and French-speaking Canadians, to name only three, have something in common with women. They have all been marginalized and excluded from full participation in economic and political life. The process by which this marginalization and exclusion takes place has been identified by feminist thinkers as the process of feminization. To be feminized is to be rendered powerless.

If I were to name all the feminized groups who continue to struggle for their fair share of the Canadian power pie, there would be only one group left unnamed: white, middle-class, middle-aged, English-speaking, heterosexual men — probably about 10 per cent of the Canadian population, if that. At first glance, this appears to be the only distinguishable group in Canada that has no history of oppression. Markedly over-represented in business, government and the media, this group can look back on its history without having to confront the spectre of its own feminization. Earle Birney is a member of this group, which helps to explain why he feels haunted by a lack of ghosts.

But is he? When I examine some of the rhetoric of white, middle-class, English-speaking men, I find it so haunted by images of the feminine that I am compelled to conclude that the figure at the centre of Canada's cultural myth is a woman. Indeed, echoes of the Greek myth of Persephone can be heard in the story of Canada's evolving relationships with Britain and the United States. As the unwilling bride of Dis, God of Hell, and the devoted daughter of Demeter, Goddess of the Summer, Persephone is the silent victim of a fierce power struggle between them. Dis invades Demeter's realm, abducts Persephone and rapes her. In retaliation, Demeter places a curse upon the earth, plunging it into deep winter until her daughter is returned to her. But this is not the end of it. The cycle of violence is repeated each year, when Persephone is required by Olympian decree to return to Hell and renew her nuptial vows. Caught between husband and mother, Persephone is the pawn in their never-ending battle for control.

The War of 1812 echoes this tale of abduction, rape and retaliation. Like Persephone, colonial Canada became the unwilling object of a quarrel between Britain and the United States. Not unlike Dis, U.S. president Thomas Jefferson was confident that the capture of Canada was, in his own words, "a matter of marching." His attempt to invade and take possession of Britain's North American colonies met with resistance, for Britain, like Demeter, was willing to do violence to prevent it. But, as in the Greek myth, this was not the end of it. Indeed, Canada seems to have internalized Persephone's fate as its national myth of identity. Many years after Confederation, Canadians were still claiming loyalty to Britain while at the same time experiencing American economic and cultural invasions, accepting them as if they were as inevitable as the return of the dreaded Canadian winter. Moreover, each agreement entered into with the United States over the years since Confederation has taken on the flavour of a patriarchal contract of marriage, complete with dowry and the forfeiture of a certain degree of Canadian independence. The reciprocity treaties of 1854 and 1935, the NORAD and NATO agreements of the mid-twentieth century, the free-trade agreement of 1988 and countless similar pieces of legislation have all inspired a Canadian nationalist rhetoric shot through with the imagery of rape, an imagery in keeping with a perception of the Canadian landscape as a vast reservoir of exploitable and exportable resources, not to mention an ideal place for the testing of American first-strike weapons. The Canadian landmass — the very body of Canada — sometimes seems to exist for the pleasure and convenience of other nations, particularly the United States.

But if nationalists have used gender terms to complain about Canada's fate, they have also used them to celebrate the nation's destiny. For example, here is a quotation from W.D. Lighthall, an Ontario politician and man of letters writing in 1889: "Canada, Eldest Daughter of the Empire, is the Empire's completest type! She is the full-grown of the family — the one first come of age and gone out into life as a nation …"(Lighthall, 1889:xxi). Canada was the daughter colony who had moved out of the imperial household, leaving her colonial siblings behind. Determined to set up housekeeping on her own, she was also resolved to remain the dutiful daughter and not betray her loyalty to Mother Britannia and her imperial family of origin.

However, to extend the metaphor, shortly after her coming-out party in 1867, Miss Canada began to flirt outrageously with her American cousin. She encouraged heavy American economic investment, permitted the establishment of American branch plants and allowed the American takeover of many Canadian-owned enterprises. Consequently, one morning, sometime after the turn of the century, she woke up to find that her virtue had been compromised. So she took what she thought was the honourable way out. Reader, she married him.

Like the poet Earle Birney, novelist Hugh MacLennan is a member of the group I have identified as white, middle-class, English-speaking male Canadians. MacLennan's rhetoric, like W.D. Lighthall's, is also haunted by a feminine figure. Here is a passage from his 1949 essay entitled "The Canadian Character" in which Canada is no longer the dutiful daughter but the compliant wife:

*This country, which once was Britain's senior Dominion and now
stands on her own, has acquired a purely feminine capacity for
sustaining within her nature contradictions so difficult to reconcile
that most societies possessing them would be torn by periodic
revolutions. Canada has acquired a good woman's hatred of quar-
rels, the good woman's readiness to make endless compromises for
the sake of peace within the home, the good woman's knowledge that
although her husband can knock her down if he chooses, she will be
able to make him ashamed of himself if such an idea begins to form
in his mind. Canada also possesses the hard rock which is the core of
every good woman's soul: any threat to her basic values calls up a
reluctant but implacable resistance. (MacLennan, 1949:5)*

That was the state of Canada's "domestic affairs" in the post-
World War Two era, a period characterized by intense feminization of
the Canadian psyche as a result of American cultural imperialism. For
example, during the forties and fifties, countless Canadian children
and adolescents were spending their Saturday afternoons in their
neighbourhood movie houses soaking up Hollywood westerns star-
ring Roy Rogers and the Lone Ranger. This period in history also
featured the onset of the Cold War, when Canada looked southward
for the appearance on the horizon of some handsome American
cowboy, who would gallop out of Texas and rescue Canada, the
damsel in distress. With his sixguns loaded with nuclear warheads, he
would have a big shoot-out with the outlaw Commies, after which
Canada would ride off into the sunset with him.

Like many women of the period who traded away the frightening
prospects of independence in exchange for male protection and the
promise of a happy ending, Canada paid the going price for its
feminine dependence. Through our involvement in NORAD and
NATO, we have become deeply implicated in American military
policy, although we are rarely consulted about what form that policy
should take. Perhaps the Canadian North can be seen as the dowry
Canada brought into this military union with the United States. By the
fifties, the North had become one big U.S. military installation, and
much of it was constructed without prior consultation with either the
Canadian government or the local inhabitants.

The imperious and insensitive attitude that characterizes the
United States as the macho man of Western culture was what
Canadian nationalists began to rebel against in the sixties and seventies, decades characterized by a struggle for Canadian self-realization
that found its mirror image in the feminism of the same period.
Indeed, those two cultural movements — nationalism and feminism
— had so much in common that they often converged. This conver-

gence was nowhere more obvious than in the literary arena, where the contents of the Canadian collective unconscious were beginning to surface.

Three English-Canadian fiction writers rose to unusual prominence during the late sixties, when Canada was undergoing the early stages of its latest national identity crisis: Margaret Laurence, Alice Munro and Margaret Atwood. They became the three most widely acclaimed writers in Canada. Their literary excellence and popular appeal made their works as important to literary scholars as they were outside the Canadian academy. In addition, they helped to put Canada on the literary map of the world. Indeed, much of Canada's international literary reputation rests squarely on the work of these three women.

In 1984, this unprecedented literary phenomenon attracted the attention of a sociologist at La Trobe University in Australia. Beryl Donaldson Langer was fascinated by the fact that even though Australia had a much richer female literary history than Canada, Canadian women writers were far more appreciated. She demonstrated statistically that this was so, and then she came to three conclusions, all of which support the image of Canada as a feminized culture vis-à-vis the United States. In her first conclusion, Langer noted that what it meant to be a Canadian in the context of economic and cultural domination by the United States was not all that different from what it meant to be a woman in the context of economic and cultural domination by men. As a result, many Canadian nationalists, who might not otherwise have been concerned with women's issues, identified positively with the oppressed heroines of Laurence, Munro and Atwood. Now, I am not saying that women's novels won all Canadians over to the feminist cause — far from it. But countless Canadian husbands got copies of Margaret Laurence's *The Stone Angel* for Christmas in 1964. Many of them even read it.

In her second conclusion about the relative acceptance of women writers in Canada, Langer articulates the Canada–U.S. difference in terms of the binary opposition of Canadian communalism versus American individualism. She argues that, unlike the U.S., Canada has not rejected all of its colonial traditions — traditions that go back to the feudal era in Europe, when the welfare of the community was more important than the rights of the individual. For example, historically, Canada has tried to emphasize the importance of social programs that balance the welfare of regional communities with the welfare of Canada as a whole. This emphasis resonates with our ideals of "peace, order, and good government," which are community ideals. They are also traditionally feminine ideals: The idealized woman is the wife and mother who tries to balance the individual needs of husband and children with the welfare of the family as a whole. But in the States, there has always been a much greater emphasis on the individual making it on his own, like the rugged, lonesome, macho cowboy who is at the heart of American cultural mythology. This is in keeping with the American ideals of "life, liberty and the pursuit of happiness," which are the ideals of individualism. Given that difference, it is hardly surprising that Langer sees Canadian culture as having been defined in terms less hostile to women.

Before I get to Langer's last conclusion, I want to finish my reconstruction of Canada's cultural myth. As history has demonstrated, nationalism and feminism as political movements wax and wane, and Canada is no longer like the woman of the late sixties and early seventies, fighting for her independence from patriarchal oppression. She has come a long way, baby, for she is now equal to her male counterpart; she can, and indeed has been, drafted to the front as a combat soldier. But despite the dubious honour of now being one of the boys, she continues to cultivate her traditional Persephonian lifestyle and renews her marriage vows as regularly as the changing of the seasons. The men who negotiated and signed the recent free-trade agreement with the United States are the same men who, as boys, spent their Saturday afternoons watching Hollywood westerns. The free-trade agreement is their long-awaited marriage contract with their American gun-slinger hero. It was therefore singularly appropriate that Ronald Reagan, that superb example of the defunct Hollywood cowboy, was the cultural stereotype with whom we negotiated that contract. Now we Canadians can all relax and live happily ever after with our American matinée idol.

I began this paper by alluding to the multicultural character of Canada, and so it makes sense to end with it. Beryl Donaldson Langer's third conclusion about Canada's cultural femininity relates to multiculturalism. She argues that the central image of a mosaic of ethnic and regional divisions creates many ways of being a Canadian, and one of those ways might thus conceivably and legitimately be female.

Implicit in multiculturalism is the concept of multiple identities analogous to the postmodern subject and an image of Canada as a culture with many subjectivities dispersed across time and space. This image is consistent with psychoanalytic models of the feminine psyche, with its fluid ego boundaries, as opposed to the more rigid ego boundaries which supposedly characterize masculine personality. The image suggests that it is probably more accurate to speak of

Canada in terms of Persephones, plural. While the American cowboy (not cowgirl) is the cultural image that has always defined what the ideal American should be like, we have had no such single cultural ideal in Canada. But we have tended to think of that as a tragedy rather than a triumph, an identity crisis rather than a positive alternative to the bourgeois humanist notion of identity.

Conclusion

Canadian cultural diversity is probably more in keeping with the definition of identity as it has come to be understood over the last few years. As my allusion to postmodernism suggests, what we are beginning to understand now is that the concept of the self as one unified entity or essence that remains stable over time is, at the very least, an oversimplified notion. The self, as the acculturated individual experiences it, is far more diverse and unstable than the previous notion of self suggests. So on the national level, perhaps it is not Canada that has unresolvable identity problems. Perhaps the problem lies with other countries, especially those that try to identify themselves with one unified static image, such as the macho cowboy. And perhaps that makes Canada at least potentially healthier than other cultures.

Note

1. This paper was originally delivered at the Annual Conference of the Association for Canadian Studies in the German Speaking Countries (GKS) in 1991, and was given at the CRIAW conference to display how Canada was presented to this conference. As the GKS conference theme was Canada-U.S./U.S.-Canada, the paper gives a comparison of the national images of these two countries. The paper is written from an Anglophone knowledge base, and the author is aware that the images might be somewhat modified if the comparisons were made with the French language.

References

Birney, Earle. *Collected Poems.* 2 vols. Toronto: McClelland and Stewart, 1975.

Coates, Kenneth. *Canada's Colonies: A History of the Yukon and Northwest Territories.* Toronto: James Lorimer, 1985.

Desbarats, Peter, ed. *The Hecklers: Canadian Wit and Humour.* Toronto: MClelland and Stewart, 1979.

Langer, Beryl Donaldson. "Women and Literary Production: Canada and Australia." *Australian Canadian Studies* 2 (January 1984): 70–83.

Lighthall, W.D., ed. *Songs of the Great Dominion.* London: Walter Scott, 1889.

MacLennan, Hugh. *Cross-Country.* 1949. Reprint. Edmonton: Hurtig, 1979.

The Challenge for Women Playwrights

Susan Stone-Blackburn

Les femmes dramaturges se heurtent à des obstacles encore plus nombreux que les femmes qui écrivent dans d'autres genres littéraires. Aucune des quelques femmes qui ont écrit des pièces à succès n'a atteint une réputation durable. Une pièce ayant pour sujet une dramaturge du XVIIe siècle, Aphra Behn, produite récemment par Maenad Productions, une compagnie théâtrale dirigée par des femmes à Calgary, a attiré mon attention sur la persistance du problème au fil des ans. Le succès de Behn au cours de sa vie, suivi par sa disparition virtuelle de l'histoire littéraire, m'ont amenée à me demander si les femmes dramaturges qui connaissent le succès aujourd'hui connaîtront un meilleur sort que Behn dans l'histoire de la littérature. Ce document examine les facteurs qui ont nui au succès des femmes dramaturges et compare la situation de Behn à celle des dramaturges canadiennes contemporaines. Il tente de répondre à deux questions : est-il dans le meilleur intérêt du féminisme d'appuyer une pièce bien structurée écrite par une femme de talent ou seulement les pièces qui correspondent aux idéaux du féminisme ? Et le phénomène maintenant répandu des compagnies théâtrales dirigées par des femmes constitue-t-il un progrès pour les femmes dramaturges ou favorise-t-il la formation de ghettos pour les pièces écrites par des femmes et épuise-t-il l'énergie créatrice des écrivaines devenues productrices ?

Women playwrights face even more barriers to success than do women who write in other genres. Not one of the few who have written successful plays has attained a reputation that lasted longer than a few decades. A play about seventeenth-century playwright Aphra Behn, produced recently by Maenad Productions, a women's theatre company in Calgary, focussed my attention on the persistence of the problem over time. Behn's success in her lifetime, followed by her virtual erasure from literary history, prompted me to ask whether the women who experience success today as playwrights are likely to fare better than Behn in future literary history. This paper examines factors that have worked against the success of women playwrights and compares Behn's situation with that of contemporary

Canadian women playwrights. It offers tentative answers to two questions raised by this examination: Is it in the best interest of feminism to support any well-crafted play by a talented woman, or only those that are in accord with the ideals of feminism? And is the now widespread phenomenon of women's theatre companies a step forward for women playwrights, or does it foster ghettoization of women's plays and drain the creative energy of the writers who become writer-producers?

Two years ago, I was still constructing my drama courses along traditional lines, and I was getting bored with them. I was including occasional plays by women in the contemporary portions of my courses; because the canon has not yet solidified for contemporary drama, there are still contemporary women's plays available. They have not all been relegated to the second-class, unanthologized and out of print, as earlier plays by women have been.

Two years ago I was not yet a feminist, but I had recently been appointed the University of Calgary's Advisor to the President on Women's Issues. The reading I needed to do for my new job was just beginning to persuade me that most women face barriers to achievement that most men do not. I became a feminist in the days that followed the deaths of fourteen women at L'École Polytechnique in Montreal, an event that changed my outlook on just about everything. One thing to be said for coming late to feminism is that it makes a terrific tonic for middle age. Everything I learned in the first half of my life needs to be reprocessed, so everything is new again.

Two fortuitous events changed my growing boredom with the drama courses I had been teaching. The first was the incorporation of a new theatre company in Calgary, Maenad Productions, whose mandate was "to promote the feminine vision through exciting and dynamic new works for theatre." The second was my colleague Susan Bennett's maternity leave, which meant that I took over the new course she had designed on contemporary British women's drama. The interplay between developments in women's theatre in my own backyard and the developments in England that I was learning about from my reading for the course gave me a sense of the universality of the challenges faced by women in theatre and the excitement of women's efforts to meet those challenges. In addition, a Maenad Productions play about seventeenth-century playwright Aphra Behn extended my sense of universality through time as well as across space. Realizing that, as an academic, I have a role to play in women playwrights' struggle to be heard gives new meaning to my teaching and new direction to my research.

The six plays that Maenad produced during its first two years were a stunning variety written by Rose Scollard or Nancy Cullen or both. Alexandria Patience, actor and director and another founding member of Maenad, joined Rose and Nancy in writing *Aphra*, which generated a lot of interest during its first run and was published in the Fall, 1991 issue of the Canadian theatre journal *Theatrum*. It centres on the failure of Behn's last play, which features a very unfeminine heroine, and on Behn's erasure from literary history because the personal notoriety of this very unfeminine author overshadowed the many successes of her prolific career.

I interviewed the three *Aphra* playwrights together, trying for an interview format in keeping with their collaborative method of work. Parts of that interview are in the Winter, 1991 issue of *Canadian Theatre Review*, a special issue on Canadian women playwrights. I wanted to know why they decided to start their own theatre company, which seems like much harder work than just hooking into existing companies. "We started from a feeling of a void," Alexandria said, "with no company in town or anywhere in the vicinity that we could make contact with that could produce the type of theatre we found very exciting. There's a lack of a female vision in mainstream theatre and even in a lot of experimental theatre" (Stone-Blackburn, 1991:28).

Maenad Productions started from the very immediate desire of a few women to make their own voices heard on stage without having to adapt to the male tastes that dominate decision making in theatres. They wanted a theatre that would welcome the theatrical exploration of women's experience and foster women's creativity. Nancy pointed out that the interviews by Judith Rudakoff and Rita Much with twelve Canadian women playwrights, published in 1990 in *Fair Play*, showed widespread feeling "that a woman's point of view isn't seen as valid by traditional theatrical hierarchies" (Stone-Blackburn, 1991:28). This is borne out by a survey of Canadian theatre seasons published in 1988 in *CanPlay*, which showed that although women comprised 32 per cent of the membership of the Playwrights Union of Canada, only 17 per cent of the plays produced were by women, and that in the fifteen largest Canadian theatres, the most lucrative for playwrights, just 9 per cent of the plays were by women (Carley, 1988).

Women's theatre companies started in England and the United States in the seventies, and they are spreading worldwide. As I read about performances of plays by Caryl Churchill, Pam Gems and Sarah Daniels in England, it seemed that women's plays were doing well there, but measured across the whole of London theatre in the seventies, the statistics were even worse than Canada's. In *Carry On Understudies*, Michelene Wandor reported a survey of London theatres in that decade that found that only 7 per cent of the plays were by women — and half of those were Agatha Christie's (Wandor, 1986:124)! Wandor's statistics also showed that in the mid-eighties, women's plays were being published as rarely as they were being performed.

The successes of individual women such as Caryl Churchill in England and Sharon Pollock here, or, more frequently, of an occasional single play by a woman, like Ann-Marie MacDonald's recent *Goodnight Desdemona*, should not blind us to the message of the statistics. We need to understand what keeps women's plays off the stage and out of the university curriculum.

In addition to the things that hold women back in any profession, there are factors unique to theatre, such as the practice of having the same reviewer, almost always a man, review any play in his vicinity, regardless of whether he has any knowledge of or sympathy with its style or subject matter. Book reviewers are more likely to review books for which they have some affinity, so books on women's experience have a reasonable chance of being reviewed by women.

Probably the most compelling reason that fewer women succeed in playwriting than in other kinds of writing is the very public and very complex nature of play production. Women's experience often gives them more familiarity with the private and personal, and the writer-reader relationship of the novel or the writer-listener relationship of the radio play is less daunting than the public exposure of a stage play (Wandor, 1986). Moreover, a great many people are required in order to stage a play — director, designers, actors, technicians — and in relation to these the playwright has to play an authoritative role or risk a production that embarrasses her. Theatre people are no more accustomed to a woman in a position of authority than are people in any other profession, and they may see her more as woman than as playwright. And, of course, the woman herself may feel uncomfortable acting authoritatively.

Even before the production stage, a playwright needs professional contacts to provide opportunities for apprenticeship in the complex art of theatre; successful scripts are not written in closets and sent unheralded through the mail. Though women do form professional relationships with men, they often find other women more approachable. Many female playwrights feel the lack of experienced female directors.

The large number of people involved in production and the preponderance of men at the top of theatre hierarchies are also factors in the politics of taste — the matter of difference in choices that women and men are likely to make in constructing plays. The more expensive a theatrical enterprise is, the fewer risks will be taken, which is why larger theatres produce fewer plays by women. Men who hold decision-making power in theatres may not find women's dramatized experience interesting or important enough to warrant production, and women's imaginative inner worlds may seem completely alien to them.

Women can learn to write like men, which probably improves their chances of success. But what if they do not want to write plays about men? (Wandor [1986:123] counted parts in Methuen's 1985 catalogue and found 908 female characters and 2,212 male ones — two and a half times as many male roles.) Not only are there fewer female characters in men's plays, but they are more likely to be stereotypes. Alexandria identified impatience with limited roles as one of her motivations for founding Maenad Productions. Actresses' sense of the inadequacies of the plays they are acting in often leads them into playwriting: Sharon Pollock, Ann-Marie MacDonald, Linda Griffiths and Judith Thompson are examples of Canadian actresses turned playwrights.

In *Feminism and Theatre*, Sue-Ellen Case speaks of the need for a poetics of drama that would "accommodate the presence of women in the art, support their liberation from the cultural fictions of the female gender and deconstruct the valorisation of the male gender" (Case, 1988:114–115). Women playwrights are quite likely to develop plots and characters that free women from cultural stereotypes and challenge men's centrality. If these plays are measured against a critical standard developed by men and based on men's plays, they will certainly be unfairly denigrated.

In contemplating the possibility of a female aesthetic, feminist theorists go beyond plot and character to consider ways in which play form may also be affected by gender. One such observation is that the standard plot line, which builds up to a single climax and then concludes quickly, seems related to male sexual experience. Another is that the assumption that the essence of drama is conflict may well reflect a male perception of what life is all about. If there is such a thing as a female aesthetic, it might reflect multiple orgasms and being in modes other than conflict.

What sort of form a female aesthetic might take is the subject of considerable discussion. In her introduction to *Women and Theatre: Compassion and Hope*, Karen Malpede suggests that in women's theatre, "the type of dramatic tension created by divisive conflict is replaced by a new, almost unexplored tension of sensual, erotic, and intellectual affinity between characters," and she observes that "the pull together, towards intimacy, is as complex and as fraught with terror and impossibility, as is the drive toward dominance" (Malpede, 1983:13). A female form might emphasize process, as Luce Irigaray suggests (Whitford, 1991:126–127), weaving itself out of fragments and maintaining ambiguities instead of seeking clarity and linearity by emphasizing a through-line. Women sometimes choose traditional play structures, but when they create other forms, they are likely to find themselves criticized for writing formless plays.

The more ways in which a woman's play is unconventional, the more likely it is to meet resistance. This is true of all departures from the traditional, of course; all experimental plays face a struggle to gain acceptance. If women want to write in ways that differ from the male tradition, they will struggle for acceptance. If a woman's play does get produced and is successful enough to be picked up by other theatres for further productions, it becomes a candidate for publication and for the next measure of success, which is survival over time. This is where getting women's plays into the classroom becomes an issue. I cannot think of any woman's play that has made it into the category of classics – not one. If they are not taught in literature classes or drama classes, they will be forgotten. Future directors and professors will not think them worthy of attention.

Quite a few women write plays, and a few even write one or more that win awards and receive multiple productions and get published, but hardly any achieve the series of successes that add up to a noteworthy career. None have attained a reputation that lasted for more than a few decades. The choices that reflect the politics of taste multiply over time, and the male bias built into the decision-making processes of artistic director and producer, of critic and editor and publisher and professor, has eventually obliterated the fame of the few women who have been successful playwrights in their own time.

The Maenad Productions play about Aphra Behn, who not only was the first woman to compete with men as a professional playwright but ranked among the foremost playwrights of the Restoration by any measure, brought the enormity of her erasure to my attention. And it made me question my assurance that some of today's successful women's plays are sure to be among those valued a century from now.

Sue-Ellen Case shattered my confidence in the inevitability of women's progress as playwrights by pointing out that there were more plays by women produced in England in the sixty-year period between 1660 and 1720 than there were between 1920 and 1980 (Case, 1988:38–39). This shook my sense that women now have equality within their grasp, but I still hoped that an examination of factors weighing against women playwrights then and now would show at least that women are fighting new battles after winning some old ones. I wound up considerably disconcerted by the suspicion that what I had at first seen as progress really amounts to a reincarnation of a problem I thought we had put behind us.

The villain of *Aphra* is moral opinion, in the form of two characters, one male and one female, who condemn Aphra Behn's every deviation from the feminine ideal. Though all Restoration comedy was denounced as immoral in the eighteenth and nineteenth centuries, the double standard meant that Behn was hit harder than were her male contemporaries. The no-win situation for the female playwright was that writing like a man was required for success but resulted in vilification. And to the extent that she exhibited an inclination to deviate from the male norm in feminist directions — by presenting an unusually masculine heroine, for instance, or declaring marriage based on economics immoral — Behn was even more vulnerable. History judged her "a mere harlot, who danced through uncleanness and dared [men] to follow" (Summers, 1967:xxx).

Now, I figured, we are past all that. We no longer have such rigid standards of femininity that acceptable behaviour for women is incompatible with success. But perhaps I was too sanguine. The Maenad Productions plays are less overtly sexual than Aphra Behn's, and the company's creators are cautious about explaining their choice to name Maenad after the Greek women of antiquity who held orgies in honour of Dionysus, god of wine and of theatre. Originally, their mandate was "to promote the orgiastic and visionary concerns of women" (Stone-Blackburn, 1991:29), but the word "orgiastic" seemed to require a lot of explanation. They treasure the celebratory, ritualistic, sensual quality of their work, but they struck the word from their bylaws "because everybody said no one will ever give you funding" (Stone-Blackburn, 1991:29). As Maureen Duffy said in her 1977 book on Behn, "In many ways emancipation hasn't yet completely caught up with her guiltless celebration of the erotic" (Duffy, 1977:291).

We may no longer be boxed so tightly in a rigid prescription for femininity as women were in the centuries between Behn's time and ours, but the issue of how to portray women on stage seems at least as problematic now because of the politics of feminism. I asked why the Maenad creators chose to describe themselves as promoting the "feminine" vision instead of the "feminist" one. They saw "feminine" as the broader term, encompassing feminism but not restricting them to a political agenda. Many of the women interviewed in *Fair Play* also commented on the tension between being judged "not feminist enough" and being constrained by a political agenda. Gender roles seem to be no less problematic for women playwrights now than they were three hundred years ago; only the terms of the debate are different.

I am left with two questions, to which I have only tentative answers. Both arise from local experience and pertain globally. First, is it in the best interest of feminism to support any well-crafted play by a talented woman regardless of content, or only those plays whose portrayal of women and women's issues are in accord with the ideals of feminism? The same question applies to choice of plays for the classroom. My tentative answer is that cold-shouldering a woman's play on ideological grounds amounts to shooting ourselves in the collective foot. Attacking women for not being feminist enough will have the same result as attacking Aphra Behn for not being feminine enough; a century from now, there will be no women playwrights in the canon, because hardly anyone measures up to a rigid ideological standard for feminism. Lillian Hellman, American playwright of the thirties, forties and fifties, is probably the best candidate for canonization since Aphra Behn, but she is likely to be lost, because she is neither male nor feminist enough. At the same time, we have to recognize that simply being talented never guaranteed anyone fame; politics of a sort always comes into play (an unplanned pun). Today, gender politics are in the spotlight, and plays that reflect gender issues are more likely to be staged, published, anthologized and taught, just as a play that deals with Canadian history is more likely to be taught in Canadian courses than is a play by a Canadian dealing with another subject.

My second question concerns the now widespread phenomenon of women's theatre companies, unheard of a few decades ago. Is this a step forward for women playwrights, or will it foster ghettoization of women's plays and drain the energies of the writers who spend time on everything from scrounging sets to staffing the box office to keep these small theatres going? The parallel question for academe is whether women's plays and other women's literature should be taught in separate courses, like mine on contemporary English women's drama, which attract few male students and take feminists away from "mainstream" teaching. My tentative answer is that at least at the moment, the opportunities provided by women's theatres to develop women's talents and confidence in their own voices are greatly needed, as are the classes to develop students' awareness of woman's voice in our culture. The success of *Goodnight Desdemona*, first produced by Nightwood Theatre in Toronto, gives us reason to hope that other plays produced in women's theatres will "cross over" to the mainstream and gain wider exposure. Similarly, what I have learned in teaching one course in women's drama will make itself felt in other courses I teach, and what students have learned will affect their future choices. As they become directors or professors, they are more likely to value plays by women.

For myself, this interest in gender politics in theatre has reawakened my interest in teaching drama. Knowing that I have a role to play in fostering women's drama and feminism gives a new sense of purpose to my work, and affects the choices I make about what to teach, from the selection of plays in existing courses to the design of new courses to the inclusion of gender politics as a subtopic, even in, for instance, a course on Shakespeare. The work feels a lot more exciting than it used to. Our only hope if plays for women to gain lasting fame is for women to move into the roles of director, producer, critic, editor, publisher and professor, as well as playwright, with increasing interest in gender politics and the determination to allow other women their own voices.

References

Carley, Dave. "Canadian Context Is Up, But Women Lose Out." *CanPlay* 5 (1988):1–5.

Case, Sue-Ellen. *Feminism and Theatre*. London: Macmillan Basingstoke, 1988.

Duffy, Maureen. *The Passionate Shepherdess: Aphra 1640–89*. London: J. Cape, 1977.

Malpede, Karen. *Women and Theatre: Compassion and Hope*. New York: Drama Book Publishers, 1983.

Stone-Blackburn, Susan. "Maenadic Rites on Stage in Calgary." *Canadian Theatre Review 69* (Winter 1991): 28–33.

Summers, Montague., ed. *The Works of Aphra Behn*. Vol. 1. New York: Phaeton Press, 1967.

Wandor, Michelene. *Carry On Understudies*. London: Routledge & Kegan Paul, 1986.

Whitford, Margaret. *The Irigaray Reader*. Oxford and Cambridge, MA: Basil Maxwell, 1991.

Furnishing a Room of One's Own

Renate I.E. Krause

Bien que cette communication soit autobiographique, sa prémisse, c'est que le personnel comporte des implications politiques, que la vision universelle se repose sur l'acte individuel. L'écrivaine examine ses propres connaissances, ses valeurs, ses attitudes et son comportement et essaie ainsi de faire face à une colère en apparence illogique contre ce qui pourrait être vu comme un refoulement. Pendant cet examen de conscience elle éprouve une forte envie de rejeter la responsabilité de cet état d'esprit lamentable sur un autre individu. Les reproches produisent des solutions de quelque sorte, mais fixer son regard sur la découverte de « solutions » a pour résultat de consolider l'état d'esprit dans lequel le problème est survenu (à voir, *The Great Code* de Northrop Frye). La vraie liberté réside dans le développement d'une capacité de permettre aux problèmes qui surviennent de mettre à l'épreuve les récits qu'on se raconte à propos de soi. Une fois compris que les récits ne sont pas « universels » et immuables, on peut décorer sa « pièce », l'espace dans lequel on aura la liberté d'assumer sa propre responsabilité, la liberté d'être guérie, d'évoluer et même de parler.

Although this paper is autobiographical, its premise is that the personal has political dimensions, that the global vision is grounded in individual action. The writer scrutinizes her own beliefs, values, attitudes and behaviour in an attempt to come to terms with a seemingly unreasonable anger against what is perceived as repression. In the process, she discovers the urge to place blame. Blame may give "answers" of sorts, but a focus on answers merely "consolidates the mental level on which the question is asked" (Frye, *The Great Code*). Freedom resides in learning to allow questions to test the stories one tells oneself about oneself. Once one understands that stories are not "universal" and immutable, one can retell those stories and appropriate them; one can create a "room" that permits freedom to take responsibility for oneself, freedom to heal, to grow and even to speak.

The spirit motivating Sir William Blackstone's legal formula that when a man and woman marry, "a husband and wife are one, and the husband is that one" (quoted in Stone, 1977:331) was the active and moving force a hundred years later, in my own life. And I do not believe that my experience is unique, or even anachronistic. This spirit was, and is yet, the moving force in the lives of many women of my generation. I had learned to define myself as property. Physically, I belonged first to my father and, after my marriage, to my husband. Spiritually, I belonged to God. This was natural, normal, the expected. I was happy. Why should I not be? I was the wife of a respected man, who treated me with great care and consideration. I was the mother of three intelligent, healthy, beautiful children. And I was a member of a church that needed my help. As the "angel in the house," I was appreciated and honoured.[1] But suddenly, after twenty years of marriage, this correct and well-ordered arrangement fell apart. Physically and spiritually, I felt that I had been subjugated; emotionally, however, I was obviously still capable of rebellion.

I had registered for a creative-writing course, and part of the course requirement was writing by free association — ten pages every week. The anger and fear, the pain of betrayal that poured from the tip of my pen onto the paper, were symptoms demanding a search for cause. The high-school English class that I taught had recently been studying Anton Chekhov's "The Darling," and comparing my life with that of Chekhov's protagonist amounted to revelation. I felt that being all things to everyone had transmogrified me, too, into a carefully designed and elaborately constructed series of masks. I was afraid to open the closet of my life and find nothing, not even a skeleton, beneath the masks I had been wearing. Pain and anger, however, forced the door open and pulled the cowering creature from her corner. And pity and anger prevented her from returning to the closet to huddle again under the debris of the now-damaged masks.

What was I to do, though, with this female being unable to survive in an environment alien and hostile to itself, one that had been infused for centuries with misogynist pronouncements such as that of St. Thomas Aquinas, who wrote that "woman is in subjugation because of the laws of nature ... Woman is subject to man because of the weakness of her mind as well as of her body" (quoted in Durant and Durant, 1950:825). I had a number of choices: I could take this creature deemed weak in mind and body and I could shove her back into the closet, repair the masks and shore up the crumbling foundations of my life. Or I could strangle her and pretend that she had never existed. Or I could accept her as myself and nurture her. The problem with this last choice was that it would require me to create a space, a room of her own, wherein she could grow and develop. Where would I find such a space and how would I create such a room? The more I examined my options, the clearer my lack of options became. I had to create this room; I had to acknowledge myself.

My experience, though the circumstances may have been unique, was, of course, not unique in itself. The recognition that women traditionally had been marginalized and cast into supporting roles by their society, their families and even themselves forms the basis of British novelist Virginia Woolf's polemic *A Room of Her Own*, published in 1929. Woolf argues that for a woman to have intellectual freedom, she needs material freedom — her own space and income. Some women have chosen to divorce themselves from "patriarchal" institutions such as marriage and religion and have found a space for themselves outside these. Others, including myself, have explored the possibility of creating a room of one's own within these institutions. Neither choice is easily made.

The first step I took in my attempt to create a space of my own was choosing to attend graduate school. Juggling the needs of a husband and family with the requirements of pursuing an education was not new to me. Our first two children were born before I was twenty-one. While they were pre-schoolers, I completed my high-school requirements by correspondence; after they started school, I enrolled in college. Graduation from college coincided with the birth of our daughter, so the decision to work on a master's degree was not as difficult as it might have been. Coming to terms with my anger, however, was.

When I graduated with a master of arts in English from Andrews University (a Seventh-Day Adventist institution), my energies were still focussed on the need to blame. Attending university during the summer months and teaching during the school year had been physically, mentally and emotionally exhausting. It had left me few resources with which to develop the space I had claimed. Moreover, I now discovered that I needed to defend that space. Blaming others, whether they were individuals or institutions, was to invite battle, and a constructive war is a contradiction in terms. War leaves no winners. Furthermore, my battle was waged with not only external forces, but with internal ones as well. The guilt over what I was feeling and doing was overwhelming. After all, my life had been stable and comfortable. I had not had to escape physical abuse in my marriage. I had not even been unappreciated. So my room, if it could even be called a room at that point, was almost uninhabitable. I was unhappy with what my life had become, and that unhappiness generated more resentment on which my anger could feed. And the angrier I became, the unhappier I was.

When I enrolled at the University of Alberta, I found that my academic survival depended upon my ability to turn handicaps, particularly the handicap of age, into assets. Competing on the doctoral level with others twenty years younger than I required changing the stories I had been telling myself. My attempts to place blame had to give way to learning my limitations and working within them. Age may mean less physical stamina, it may even mean some loss of memory, but it also means greater experience; so went the new story. And it worked! Furthermore, I discovered that my need for blaming was rooted in my need for answers. But the seminar format of my classes was more conducive to generating questions than answers. In fact, I learned to understand Northrop Frye's contention that a focus on answers merely "consolidates the mental level on which the question is asked"; I needed to "break down the powers of repression" in my mind that kept me from making my space my own (Frye, 1982:xv). And these powers of repression could be defeated only with questions, not with answers.

This point is illustrated by Hélène Cixous in her retelling of Franz Kafka's story "Before the Law."[2] The story begins, "Before the law, there stands the doorkeeper." Once a peasant came to ask for admittance to the law, but the doorkeeper informed her that she could not go in. The humble little woman from the country, in awe of the bearded, fierce and large doorkeeper, humbly asked when she would be able to enter and was told, "Perhaps later." The woman waited and waited. As she waited and waited, she grew smaller and smaller while the doorkeeper grew larger and larger. The years passed. As the woman finally changed from the size of a pea to that of a pinhead, she realized that during all the time she had been waiting, she had seen not one other person aside from the doorkeeper. Quickly, before shrinking into nothingness, she addressed the doorkeeper once more to ask why no one else had come. Shouting very loudly, because the woman now was dead, the doorkeeper answered, "Because this was your own door."

Cixous, commenting on this story, points out, "We behave as country people when we read Kafka's fable. Because we read, 'Before the law stands the doorkeeper,' and we go on reading and staying in the front of the door of the text, and go on and die. And suddenly we ask, we can wonder, But what is the law?" (Cixous, 1987:5). The reason we have not thought about it before is that there is apparently nothing to think about. Law is law. One does not question the law — or does one? One must obey the law — or must one? Kafka's little peasant spent her life in obedience to what she was told. She may have grown angrier and angrier while she was waiting. She may even have felt betrayed, but she sacrificed her life to a story — a story of the law's immutable omnipotence — because she did not recognize the liberating power of questions. When she finally did question, it was too late.

Storytelling has long been an essential human activity. We tell (and write) stories in an attempt to order the world, to understand and make ourselves capable of action by, as literary critic Peter Brooks observes, "reassessing the meaning of our past action," so that we may plan future projects and anticipate their outcomes (Brooks, 1984:3). Stories both determine and reflect our expectations of what life is, or ought to be, and thereby aid in forging societies from individuals. We would all agree, however, that some of the stories we have been told, and some of the stories we have learned to tell ourselves, are pernicious. Yet our own experiences, as well as the experiences of others, have demonstrated that the individual who refuses to model his or her behaviour to conform to the basic stories of a particular society is threatening to that society unless some sort of adaptation or modification takes place, either on the part of the individual or on the part of the society. And history demonstrates that society usually changes not only very slowly, but very reluctantly. It is up to us, then, to start telling new stories. And that cannot be done unless we question the old stories thoughtfully, not focussing on answers that will consolidate the mental level on which the question is asked, but asking questions to deconstruct and then formulating more liberating stories.

I learned that no one can escape the process of acculturation. The attempt to place blame, therefore, is futile. Acculturation begins at infancy, for the individual as well as for a culture. As a society develops, its absorption of the basic narratives that have given birth to it will breed additional ones which not only shape further development, but also reflect it. In Northrop Frye's terms, "Its mythology tends to become encyclopaedic, expanding into a total myth covering a society's view of its past, present and future, its relation to its gods and its neighbours, its traditions, its social and religious duties, and its ultimate destiny" (Frye, 1971:36). My absorption of these acculturated stories shaped my acquisition of my society's culture. Because acculturated stories are so basic to the philosophy of a culture (in both the collective and individual sense), it was no wonder that I had not recognized them as being stories, much less questioned them. But I found that totally breaking out of the mental habits formed by the framework of acculturated stories is difficult, if not impossible. There will always remain some blindness in the midst of the insight we achieve. "One cannot," according to Frye, "be without preconceptions" (1971:43).

Yet my attempt at creating a room of my own meant that I could not afford to be like Kafka's peasant; I could not accept the "universality" and immutability of the stories (or even the stories about stories) that I had been told. I had to learn to question not only the stories themselves, but also the manner in which they were told, for they can blind one to the possible validity, perhaps even the existence, of other stories or other ways of telling. Only as I learned to challenge the received cultural codes, only as I questioned the stories my society has told itself, could I truly create a space for myself that was conducive to constructive and healing work. Coming to terms with any anger and channelling it to constructive ends meant recognizing that the prevailing laws, mores, customs, traditions and attitudes are social constructs, stories that can be deconstructed, appropriated and reconstructed by simply questioning their seeming intractability, inevitability and unchangeability.

And so, through a process of trial and error, advance and retreat, ups and downs, I built a room in the space I had claimed. At first, it was in the attic. Its walls were impregnable, its windows narrow slits and its door heavily studded oak, secured by a huge lock. In short, it was a fortress. I found myself uncomfortable, however, in my self-assigned role as defender. Little time or energy was left for anything else. Nor could I lock myself in and be like Tennyson's Lady of Shalott, "embowered" on a "silent isle," isolated from life. Now my room is on the ground floor. Its windows are large, and its door is often open.

Rooms, however, require furnishings. An empty room is an incomplete room. But what does one do with such traditional furnishings as the bed and the cradle, the bookshelf and the desk, the kitchen table and sink? A number of possibilities presented themselves. I could accept and use the furnishings as intended. But that would require imitation and internalization of the same traditional male values that had taught me to wear masks in the first place. I could also demolish these furnishings or, at the very least, refuse to allow them into my room. As I looked around, though, I saw no materials with which to construct new furniture. It thus seemed only reasonable to bring them in so that I could adapt and shape them to fit my preferences and needs.

Only when one realizes that one can appropriate and reinterpret the images traditionally used to marginalize and colonize women can these very images, which at one time enforced bondage, liberate. I do not need to accept the story implied in Rousseau's *Emile*, which claims that the "body of woman is made expressly to please Man." Freud's assertion that "some means of sexual bondage" is "indispensable to the maintenance of civilized marriage" is not irrefutable. The marriage bed that signified male power need not continue to play that role, because I can change the story. I now have a room of my own. And so whether or not a heterosexual relationship results in a power relationship is determined by me. Emotionally, another person can have power over me only if I allow him (or her) to have it.

The metamorphosis I can effect on the bed, I can also effect on other furnishings. Until I realized that I do have that ability and gained confidence in using it, I was in bondage even to the *absent* bed, or table, or kitchen sink, because fear is always debilitating. Now I can choose my furnishings freely.

I would not want to suggest that I found the appropriation and reinterpretation of images simple. The clock, for instance, gave me great trouble. Thinking of time as other than what Ewa Gunnarsson and Ulla Ressner call "collective" was difficult (quoted in Davies, 1990:15). All my life, I had been taught that the needs of my church, my family and my friends should come before my own. I had adjusted even my career accordingly. I had taught school so that my hours away from home coincided with my children's. Temporal servitude had become part of my make-up. Another difficult image was the mirror. In Virginia Woolf's words, I had made myself a looking-glass, one that "possess[es] the magic and delicious power of reflecting the figure of man at twice its natural size" (Woolf, 1929:35). In fact, to reflect and enlarge more effectively, I had polished the surface by adopting my family's and my church's interests and goals as my own.

And that brings me to the most difficult task I faced: the metamorphosis of the kneeling bench under the crucifix. Finally realizing that the kneeling bench and the crucifix were not one and the same, I took the kneeling bench apart to look more closely at its construction, and I found that religion must be contextualized. The Judeo-Christian tradition is based on a book that, though I believe it to be inspired, was nevertheless written by men for men. Truth, as it is embodied by God, is different from revealed truth. And even revealed truth is different from perceived truth. One's perceptions are actuated by one's acculturation. More significant yet, the truth operative in one's life (i.e., existential truth) is other than even perceived truth. Therefore, the record of the revelation of God in the Christian Bible is to a large degree culturally determined; further-more, the reading and living of that record is culturally determined as well. I found that the biblical text, when read in its entirety, allows a rereading of old stories, a practice Christ Himself encourages.3 And so, as long as my church insists on the authority of Scripture rather than the authority of tradition, and stresses the need for a relationship with God rather than blind obedience to its own precepts, I am glad that the kneeling bench can remain a part of the furnishings of my room.

Too long was this room of my own furnished for only one person. I have recently moved several comfortable chairs into it because I need community. Sometimes, I will admit, I close the door rather abruptly and rather hard. For instance, when my husband talks of a certain household chore as "your job," I retreat to my room. It keeps me from rushing to the closet and digging out the appropriate mask. Or when I walk into an ad hoc committee meeting and the chairman tells me that he and the rest of the male members are glad to have a woman assigned to that committee because now they have someone to take the minutes, I call up the strength that I find within my room. Recently, I not only closed the door but pulled the blinds when my church legislated against the ordination of women. One writer graphically delineates the attitude of many members in a letter to the editor:

> In God's original plan, a mother's special role is to furnish physical nourishment, and the father's special role is to nourish spiritually through the priesthood of the family and the church. For some of us the idea of a woman being our minister is about as unacceptable as a man attempting to nurse his child physically. (Crosby, 1990:2)

At times like these, I realize that my ownership of that room is still essential to my freedom. There, I am surrounded by evidence that I have the freedom to question even my church, the freedom to take responsibility for myself, the freedom to heal, the freedom to grow. And these give me the freedom to speak.

Notes

1. The phrase "angel in the house" is taken from Coventry Patmore's poem of that name. It refers to what Elaine Showalter calls the "phantom of female perfection who stands in the way of freedom" (1977:262).
2. With apologies to both Kafka and Cixous, I have changed the gender of the protagonist.
3. Rosemary Radford Ruether's essay "Renewal or New Creation" identifies Christ's commentary on Isaiah 61:1–2 in Luke 4:17–27 as a retelling of an old story. Isaiah, Ruether points out, had been read by the Jews as Israel triumphing over its enemies; Jesus uses the Isaiah text to condemn the ethnocentric complacency of the Jews. Many other instances are recorded of Christ appropriating stories from the Old Testament. A well-known one is his retelling of a number of laws (including the seventh commandment from Exodus 20:14) in Matthew 5.

References

Brooks, Peter. *Reading for the Plot: Design and Intention in Narrative*. New York: Alfred A. Knopf, 1984.

Cixous, Hélène. "Reaching the Point of Wheat or a Portrait of the Artist as a Maturing Woman." *New Literary History* 19, no. 1 (Autumn 1987): 1–21.

Crosby, Ellen. Letter to *The Adventist Review*, p.2 [Silver Spring, Maryland], 14 June
1990.

Davies, Karen. *Women, Time, and the Weaving of the Strands of Everyday Life*. Aldershot: Avebury, 1990.

Durant, Will and Mary Durant. *The History of Civilization*. Vol. 4, *The Age of Faith*. New York: Simon and Schuster, 1950.

Frye, Northrop. *The Critical Path*. Bloomington: Indiana University Press, 1971.

— . *The Great Code*. Toronto: Academic Press, c. 1982.

Ruether, Rosemary Radford. "Renewal or New Creation." In *A Reader in Feminist Knowledge*, 277–289. Edited by Sneja Gunew. London: Routledge, 1991.

Showalter, Elaine. *A Literature of Their Own: British Women Novelists from Bronte to Lessing*. New Jersey: Princeton University Press, 1977.

Stone, Lawrence. *The Family, Sex and Marriage in England 1500–1800*. New York: Harper and Row, 1977.

Woolf, Virginia. *A Room of One's Own*. London: Triad Grafton, 1929.

CREATING A LIFE, PUSHING AGAINST THE BARRIERS

CRÉÉR UNE VIE, REPOUSSER LES BARRIÈRES

In her book *Composing a Life,* Mary Catherine Bateson (1990:1) speaks of "that act of creation that engages us all — the composition of our lives. Each of us has worked by improvisation, discovering the shape of our creation along the way, rather than pursuing a vision already defined." Bateson describes this as a complex task, because compared with lives lived in more stable societies, "the materials and skills from which a life is composed are no longer clear" (Bateson, 1990:2). This is especially true for women, whose lives-in-progress tend to resemble patchwork quilts more than they do the "purposeful and monolithic" carvings of lives shaped to assert a unitary, typically male, vision (Bateson, 1990:4).

The writing in this section describes the kinds of patching and stitching that four women are doing in creating their lives, and the designs that are emerging from this work. This is not the calm, peaceful work one normally associates with quilt-making. Rather, these women struggle to create something practical yet beautiful, with materials that do not fit the conventional frames and patterns of their society. They push against these barriers, reshaping the frames and redesigning the patterns.

For Sylvia Vance, whose poem opens this section, the frame is that of giving birth, the act that creates one's own life anew in the creation of another. Birthing is labour, hard and painful work, but worth every wrenching minute, according to the conventional pattern. Vance's words and images, however, take us into the world of the mother for whom the pain never goes away. The design lives on, but as memory only, as a "sorrow that does not end."

Karen Blackford's frame is also pain and motherhood, but the materials are a mother's progressive debilitation by multiple sclerosis and the family's responses. In the conventional pattern, the illness takes centre place not only in the woman's life but in her family's as well. Through interviews with other MS mothers and their children, and readings in the literature of opposition to domination and oppression, Blackford finds another pattern. In this pattern, chronically ill mothers regain their central, leadership role in their families. Along with their families, these women become part of community networks of mutual support rather than victims of illness, no longer confined by frames of reference that are built from historical notions of disability and disempowering social relations.

As a young feminist, Danielle Forth's hope is to take part in building a support network that has a slightly different focus, one that expands the existing frame of feminism to include the experiences and needs of young feminists. Using the image of "diving deep and surfacing," Forth argues that by engaging in a genuine dialogue with young women, older feminists can support younger ones in their dives into the depths of history and theory. At the same time, listening to their younger colleagues can help older feminists once again break through to the surface, where they can learn more about the patterns that constitute reality for women now in their second and third decades of life. To extend Forth's image a little further, however, perhaps she should also be urging older feminists to use their (our) experience and knowledge as a diving platform rather than a deck chair. From the comfort of poolside we can survey the surface, but it is only by continuing to dive with our younger sisters that we can hope to know the deep thoroughly enough to be able to transform its surface patterns in any lasting way.

Pauline Fahmy confronts another issue in the lives of women who are struggling to create their lives: Why do so many women forsake professional life and lack a career perspective in their working lives? Fahmy meticulously reviews the reasons that have been advanced in the literature: job ghettoization, gender stereotypes, fear of success, lack of feminine role models. The responses of the women in Fahmy's sample (all from the Quebec City region) indicate a much more profound set of reasons for their rejection of the dominant, uni-dimensional, male model of "career" that demands an excessive proportion of their day given over to work at the expense of their personal and domestic lives and is characterized by the exercise of power, aggressive competition and identification of self with the business. These women do aspire to progress in their careers, but they see that progress in terms of taking on more useful and interesting tasks, enhancing their knowledge, improving their status, obtaining more decision-making power and safeguarding the balance between their private and professional lives. One gets the feeling that this holistic approach could transform the academic world of research into women's relation to the labour market. We feel privileged to be able to publish it.

Reference

Bateson, Mary Catherine. *Composing a Life*. New York: Penguin Books, 1990.

On My Daughter's Twenty-Third Birthday

Sylvia Vance

I hardly remember you, really.
Chubby hands and cheeks,
dimpled knees
have been lost with hazy blue eyes
among the reflections of
the many babies
I have held on my knee.

But your black hair
remains vivid —
so shocking that out of
my pale body
this dark-haired creature
would be born.

And your blue-veined
translucent eyelids
that I inspected as you slept,
with the hope that in their
mapping, their travelling
through the thinnest of skins,
I could read your life.

Now, I know
the ordinary truth
about sorrow —
that it does not end.
Not with time,
not with experience,
not with laughter.

Then, I could not believe
the pain in my arms.
The veins were on fire.
The muscles twisted
as if being tourniqueted.

This other kind
of phantom pain,
where the limb remains intact,
racks my arms
in the exact same way
it did twenty-three years ago,
when I lifted you for the last time
to someone else.

This poem was previously published in *Dandelion* 18, no. 1 (1991): 19.

Can Others Really Do Our Marching for Us?

Karen A. Blackford

Ce document se penche sur les contraintes dans la vie des mères atteintes de maladies chroniques et dans celle de leurs enfants. La méthodologie se fonde sur l'action de féministes canadiennes qui préconisent la reconnaissance du vécu des chercheuses et la divulgation des complexités inhérentes à la vie personnelle de ces femmes. Les entrevues avec ces enfants et leurs mères atteintes de sclérose en plaques sont analysées à l'aide des principes de la théorie sociale et des souvenirs des expériences personnelles de l'auteure atteinte d'une maladie chronique. La colère et l'apathie y sont considérées comme le résultat de relations sociales qui cantonnent les femmes malades et leurs enfants dans un état démuni de pouvoir. Les membres de la famille y sont montrés comme des agents qui résistent aux notions prépondérantes d'incapacité, de maternité et de caractère privé de la famille nucléaire. Ironiquement, cette résistance donne lieu à des conséquences inattendues. Les souvenirs mêmes de l'auteure expliquent certaines notions de rejet de soi et de douleur inhérente au handicap et contribuent à mieux comprendre les principes de la surveillance de soi et de la reproduction de relations sociales dominantes.

This paper explores constraints in the lives of chronically ill mothers and their children. The methodology is informed by Canadian feminists who advocate recognizing the researcher's experience and reporting the complexities in the personal lives of women. Interviews with children and with their mothers who have multiple sclerosis are analyzed using social theory in conjunction with reminiscences from the author's personal experience with chronic illness. Anger and apathy are seen as a result of social relations that keep ill women and their children in a powerless position. Family members are shown to be agents resisting hegemonic notions of disability, motherhood and privacy of the nuclear family. Ironically, resistance results in unexpected consequences. The author's own memories bring clarification of the self-rejection and pain associated with disability, and contribute to a better understanding of self-policing and the reproduction of dominant social relations.

Introduction

This paper is about the importance of being involved so that you can tell your own tale. It is a plea for making space in the academy for people's lived experiences as a basis for theory building.

Not until I came to write about children with chronically ill mothers did I begin to appreciate the importance personal experience can bring, especially to the study of a group about which very little is known. My concern for my own son, my anxieties and joys about our relationship in conjunction with my chronic illness, have tuned me in to the importance of studying the situation of children with ill mothers. In addition, my self-reflections are proving valuable in terms of my understanding of the theory I read and as a catalyst for new theory building.

In my approach to studying children whose mothers have multiple sclerosis, I have varied sources of information: children, their chronically ill mothers, their well fathers (where they are present) and staff of the MS Society. I am therefore pursuing the triangulated approach, as Glaser and Strauss (1967) have advocated. But even without that variety in field data, I have three sources that ensure triangulation: readings about theoretical constructs, my field observations and my own memories. It is out of all three that I have built my own constructs. In this paper, I want to share what for me is an exciting experience and also a discovery of how to do creative work in the social sciences.

Beyond my own experiences and self-reflection, I have been encouraged by the writings of two feminists: Patricia Marchak and Kathleen Rockhill. From Marchak's work, I draw the courage to face critics who would claim that my work is flawed, since I may be insufficiently distant or objective in my perspective. Marchak (1991:5) lamented, "If only it were so simple to divide the labour: we write the scholarly text books; others do the marching." To be relevant, she suggests, we must abandon hands-off objectivity; location is a critical element in relevant academic work. My message, however, is slightly different from Marchak's. She speaks to the importance of pursuing explorations in territories she happened to find herself in, through her professional or public life. I am talking about the importance of pursuing explorations in territories that are part of our private lives.

Rockhill expresses support for the notion of self-reflection and uses her "subjectivity as a basis of inquiry" (1987:15), exploring gender relations through the prism of her own experience as a child who was sexual abused. She takes what I see as a bolder step, however, when she explains the necessity of reporting *all* the data gathered. As an example, she explains that her interviews with Mexican-American women revealed that some of these women were in abusive spousal relationships. Since abuse was not the focus of her study of literacy practices, and as she did not wish to "perpetuate and contribute to negative, class-based racist stereotypes about the Mexican community" (1987:15), Rockhill chose to withhold these findings. In a retrospective critique of her own work, she comments:

> *Far from being peripheral to the problem of literacy in their lives, the violence the women experienced was central ... The women ... experience literacy in the context of their oppression as women in the family. In the power relations between themselves and their husbands, literacy is highly charged and it is experienced as both a threat and a desire. (Rockhill, 1987:15)*

This discussion was especially important for me. In my previous work, I had carefully taken a pro-active stance toward the investigation of children with chronically ill mothers. This stance was my attempt to counterbalance what I saw as the overuse of terms such as "dysfunctional," which have restricted the parameters of what can be considered healthy family life. Functionalist family theorists (Sullivan, 1980) have postulated negative assumptions about parents with disabilities and their families in unnecessary, distorted and possibly destructive ways. In spite of this very real concern, I read in Rockhill's work permission not only to explore strengths of children and parents in such families, as I have done in the past, but also to examine areas of discomfort, even domination, in relationships. Only through recognizing, reporting and seeking an understanding of constraining as well as empowering phenomena in populations we study will the complications of a person's particular experience be uncovered. It may be possible in this instance to identify where and how children with ill mothers are in one sense constrained, even while demonstrating individual agency. Perhaps through greater insight into this process we will come to understand how social relations, in which the powerful control those with less power, can be transformed.

This paper is my first attempt at trying to understand the constraining side of living with a chronically ill mother. Space does not permit a complete discussion of the families interviewed, so at the outset I can promise that the paper will not be balanced. In some senses, this approach is an attempt to confront a personal dragon, a worry that perhaps I was not, using Little's (1992) terms, in every instance a perfectly "fit and proper" parent.

The Benefits of Interviewing

I have been carrying out private interviews with children aged nine to seventeen years old, and separately with each of their parents, when the mother has multiple sclerosis. This method permits parents and their children to define their situation in their own words (Glaser and Strauss, 1967).

In all of the families I visited, parents worried about how the mother's illness might affect their children, and most went to great lengths to ensure that the illness impinges as little as possible on their children's lives. There was concern, but there was also an abundance of caring. Many of these people described the importance of living in the present and wanting every day to be quality time. However, two signs were apparent which suggested that parents were overwhelmed by their circumstances. In some instances, both the children and their parents were angry; in other instances, they were resigned.

"MS Rage"

Some mothers explained that they were aware of what happened when they became overwhelmed with a combination of fatigue, pain and, primarily, frustration with their circumstances. One woman talked about her urgent need "to crash" when the day had one too many unsolved problems: she would "lose her cool" and need to lie down. Another described an article she had read entitled "MS Rage." This was her first hint that other people with MS also experienced feelings of being overwhelmed. These two mothers described criticizing and shouting at their children, assuming that the children were being deliberately provocative. Although social circumstances clearly played a large role in their bouts of anger, frustration and fatigue, these women somehow believed that people without MS would not get so irritable. Therefore, biology and themselves as imperfect biological bodies were to blame for discord, or even unfairness, with their children. These mothers explained that when they go through such an episode, they end up apologizing to their children for their own behaviour.

The children were left with a global notion that the illness was at the root of their mother's anger. A son reported that when his mother "needed to crash," it was wise to be "outside playing." The adolescent daughters of the mother describing "rage" explained that Mom sometimes kicks out at them "but she hurts herself more than me." This mother has lost muscle strength and uses either a wheelchair or a walker. Since parents could usually describe particular external events that led up to a given episode of "losing their cool," why did they end up apologizing for their behaviour? How did children come to decide that this behaviour was entirely attributable to maternal MS?

That's Life!

I also observed that some parents and children appeared to be resigned to their circumstances to the point of almost policing themselves in terms of social expectations. For example, a single mother using a scooter, who lived with her three children in a two-bedroom low-rental housing unit, reported that homemaking services had been reduced and physiotherapy services had been stopped outright. "They showed my kids how to help me with exercises and said physiotherapy visits weren't needed. So I don't do much exercise. I can't do it myself and I hate to ask the kids. They're already so busy. Their school work should come first."

Adolescents in this family explained that the homemaker came only half a day rather than three days per week. The homecare assessment staff had decided that "we're old enough to do most of the work." This assessment, however, did not take into account that one teenager already swam for his school team every morning before classes and cooked supper promptly after school so he could do his homework. This young man has dreams of being an astronomer. Nor did the staff acknowledge the difficulties that his sister was having in adjusting to a new high school social environment and negotiating a university-preparation course load. She explained that teachers assumed that students like herself (from low-income housing or with a chronically ill mother) should take courses to prepare for employment, not university. Time, energy and skill were needed within this family so that this adolescent girl could get the counselling and support she needed from her mother and older brother. Additional housework chores, particularly at this stage in her development, did not improve the chances of her receiving such support or completing her homework tasks.

I was puzzled about why this ill mother and her children would put up with such a situation. Why give in to what were obviously decisions convenient to an agency and contrary to the family's needs?

The Benefits of Theory

Paul Willis provides a number of useful ways in which to put into words the relations observable within these families with ill mothers. Willis has shown how individual agency is embedded within larger structural class dynamics. He uses the term *partial penetration* to explain that individuals within oppressed cultures may only partially understand their circumstances and fail to see the power they hold to change the system. In this situation, ironically, oppressed agents tend to confirm the values of the larger system (Willis, 1977:161–162). Willis also explains that dislocation can occur when members of oppressed groups choose to separate themselves from each other into racial, gendered or other subgroups. Resistance is clearly weakened through divisions within oppressed ranks. To the extent that children and their parents with MS could identify structural arrangements or decisions on the part of more powerful others as the source of their oppression and the catalyst for what might be seen as their verbal revolt into anger, they were demonstrating penetration.

Raymond Williams (1973) categorizes attempts at change made by the dominated, using the terms *residual* and *emergent* oppositional actions. In his description of emergent actions, Williams describes holding on to the practices, ideas, meanings or beliefs of a previous time as an active, almost purposeful behaviour, in order to achieve an alternative to the full adoption of current hegemonic practices, thus preserving an outdated mode of thinking. Ironically, although holding on to traditional practices is usually seen as, and may often actually constitute, a conservative act on behalf of the status quo, Williams suggests that the inverse is possible — that holding onto the past is an alternative way of displacing the status quo, as a form of resistance to current hegemonic practices.

Pierre Bourdieu (in Snook, 1990) explains that a leader, a person in authority, is given that authority when designated by "the dominated" as speaking for them. It is the action of the individuals who are dominated that constructs and agrees to the construction of the *minister* as representing them, speaking on behalf of them and naming them. Bourdieu is clear that the power of the minister is effective only when it involves hidden dominance and is presented as being for the good of others or for that of the group as a whole. "The mystery of the ministry only acts on the condition that the minister disguises his usurpation and the imperium which it confers to him, by presenting himself as a simple minister" (quoted in Snook, 1990:175). Bourdieu also explains that the dominated stay in their designated places and do not question their designation for long, or in a loud voice, because they feel guilty: "The priest uses a language shared by the faithful in order to control them by making them feel guilty. He uses his language as a strategy to bring about guilt" (quoted in Snook, 1990:175). The dominated experience this guilt because they view their own protest against domination as a cry for self-interest. They compare this self-interest to the evidently universal, paternalistic interest of the dominator, who works for the good of all. The dominated therefore feel ashamed of and guilty for their self-serving request for an individual voice and recognition.

The Benefits of My Own Memories

These theoretical constructs became easier for me to understand as I recalled my own experiences as a sole-support mother raising a six-year-old son and feeling overwhelmed. This journey back through my memory brought tears of regret for what some of the experience was like and, again, a feeling of frustration about what could and should have been different.

I remembered wanting my son to have the link to a northern Ontario community that comes with being on a hockey team. (My current ideas about the benefits of hockey for young boys are quite different.) I wanted him to have exposure to adult males, since all the psychology books said that he would certainly be deprived if there were no men in his life. I could not take him to the arena myself because I was too weak; I could not even tie his skates because my finger joints were too sore. Money was a problem on a disability pension, so I could not afford to hire someone else to accompany him.

Looking back on this experience helped me understand why ill mothers blame themselves and their illness for barriers they experience, and why children come to believe them. I remembered that it was not the pain or lack of energy that caused me to feel overwhelmed and irritable, but the frustration of finding no solution to our social and economic circumstances. The pain and fatigue were exacerbated by this frustration, rather than being its sole cause. In spite of this realization, when I was "at the end of my rope," I explained my feelings to my son in terms of my body: "I don't feel good. My pain's getting worse."

This was a simplistic and somewhat distorted explanation of what was actually going on. In part, it was offered as an adult with the intention of making something clear to a six-year-old. However, it was also easier to admit to bodily weakness than to explain what I felt more ashamed about. It was difficult to explain that "the system" — the authorities, the adult world — had me stymied.

In revealing that I did not have enough clout to negotiate with others for our needs, I would have had to acknowledge that this was in part due to disrespect from others who were prejudiced against imperfect bodies. Others could not see what we knew to be true: ill mothers, in spite of physical limits, can maintain their skill as family leaders and caregivers worthy of respect. If I verbalized this lack of respect from others, I might lose face with my son and show weakness. Nor did I want to teach my son prejudice by pointing out the reality of other adults' prejudice. If I avoided the topic, perhaps the prejudice would go away.

In retrospect, I was also avoiding a topic that was difficult for me because of my own prejudice against that imperfect part of my body. On one side, I observed my experience of being an effective parent in spite of my illness. On the other side, I was assuming that I must be less valuable than other adults. My ideas about disability stemmed in part from the same historic sources as theirs. Had I shared with my son my analysis of social factors related to parental disability, I would have provided him with an alternative view. Instead, my reference to my pain and fatigue confirmed for him the dominant view (Willis, 1977).

My explanations to my son had the additional effect of what Willis terms *dislocation*. The value of solidarity within our family could be challenged by the dominant ideology of individualism (Ryan, 1981), the rigid criteria for the perfect body (Spakeman, 1989), notions about the perfect mother and the perfect family. Instead of using what power I had to expel these impossible ideals, I confirmed them. By highlighting myself as disabled, I became "other" to my son, who could claim a healthy body. I dislocated whatever solidarity as a family "together against the world" we had achieved.

This analysis based on memories helped me to understand why mothers I interviewed pointed to their disease as the culprit for their irritability, fatigue and feelings of being overwhelmed. It also showed me why children learn that mother is different because of her illness. Mother learns through social relations that she is devalued because of her disability, and the child hears her message.

My memories, in conjunction with theory, also served to clarify why ill mothers and their children were apparently willing to forgo the struggle for vital social and health services. My own experience with such a struggle could be partly explained by guilt and by Bourdieu's ministerium. In my case, I started to put out gentle feelers for help to members of our extended family. Hints to my brother, a high-school teacher, that he might accompany my son to the arena were not taken up. Nor were queries to my father, who was retired but preoccupied with escorting my mother to bowling. My sister, who was an almost full-time "hockey mom," saw only her own financial burdens associated with getting her son to games she did not see how she might be able take an extra passenger at the same time. When informal inquiries were not successful, I tried to get Big Brothers involved. Unfortunately, the waiting list for a Big Brother volunteer was four years long.

Finally, biting my lip with embarrassment and shame, I approached a social organizer in my community and asked her to visit. I had written out what I thought would be costs associated with the hockey — a person's time and transportation costs — and I asked, "With all of those charitable organizations, the Legion, church groups, would there not be some way of funding this?" Unfortunately, my request did not seem to meet the criteria for funding agencies. Only if I needed funds for a wheelchair might help be available.

Eventually, I came to realize that, of course, no help was there because as an individual parent I was solely responsible for my own nuclear family. I stopped expecting or even hoping that others would take some responsibility for assisting in our lives. I gave up the dream of a caring community network.

Structural forces embedded in the middle-class notion of the private nuclear family (Ryan,1981) and the Enlightenment notion of individualism were being presented and personified by the ministerium, those authorities in my extended family and the community. It was apparently for the good of all that individual families are self-sufficient, although family isolation didn't quite bring the feeling of the most good for people like us. I felt guilty about asking for assistance in our own self-interest.

I managed to communicate this new knowledge, which I now see as a "warped" perspective, to my son, who has matured into a most independent young man. He stopped asking a long time ago for family life to be different and for his own needs to be met. Unfortunately, he stopped believing that his needs are important, or that he deserves a support network.

In remembering these incidents, I can understand how and why the mother in my study started to believe that it was up to her to do her own exercises. I could see how she did not have the energy to continue on her own, and how she hated to rob her children of their study or play time. She did not want to put her own needs before the good of the family. I could see why both son and daughter were not bound by gendered division of labour. They both took on household chores, although these chores reduced their time with friends and sports activities. They did not want to feel selfish for putting their needs above the family's, nor did they want to challenge their mother's decision-making role as family leader. Furthermore, those outside "ministers" — homemaker, nurse and physiotherapist — had named them as able to perform and be responsible for these chores. They had labelled responsibilities within the nuclear family unit as separate from those of the community. To a large extent, this thinking had a direct effect on these children's definitions of their own situation.

Professionals such as physiotherapists and nurses come with university educations and middle-class values. Many also come with the notion that hospitals are factories for warehousing persons with chronic illnesses or factories for curing them. With policy changes regarding deinstitutionalization, the same expectations are now held about the home where a chronically ill person resides. These assumptions suggest that the family's purpose should be (as the hospital's purpose had been) to keep medical schedules and regimes, and to chase the illusive dream of a cure. Whereas in other middle-class families, mothers and their daughters are expected to care for fathers and brothers, the assumption here is that the "needs of the disabled" should take precedence even over the power of patriarchy and the gendered division of labour. Indeed, persons with disabilities are seen as so needy that their rights must exclude the needs of all others, just as their position as family leaders must be set aside.

In not continuing her exercises, this woman was creating disadvantage for herself. From her own perspective, however, perhaps she was also gaining something. She was in league with her children in a revolt. By not conforming to the exercise regime, this family was insisting that she was a mother first, with responsibilities for children, and not just a patient. Family members were offering residual oppositional action (Williams, 1973) against the relatively recent middle-class notion (Hutter, 1985) that the purpose of family life should be focussed on individuals (such as a sick person). Instead, the strength of family life for them was in the collectivity of a previous era. Furthermore, they were resisting the newly imposed definition of mother as patient, of themselves as caregivers and of their home as an extension of the hospital. Instead, they were insisting on mother as family leader, and on family as a place where all members would help all other members to achieve whatever was possible.

Conclusions

So what does this combination of reminiscence, observations and theory tell us? It shows how notions of family and disability become part of our personal understanding of the world. We learn not so much about their truth, but about their power, through our relations with more powerful others. They are filtered down to our children, colouring their own notions of what family life should be, of what their own place is in the world, as a child of a chronically ill mother. So we not only learn, we reproduce what we learn.

This exploration has also given a hint of where insights are achieved, even by oppressed groups, and where resistance lies in everyday lives. People are not just shaped by ideology and social relations, they are also actors in the creation of those relations.

In this paper, I set out to demonstrate constraint in the lives of family members dealing with chronic maternal illness. The examples I have used from my own experience, and from the lives I have observed, suggest that constraint is often present. In spite of partial insight, there are unintended consequences to our oppositional actions.

While my son has learned that the community is not there as a collective support, and has learned assertiveness skills as a protection, he is now reproducing the ideology of individualism. Furthermore, he is caught in the web of self-blame when that world sends him an unexpected, overwhelming challenge.

While the interviews showed a family seeing through and reject- ing the gospel of individual rights and of sacrifice to an illness regime, the outcome of their resistance was disadvantage for all family mem- bers. The outcomes include a daughter who may underachieve at school, a son who may leave school early to increase the family income, and a mother whose illness will become more debilitating without physiotherapy or housekeeping services. Ironically, these outcomes of resistance have the potential for reinforcing the notion that women with chronic illnesses really are not "fit and proper" mothers and deserve to be relegated to the historical category of impotent and infirm (Stone, 1985).

Still, I hesitate to leave the discussion here. While social relations have worked together with notions of gender, disability and family to constrain family members in these particular examples, the unique notions that their situations raise may also serve to empower these actors at other times or locations. In addition, some of the partial insights they achieved and their oppositional actions may have spin- off effects on the social actors whose lives they touch. Their suggestion that other family forms are possible, that division of labour or respon- sibility based on age, gender or physical condition may be changeable and that alternative views of disability may be valuable could spark innovation in social relations.

Some people are overwhelmed by the life circumstances sur- rounding their illness. Note that I am *not* saying "overwhelmed by their illness." Circumstances around the illness, many of which can be altered, are part of the relations located within structures and arise from historical notions of disability, gender and family, creating a pattern that is a maze of circumstances. It is this maze that can become overwhelming.

This paper was informed by theorics offered by Willis (1977), Williams (1973) and Bourdieu (Snook, 1990). In accounting for insights, oppositional actions and power relations, application of these theories explains to some extent how and why children and their ill mothers may police themselves and see themselves as unworthy. However, the language and examples used by these theorists fail to capture the power and complexity of the social relations associated with ill mothers and their children.

Ill mothers (and their children) see that they can be worthy family leaders and recognize possibilities for a more collective community network, but are held back by loathing of the disabled self (and the disabled mother), by thinking of the self (and the mother) as "other." Such thinking arises from historical notions of disability and from disempowering social relations with more powerful players. In using my own experience as data, as Marchak (1991) and Rockhill (1987) suggest, I can see that this is an area that demands further consideration by researchers and theorists.

This exploration of self, others and theory has also taught me to trust my own feelings. Personal perspectives decentred from mainstream positions are relevant to the more global notions of family, gender and disability.

References

Boudreau, F. "The Making of Mental Health Policy: The 1980's and the Challenge of Sanity in Quebec and Ontario." *Canadian Journal of Community Mental Health* 6 (1987): 27–47.

Glaser, B., and A. Strauss. *The Discovery of Grounded Theory.* Chicago: Aldine, 1967.

Hutter, M. "Symbolic Interaction and the Study of the Family." *Symbolic Interaction.* Supplement No. 1, *Foundations of Interpretive Sociology: Original Essays in Symbolic Interaction* (1985): 117–152.

Little, M. "A Fit and Proper Parent." Paper presented to the Feminist Lecture Series, York University, 1990.

Marchak, M.Patricia. "Relevance: Panel Presentation to the Social Science Federation of Canada." *Society/Société* 15, no. 1 (1991): 1–6.

Rockhill, Kathleen. "The Chaos of Subjectivity in the Ordered Halls of Academe." *Canadian Woman Studies* 8, no. 4 (1987): 12–17.

Ryan, M. *Cradle of the Middle Class.* Cambridge: Cambridge University Press, 1981.

Snook, I. "Language, Truth and Power: Bourdieu's Ministerium." In *An Introduction to the Work of Pierre Bourdieu,* 160–180. Edited by R. Harker, C.

Mahar and C. Wilkes. London: MacMillan, 1990.

Spakeman, B. *Decadent Genealogies*. Ithica, NY: Cornell University Press, 1989.

Stone, Deborah. *The Disabled State*. London: Macmillan, 1985.

Sullivan, J.A. "Family Members' Perceived Level of Family Adjustment and Symptomatology in Other Members in Families with a Chronically Ill Patient." Ph.D. diss., New York University, 1974. Ann Arbour, MI: University Microfilms International (University Microfilm No. 75-8566).

Williams, R. "Base and Superstructure in Marxist Cultural Theory." *New Left Review* 82 (December 1973): 3–16.

Willis, Paul. *Learning to Labour*. New York: Columbia University Press, 1977.

Diving Deep: the Generation Gap Between Older and Younger Feminists

Danielle M. Forth

La littérature féministe semble indiquer que les jeunes femmes n'apprécient tout simplement pas les efforts déployés par des femmes moins jeunes pour améliorer la situation de la femme dans notre société. Les différences d'âge et d'expérience ont entraîné des vues très différentes du féminisme et bien que ces différences semblent diviser jeunes et moins jeunes et leur définition du féminisme, il existe dans leurs expériences des similarités qui comblent l'écart des générations et offrent un terrain d'entente où jeunes et moins jeunes pourraient se rencontrer. Cet article examine les expériences qui contribuent au développement d'une conscience féministe chez les jeunes femmes et essaie de définir le processus qui consiste à se définir comme féministe.

Feminist literature suggests that younger women simply do not appreciate older women's efforts to improve the status of women in our society. Differences in age and experience among women have resulted in differing views of feminism. Although these differences appear to divide older and younger women and their definitions of feminism, there are similarities in experience that bridge the generations and offer a common ground where younger and older women may meet. This article explores the experiences that contribute to the development of a feminist consciousness in young women and attempts to define the process of labelling oneself as feminist.

Born in the late sixties, I have grown up in the midst of the feminist movement; for almost as far back as I can remember, my thinking has been feminist. Feminism is one of the important influences in my life and has contributed, both directly and indirectly, to how I think and how I have come to define myself. I am a second-generation feminist. Many young women of my generation are both the children and the pupils of feminism.

Finding a Voice: The Second Generation's Search for Language

When I search through the pages of periodicals, books and articles for accounts of other young women's experiences, I see that writings by women of my generation are almost totally absent. The feminist vocabulary does not include words to describe the experiences of a generation raised on a diet of feminist rhetoric, whose mothers went to consciousness-raising classes and pursued university degrees or pushed open the corporate doors while raising a family. How strange that the generation of women ahead of me, who have worked (and continue to work) to tear away the patriarchal structures and change society's values and beliefs, should neglect to look behind them at the generation following in their footsteps. And now the generation behind mine is also absent in feminist literature.

Literature written by older feminists about young women is frequently critical. Young women are criticized for not labelling themselves as feminists, even though the term *feminist* has become so distorted over the decades that it no longer holds the same meaning as it did in the sixties. As a label, feminism has been rejected by many young women of my generation because it does not adequately express what we mean or experience.

It has been my experience that I have been more able to articulate what I am *not* as a feminist than what I *am*. I am not a parent, nor am I disabled. I am not married, separated or divorced. I am not a member of any class, race or religion that feminism is now addressing, although I acknowledge that I have privileges that other women do not. I have not experienced the pain of any form of physical, sexual or psychological abuse.

But I am a young woman. As feminism becomes more cognizant of other women, young women get lost in the shuffle. And so, as a feminist who "is not," I have spent much time and energy trying to locate myself in feminist vocabulary. I have tried to speak words shaped for the mouths of those whose experiences differ greatly from my own. These words describe situations and experiences that are not my own and may never be: they are descriptions of the experiences of older women.

Feminism has become a loaded word. Its media-perpetrated image of shrill, humourless, man-hating women with hairy legs is a real turn-off for young women who are involved in the process of seeking and developing their own identity. Given this image of feminism and feminists, who would want to become one?

Young feminists are also criticized for our lack of experience, so that even if we did label ourselves as feminists, we would be denied membership (i.e., validation of our experiences) on the basis of our age. "Young women haven't been through enough yet to appreciate the women's movement. When they hit thirty-five or so, feminism isn't such a bad word any more" (Corelli, 1987:44). Is it possible for a young woman to be a feminist given the definition of feminism used by older feminists and the media? The many types of feminism make it difficult for me to define myself. Where do I fit? If I do reject the media's misperception of feminism and I am rejected by older feminists, where does my reality fit in? Young women must persist to find their place in feminism.

Older feminists (approximately thirty-five years and older) were involved in a creative process, questioning their society and laying a foundation for change that has provided them with a bond with one another. And what has followed is an explosion in feminist literature over the last thirty years. Older feminists created a new way of looking at society, and they created a language to describe themselves and their society. The vocabulary was derived from their common experiences with such things as blatant sexism and discrimination and their common knowledge base, due to the limited number of feminist books published in the sixties.

Feminism has made women more visible than they were in the past and has given them a language of their own to describe their experiences. So what are the results of this increased visibility and new language? If we look at adolescent girls and young adult women, we find that feminism has contributed to their life experiences, sometimes in very unexpected ways. My generation and the one behind mine can attest to the fact that feminism is alive and doing well but that it could use a little help.

Adolescent Girls: Romance or Reality?

Adolescent girls are sometimes criticized for being romantics, without ever understanding how they have come to be regarded this way or if their perceptions are really romantic. In the Canadian Advisory Council on the Status of Women publication *What Will Tomorrow Bring? A Study of the Aspirations of Adolescent Women*, Maureen Baker (1985:113) comments of adolescent girls, "We have seen that their lack of awareness of potential barriers to accomplishing their goals and of opportunities available to them has led to some very romanticized ideas about the future." However, there are some important factors that contribute to this romantic view which may, in the life experiences of these young women, be more real than romantic.

My generation has a number of advantages. We have access to

birth control for purposes other than regulating our menstrual cycles, and thus to a reproductive freedom that was not available to the generations before us. Feminism has certainly contributed to creating alternatives for young women, both career and personal, that were not available to generations before ours. Women are more visible in the public sphere, making contributions in sports, politics, law and business. For example, the leader of the New Democratic Party and two of Canada's Supreme Court judges are women. We see women on the television news as reporters and anchors, and the portrayal of women in television programs is often positive. Women have increased their numbers as both students and academics in universities. We have become an area of study; students can earn a degree in women's studies. There are bookstores whose shelves are filled with books written by, about and for women. Young women are inspired by this visibility, and yet we take it for granted; it is normal to us. A superficial look at the world reveals that women have indeed come a long way. Given women's high visibility, why would we think any differently? Young women have reaped some incredible rewards from the feminist movement, which have become part of our acculturation.

With the removal of unacceptable and problematic materials from the curriculum and the emergence of textbooks utilizing nonsexist language, as well as women's higher visibility in the public sphere, came the picture of a world in which minority groups and women are portrayed in a variety of roles and which ultimately gives the impression "that discrimination is no longer a problem" (Neitz, 1985:347). The curriculum, for example, serves to perpetuate the misconception that women have progressed to the point of being equal with men, and that it is possible to combine career and family goals easily. While this does seem rather romantic to those of us who have experienced the discrimination and sexism that operate on all levels of our society, it is this perception of the successes of feminism that has been portrayed to adolescent girls. This is the reality that they relate to in the creation of their self-identity.

If older women have had a limited number of alternatives, feminism has opened a range of options for young women. Some are unable and unwilling to explore these alternatives, while some feel the contradiction between their own realities and the reality created by gender-neutral textbooks that "portray a nonsexist world that does not yet exist" (Neitz, 1985:340). And perhaps it is these very contradictions that lead adolescents to feminist thinking. A young feminist is someone who sees the contradictions between surface and deep realities.

Equipped with this realistic/romantic view, many adolescent girls will emerge from their gender-neutral high schools into a world that offers many experiences which vary significantly. Depending on factors such as class, ethnicity, race, socio-economic background, the relationship with their parents (specifically their mothers) and their own self-reflections, these experiences may determine whether or not they come to embrace a feminist agenda.

Second-generation feminists want to take feminism somewhere, into more places where sexism and racism hide, and into the institutions of our society that pay lip service to women without really addressing the issues. We have life experiences that enable us to take on this task. Some of our experiences are quite different from those of older feminists — which is to be expected, as it is almost thirty years since the resurgence of the women's movement in the sixties. Times have changed, but our experiences deserve recognition and validation just the same.

Bridging the Gap: Somewhere Between the Surface and the Deep

A popular metaphor used by feminists is that of diving deep and surfacing. Many young women are involved in the process of leaving the surface reality in order to dive into the underlying reality that they know exists. At this level, we engage in the same sort of questioning process that older feminists did (and do): Why are we discriminated against? How can I change the structures of patriarchy affecting my generation?

Many older feminists seem to have dived deep and not resurfaced. What they see from this perspective are those young women comfortably situated at the surface level. These women should not be so harshly criticized; older feminists made this level comfortable, so why should young women move beyond it? But second-generation feminists have also been diving deep, unrecognized by older feminists, in an attempt to understand society's contradictions. Older feminists do not talk to us; they talk about us. So we return to the surface. We are trying to create a language that describes and validates our own experiences and that could possibly bridge the generation gap that clearly exists. When this is done, maybe we can talk with one another without alienation.

What makes a young feminist? Perhaps it is the ability to see the contradictions between the reality presented to us in our adolescence and the reality that greets us when we become women. Perhaps, as one young feminist suggested, "All little girls are born feminists:

self-identified, curious, strong. They just get tampered with along the way" (Brodsky, 1990:99).

Younger feminists are a new breed. We look different from older feminists and we speak a different language. As we dive, we are dressed in lightweight scuba-diving suits that give us the mobility to dart around, back and forth between the surface and the deep. Young feminists dive deep as individuals. Our experience has not made it necessary to travel in groups. We do not share the same sorts of bonds with one another as older feminists do. Older feminists, wearing the more cumbersome diving suits with hoses that link them to each other and to the "breathing apparatus" they share (i.e., their common knowledge base), have less mobility. The weight of their suits keeps them at the bottom, in the deeper reality.

Because older feminists are looking for younger women who look, talk and behave like themselves, they do not recognize young feminists. For older feminists, the experience of being a token woman in academia or in a profession was very real, but this is rarely the younger feminist's experience. For example, while women make up the majority in most of my classes, older feminists are unable to relate to this. They ask younger feminists, "Don't you see how precious that is?" Younger feminists can only respond that we have never experienced anything different.

Young feminists are talking openly about date rape and family violence, issues that previously were never addressed. Their discussions of these issues give them a visibility that yields the illusion of things being worse than they used to be. We see the contradictions between what we aspire to and expect to achieve and the limitations that society has placed on women and maintains through patriarchy. We dive deep, exploring the reality that we have come to recognize exists below the surface.

Younger feminists need to move beyond recognizing the contradictions of their society to developing the ability to act on these contradictions. Older feminists can help. They have links with one another and share a history that has nurtured these links. They can help us learn their history so that we may appreciate their efforts and develop our own links among ourselves. An appreciation of our history is vital to all women who seek to improve women's status. More recent history comes from talk/discourse, but older and younger feminists are not talking with each other. The generation gap is a barrier between us that must be overcome.

Younger feminists' experiences are primarily lived in the surface reality. For many older feminists, this is problematic because they do not recognize the surface reality as real. The surface reality is perceived by older feminists, sitting at the deeper reality, as "romantic." As a result, older feminists invalidate the experiences of younger feminists. They do not recognize the similarities that older and younger feminists share. For example, women's studies as an academic discipline has been regarded by some as controversial. As a women's studies student I have been regarded as a curiosity by other students; they do not fully understand why I would want to study women or why women should be studied. Both in and out of the classroom, I have been called upon to represent feminists, and the experience of tokenism did not feel good.

As a younger feminist, I am asking older feminists to share nonjudgmentally their recent history with us. I agree that there are numerous differences between us. Some of these differences will never be overcome, but we have to appreciate and understand them. Just because younger feminists look and behave differently from older feminists does not mean that we are any less committed to the feminist movement. Older feminists must also avoid blaming younger women who do not see the contradictions that exist beneath the surface reality. We must develop tolerance and respect for one another. In return, young feminists can share our history, our experiences of life on the surface, with older feminists. And perhaps we can meet at some place between the surface and deeper realities where we can come to an understanding and appreciation of one another and take feminism one step further. Together.

References

Alberta Education. *Teacher Reference Manual for Learning Resources Identified as "Unacceptable" or "Problematic" during the Curriculum Audit for Tolerance and Understanding*. Edmonton: Alberta Curriculum Branch, April 1985.

Baker, M. *What Will Tomorrow Bring? A Study of the Aspirations of Adolescent Women*. Ottawa: Canadian Advisory Council on the Status of Women, 1985.

Brodsky, M. "Journeys in Our Lives: Learning Feminism." *NWSA Journal* 2 (Winter 1990): 79–100.

Corelli, R. "What Women Want Now." *Maclean's*, 16 November 1987: 42–44.

Kostash, M. *No Kidding*. Toronto: McClelland and Stewart, 1989.

Neitz, M.J. "Resistance to Feminist Analysis." *Teaching Sociology* 12, no. 3 (April 1985): 339–353.

Les femmes et leur carrière : quelques résultats d'une recherche auprès de travailleuses de la région de Québec[1]

Pauline Fahmy

Recent statistics on the working population and research on women's work lead us to conclude that neither the rate of participation of Canadian women in the labour market nor the levels they reach within it are satisfactory. Women still have to face a large number of structural and psycho-sociological obstacles, which prevent them from fully utilizing their potential. The theoretical framework for this study is psycho-social and makes use of new studies on the psychology of women. The research focusses on some of the elements that mediate the relationship between individuals and their society: the perceptions, aspirations and values of women concerning their professional lives. In-depth interviews were conducted with a limited sample of working women on salary or running their own enterprises. The results presented here concern only the former. Analysis of the data shows that these women feel that the obstacles they encounter in their professional lives are related to workplace organization and culture, and that at the heart of these obstacles, as at the heart of their aspirations and values, lies a desire for more decision-making power, a serious questioning of the predominant model for exercising power over individuals, and a desire to build and preserve an adequate balance between their personal and professional lives.

Les statistiques sur la population active et les recherches sur le travail des femmes nous apprennent que ni le taux actuel de participation de celles-ci au marché du travail, ni les niveaux auxquels elles accèdent, ne peuvent être considérés comme satisfaisants. Les femmes se heurtent encore à des obstacles d'ordre à la fois structurel et psychosocial, qui entravent la pleine utilisation de leur potentiel, et qu'il importe, par conséquent, de bien comprendre. Notre approche de la question se situe dans le nouveau cadre théorique de la psychologie des femmes. Elle est aussi résolument psychosociale, dans la mesure où nous avons consacré notre recherche à l'étude d'un certain nombre d'éléments qui médiatisent le rapport individu-société, en l'occurrence : les représentations, les aspirations et les valeurs des femmes relatives à la vie professionnelle. À cet effet, nous avons procédé à des entrevues en profondeur auprès d'un échantillon limité de travailleuses, comprenant à la fois des salariées et des entrepreneures. Les résultats présentés ici concernent uniquement les salariées. Il ressort de notre analyse, qu'aux yeux de ces femmes, une part importante des contraintes et obstacles qui jalonnent leur vie professionnelle est liée à la culture et à l'organisation du monde du travail, et qu'au centre de ces obstacles, tout comme au centre de leurs aspirations et de leurs valeurs, se trouvent le désir d'obtenir plus de pouvoir décisionnel, la remise en question du modèle dominant d'exercice du pouvoir sur les individus, et la construction et le maintien d'un équilibre entre la vie professionnelle et la vie personnelle.

Les femmes, au Canada, participent en nombre grandissant au marché du travail. Les données de Statistique Canada nous apprennent qu'en 1990, le pourcentage de Québécoises qui font partie de la population active est de 55,5 — comparativement à 47,5% en 1981, 35,1% en 1971 et 25,0% en 1951. Selon Travail Canada, il s'agit là d'un phénomène commun à plusieurs pays occidentaux, et destiné à prendre encore plus d'ampleur dans les prochaines années. Toutefois, et en dépit de cette progression sur le plan quantitatif, la situation des femmes sur le marché du travail continue, à l'examen, de se révéler des plus insatisfaisantes. Elle se caractérise par le regroupement des participantes dans quelques « ghettos » d'emplois (vente, services, travail de bureau) (Armstrong et Armstrong, 1983, 1984; CSF, 1978). Les occupations dans lesquelles elles sont cantonnées (secrétaires, serveuses, caissières, vendeuses) sont sous-payées et rapidement plafonnées (David, 1986 ; Descarries-Bélanger, 1980 ; England, 1985). Enfin, les femmes ne se retrouvent que très rarement à des postes de prises de décisions (Travail Canada, 1982). Bref, elles n'ont pas ce qu'il est convenu d'appeler une carrière, mais de simples emplois.

De plus, même lorsqu'on examine la tranche d'âge dont le taux de participation est le plus élevé — c'est-à-dire celle des femmes âgées de 25 à 44 ans — on constate que 30% d'entre elles ne font pas partie de la population active, alors que pour les hommes le taux correspondant est de moins de 8% (Paquette, 1989). Or, même dans le schéma traditionnel de la répartition des rôles, on s'attend à ce qu'une jeune femme occupe un emploi rémunéré tant qu'elle est célibataire, ou sans enfant. Il est donc permis de penser que ces femmes ont été un jour sur le marché du travail et qu'elles s'en sont retirées.

Ces phénomènes, que nous venons de décrire, de l'abandon de la vie professionnelle et de l'absence de perspective de carrière, ont été étudiés sous l'angle de l'absence d'aspirations manifestes à la carrière chez les adolescentes, et sous celui du conflit de rôle. Ils ont aussi été étudiés sous l'angle de la socialisation première ainsi que de la socialisation qui s'exerce tout au long de la vie par les media et par les attentes stéréotypées de la part des « autruis significatifs» — conjoints, conseillers, etc. (Bardwick et Douvan, 1971 ; Bourbonnais, 1985 ; Crealock, 1979 ; Fahmy, 1980, 1982 ; Herman et Gyllstrom, 1977 ; Kergoat, 1984 ; Leith et Fitzsimmons, 1978 ; Long-Laws, 1978 ; Richardson, 1981 ; St-Onge, 1983). Ont été finalement soulignés, en rapport avec cette question des aspirations des femmes à la carrière, les points suivants:

- les difficultés, sinon l'impossibilité, d'accès à un certain nombre d'occupations réservées aux hommes, sans oublier bien sûr la minceur, sinon l'inexistence, des possibilités d'avancement dans certaines occupations ;

- les stéréotypes et préjugés qui marquent les attitudes des employeurs et des collègues masculins à leur égard, ainsi que les jugements stéréotypés relatifs à leurs compétences de la part des personnes susceptibles d'y avoir recours ;

- la peur du succès ou plus précisément la peur du rejet et des sanctions sociales ;

- l'absence de modèles identitiels féminins dans des occupations investies massivement par les hommes ainsi que la difficulté d'y affirmer des valeurs et une identité vécues comme « féminines » (Chanlat, 1988 ; Fahmy, 1980 ; Huppert-Laufer, 1982 ; Plasse et Simard, 1989 ; Simard et Tarrab, 1986).

Ces obstacles se combinent évidemment à ceux liés à la structure et à la gestion de l'emploi ainsi qu'aux lacunes dans l'infrastructure des services collectifs.

Il importante de noter ici qu'il s'agit d'obstacles auxquels sont exposées toutes les femmes dans notre société, à des degrés divers bien sûr, compte tenu des autres déterminismes qui influencent la mobilité sociale par le travail. Cependant, que cela tienne aux caractéristiques psychologiques des personnes en cause ou à des variables de leur environnement social, force est de constater que ces obstacles n'empêchent pas un certain nombre de femmes d'inscrire leur engagement professionnel dans la perspective d'une progression dans une carrière.

Mais, est-il nécessaire de le rappeler ? Le fait d'envisager son activité professsionnelle sous l'aspect d'une carrière à poursuivre, ne signifie pas que l'on puisse forcément réussir sa carrière. On peut en être partiellement ou totalement empêchée, et ceci malgré le désir qu'on en a, les compétences que l'on possède et les démarches qu'on entreprend. Il n'y a certes pas à s'en étonner, compte tenu de la structure de l'emploi. Les obstacles à la progression, inhérents à cette structure, peuvent cependant amener les personnes qui s'y heurtent à se désengager, c'est-à-dire à adapter leurs aspirations à leur estimation de leurs chances de les voir se réaliser (Long-Laws, 1976). Kanter (1977) affirme que ce genre d'évaluation, et le désengagement qui en résulte, sont plus souvent le fait des femmes que des hommes dans les organisations. Herman et Gyllstrom (1977) estiment, pour leur part, que les femmes qui se résignent ainsi à réduire leurs aspirations n'en sont pas pour autant satisfaites.

Il arrive aussi que les aspirations à progresser ne débouchent pas sur des démarches destinées à les réaliser, ce qui amène facilement à conclure à l'absence d'aspiration à la progression dans la carrière. Cette interprétation me paraît suspecte sur le plan politique — parce qu'elle sert trop bien à maintenir le statu quo quant aux places respectives des femmes et des hommes dans la société — et inacceptable sur le plan théorique parce qu'elle ignore le lien qui unit les aspirations aux représentations que les individus ont d'eux-mêmes et de la société y compris les obstacles, les contraintes et les possibilités qu'ils y décèlent. Que ces obstacles soient considérés comme insurmontables ou engageant des actions incompatibles avec des éléments-clés de l'image de soi (e.g. des valeurs centrales) et l'aspiration ne pourra émerger ; elle restera latente (Fahmy, 1980 ; Long-Laws, 1976 ; Veress et Veress, 1972). Par contre, une aspiration manifeste, ressentie avec force et partagée par un grand nombre de personnes capables de s'organiser en vue de l'action, peut déboucher sur la revendication — et ceci même si ces personnes ne représentent qu'une minorité (Moscovici, 1979).

Mon approche de la question s'appuie aussi sur un certain nombre d'autres éléments théoriques et empiriques qui vont tous dans le sens d'une critique du modèle de développement masculin comme référent pour le développement des femmes. En effet, les remarques de certains conseillers œuvrant auprès des femmes (Baron, 1985) ainsi que les études sur des femmes engagées dans des sphères d'activités aussi diverses que le travail ouvrier (Armstrong et Armstrong, 1983), l'enseignement primaire (Goulet, 1982) ou la direction d'entreprise (Aubert, 1982 ; Grisé et Lee-Gosselin, 1987, 1988 ; Laufer, 1984) semblent indiquer qu'elles ne veulent pas d'une réussite

« à tout prix » : elles refusent le développement unidimensionnel qu'entraîne une proportion excessive du temps quotidien dévolu au travail, le modèle dominant (et masculin) d'exercice du pouvoir, la compétition agressive et l'identification à l'entreprise.

Enfin des recherches entreprises au Canada auprès de femmes cadres insistent sur le fait qu'on ne peut étudier la carrière de celles-ci sans tenir compte des exigences et des contraintes qu'elles ont, en relation avec leur vie personnelle et domestique (Andrew ; Andrew, Coderre, Daviau et Denis, 1988 ; Denis 1987) ainsi que sur la pluralité des modes d'intégration des intérêts, valeurs et compétences qu'elles investissent dans leur vie professionnelle et personnelle.

De leur côté, les nouvelles théoriciennes du développement (Gilligan, 1986 ; Roberts, 1985 ; Ryff et Mygdal, 1984) insistent sur la nécessité d'étudier le développement des femmes dans sa spécificité et non — ainsi qu'on l'a trop souvent fait — à travers des généralisations tirées de l'étude du développement des garçons. Gilligan estime que les filles et les garçons se développent selon des modèles différents et qu'il est vain de prétendre à la supériorité absolue de l'un par à rapport à l'autre. Chacun des deux modèles obéit à sa propre logique et comporte ses limites spécifiques en terme d'adaptation sociale. Mais il n'y a aucune rigidité ou aucun surdéterminisme attachés à ces développements spécifiques, puisque des valeurs, des attitudes et des comportements nouveaux peuvent être appris en cours de socialisation. Il n'en demeure pas moins, qu'en dépit des grandes variations entre les individus de même genre, Gilligan constate globalement des différences psychologiques entre les hommes et les femmes. Différences qui font que les femmes, en général, valorisent, comme fondement de leur action, l'empathie, l'inclusion, l'intégration des divers éléments du vécu, la prise en compte du concret, du particulier, la prise de décision consensuelle, alors que les hommes ne répugnent pas à l'exclusion et valorisent la non-prise en compte du particulier, du concret (au bénéfice du principe abstrait), la compétition, la décision majoritaire, et la séparation des divers éléments du vécu. Ainsi donc, les hommes se trouvent à développer des caractéristiques qui collent au modèle dominant du pouvoir dans le monde du travail, ce qui n'a en fait rien d'étonnant, ce modèle ayant été forgé par et pour des hommes.

Mais, comme le rappelle Gilligan, différence ne veut pas dire inégalité. Il n'empêche que dans la pratique, la dominance du modèle masculin marginalise les femmes, les place dans une position désavantagée. Il importe, par conséquent, de se pencher sur les critiques que les femmes adressent à ce modèle, sur la façon différente dont elles désireraient exercer le pouvoir dans le travail ainsi que sur leurs conceptions de la réussite professionnelle, dans ses rapports avec la réussite dans d'autres domaines de l'existence. Il ne s'agit plus ici de simple conflit de rôle mais de l'expression ou de l'aliénation de son identité. Une telle démarche s'impose parce qu'elle permettrait une meilleure compréhension des obstacles qui interfèrent avec une pleine participation des femmes au marché du travail.

C'est dans cet esprit qu'a été entreprise la recherche dont je me propose d'exposer ici certains résultats. Cette recherche avait pour principal objectif l'étude et la compréhension des éléments d'ordre psychosocial qui médiatisent le rapport des femmes au marché du travail. Plus précisément, nous nous sommes attachées à faire ressortir :

- les représentations d'un échantillon réduit de femmes de la population active, âgées entre 30 et 40 ans, des obstacles et contraintes qui entravent leur progression dans leur carrière;
- leurs aspirations et leurs valeurs relatives à la progression dans la carrière, ainsi que leur définition de la réussite de la vie professionnelle.

Je me propose de présenter ici quelques unes des réponses que nous avons obtenues aux questions que nous leur avons posées sur ces thèmes. Mais avant d'aller plus loin, il me faut fournir quelques informations sur l'échantillon et sur la méthodologie que nous avons utilisée.

Échantillon et méthodologie

Nous avons interviewé en tout 55 femmes âgées entre 30 et 40 ans, toutes francophones résidant dans l'agglomération urbaine de Québec. De ces femmes, 47 étaient des salariées et 8 des propriéraires dirigeantes d'entreprises. Parmi les salariées, 37 étaient à l'emploi et 10 en chômage. Ces sujets salariées se répartissaient également en trois grandes catégories socioprofessionnelles, obtenues par le regroupement des catégories de l'échelle de Blishen (1965) en trois niveaux : supérieur, moyen et inférieur. Sauf pour de très rares exceptions, nous avons composé notre échantillon par tirage au hasard dans les listes électorales de l'agglomération urbaine de Québec, en respectant toutefois la représentation en proportions égales des trois catégories sociales. Pour le repérage des femmes en chômage, nous avons eu recours à l'affichage dans les centres d'emploi. Sans prétendre obtenir ainsi un échantillon représentatif, nous voulions, en nous astreignant à cette méthode de constitution de notre échantillon, éviter le plus de biais possibles et obtenir l'éventail de réponses le plus large possible pour la construction du questionnaire de la prochaine étape.

La cueillette des données s'est faite au moyen d'entrevues en profondeur, réalisées à l'aide d'un guide d'entrevue de type semi-directif. Un court questionnaire, destiné à recueillir des précisions supplémentaires relatives aux conditions objectives de vie, a été administré à la suite de chaque entrevue.

Les entrevues, de trois heures environ chacune, ont été enregistrées et retranscrites intégralement, par la suite, en vue de leur analyse.

Cette analyse essentiellement qualitative a été accompagnée d'un traitement quantitatif des données destiné à nous fournir un portrait d'ensemble des répondantes et à repérer d'éventuelles relations significatives entre les principales variables. C'est le portrait d'ensemble des travailleuses salariées que je veux présenter ici, et dont je me propose de commenter les principales caractéristiques.

Résultats

1. Le statut de l'emloi actuel ou, dans le cas des sujets en chômage, du dernier emploi occupé :

- 35 emplois permanents dont 33 à temps plein et 2 à temps partiel ;
- 12 emplois temporaires.

2. Secteur de travail :

- 44,7% de ces emplois sont dans le secteur public (et para-public) et 55,3% dans le secteur privé.

3. L'évaluation que font les sujets de leurs conditions actuelles de travail ou, dans le cas des chômeuses, du dernier emploi occupé :

Il est à noter que les thèmes du salaire, des avantages sociaux, du pouvoir décisionnel (c'est-à-dire la possibilité de participer aux décisions qui se prennent et qui affectent les orientations ou l'organisation du travail dans l'entreprise) du pouvoir d'autonomie (celui d'organiser son propre travail, d'y avoir une certaine marge de manœuvre, d'initiative) de l'augmentation des compétences et celui de la possibilité d'utiliser les compétences accrues sont abordés par la quasi totalité des sujets. De plus, si l'on excepte la question des avantages sociaux et celle de l'autonomie, la très grande majorité des répondantes (les taux varient entre 60,9% et 87,8%) trouvent ces aspects de leurs conditions de travail à peine acceptables ou carrément insatisfaisants. Or, il s'agit là de dimensions que l'on prétend souvent être secondaires aux yeux des femmes, du moins si l'on en croit le cliché qui veut qu'elles travaillent pour un salaire d'appoint et sont peu intéressées par le pouvoir ou la progression dans la carrière. Bien sûr, elles se montrent aussi très intéressées par la question des relations interpersonnelles : relations avec les patrons, avec les collègues et, le cas échéant, avec le public (les usagers et usagères de leurs services). Le souci qu'elles en ont correspond bien aux intérêts que l'on s'accorde à reconnaître aux femmes. Cependant, ce thème des relations interpersonnelles, même s'il est persistant, ne revient pas plus souvent dans leurs propos que les thèmes du salaire et des avantages sociaux ou celui du pouvoir décisionnel ou encore celui de l'augmentation des compétences (ou de l'acquisition de connaissances nouvelles) et ceci tant dans leur évaluation de leur progression dans leur carrière que dans les aspirations concernant cette progression ou encore dans leur définition de la réussite de la vie professionnelle.

4. Les représentations relatives à leurs perspectives actuelles de progression dans leur carrière :

Nous leur avons demandé d'abord de nous parler de leur progression dans leur carrière jusqu'à aujourd'hui. L'analyse de leurs réponses à cette question donne les résultats suivants : 37,0% des sujets parlent de leur carrière en termes de stagnation, sinon de regression, ou bien estiment qu'elle a été tellement morcelée qu'elles ne peuvent pas y déceler une quelconque progression ; 63,0% estiment qu'elles ont progressé. Cependant, l'analyse nous révèle qu'en fait, 41,3% des sujets décrivent une progression uniquement « horizontale » (un bon nombre d'entre elles la qualifient ainsi elles-mêmes) ; elles ont acquis des connaissances ou des compétences nouvelles — sans la possibilité de les faire reconnaître par leur employeur et encore moins de faire traduire cette reconnaissance par une amélioration de leur statut ou de leur salaire — ou bien encore elles ont obtenu des emplois plus en accord avec leurs goûts et intérêts. Seulement 21,7% des sujets estiment qu'elles ont connu une quelconque progression verticale.

Quant à leurs perspectives actuelles de progression, voici comment les évaluent celles qui en parlent:

TABLEAU 1
LES PERSPECTIVES ACTUELLES DE
PROGRESSION DANS LA CARRIÈRE

Perspectives	Bonnes ou très bonnes (%)	Faibles ou mauvaises (%)
globale (89,4%)[2]	11,9	88,9
amélioration du salaire et autres avantages matériels (74,5%)	17,2	82,8
amélioration du pouvoir décisionnel (72,3%)	14,7	85,3
augmentation des compétences ou des connaissances (91,5%)	30,2	69,8
utilisation des compétences accrues (74,5%)	22,9	77,1

Les chiffres placés entre parenthèses dans certains tableaux renseignent sur les pourcentages de répondantes qui ont abordé tel ou tel thème sous l'angle présenté dans l'analyse.

Ainsi qu'on peut le constater, la très grande majorité des répondantes abordent la question de leurs perspectives de progression dans leur carrière sous l'angle du salaire, du pouvoir décisionnel, de l'augmentation des compétences ou de l'acquisition de connaissances, et de l'utilisation des compétences accrues. Et parmi elles, une très grande majorité estiment que ces perspectives sont « faibles » ou bien encore carrément « mauvaises ». Les résultats exposés au tableau 1 sont, à cet égard, fort éloquents. Ils le deviennent encore plus lorsqu'on raffine l'analyse pour tenir compte des divers niveaux d'insatisfaction. On constate alors qu'en ce qui concerne les perspectives relatives à l'augmentation de leur pouvoir décisionnel, le pourcentage de celles qui les qualifient de « très mauvaises », sinon « nulles », se monte à 70.6, et qu'en ce qui concerne l'utilisation des compétences accrues, le pourcentage des répondantes « très insatisfaites » est de 62,9. La question de leurs aspirations relatives à la progression dans leur carrière n'en devient que plus importante.

5. Les principales aspirations relatives à la progression dans la carrière :

Une fois de plus, on voit apparaître dans des proportions très importantes les thèmes de l'amélioration du salaire et avantages sociaux (83% des sujets), du pouvoir décisionnel (89,4% des sujets) et de l'augmentation des compétences ou des connaissances (89,4% des sujets). L'aspiration à occuper un emploi plus en accord avec ses goûts et intérêts revient dans le discours de plus de 89% des salariées interviewées. Finalement, 80,9% d'entre elles disent aspirer à plus d'autonomie dans l'exercice de leurs fonctions, ce qui ne laisse pas d'étonner étant donné le pourcentage élevé de celles qui s'étaient déclarées satisfaites des conditions qui leurs étaient faites, à cet égard, dans leur travail. On a l'impression, à la lecture de leurs réponses, que nombreuses sont celles qui estiment qu'elles ne pourront jamais avoir assez d'autonomie.

Un autre résultat a suscité aussi notre étonnement, c'est le pourcentage relativement élevé de répondantes qui aspirent à devenir entrepreneures (près du tiers des sujets). Nous devons toutefois préciser qu'un bon nombre de ces aspirantes à l'entreprenariat sont des femmes en chômage ou qui connaissent depuis des années des conditions précaires d'emploi. Fonder sa propre entreprise semble être devenu un mot d'ordre fort populaire ces dernières années, en réponse au chômage. C'est une réponse qui permet d'échapper à la démoralisation et au sentiment d'impuissance qu'induit la multiplication des recherches infructueuses d'emploi.

6. Les représentations des obstacles à la progression dans la carrière :

Les obstacles d'ordre structurel sont mis en cause par 42,6% des sujets. Ils sont évoqués, comme on peut s'en douter, par les répondantes coincées dans des types d'emplois qui n'offrent que des possibilités dérisoires de progression. L'emploi de secrétaire est, à cet égard, exemplaire, et les propos que tiennent là-dessus les répondantes sont d'une exceptionnelle amertume : « C'est comme si tu avais le mot secrétaire tatoué sur le front, tu ne peux pas t'en sortir » ; « Tu peux suivre des cours, obtenir des tas de crédits, ça sert à rien » ; « Parfois, ils le savent bien que ce n'est pas du travail de secrétaire que tu fais, ah ! ton patron te le répète assez souvent que tu es son adjoint, son bras droit, mais ça reste là, tu restes une secrétaire et "rien qu'une secrétaire" ». D'autres se révoltent contre l'emploi même du mot carrière dans leur cas. Non point parce qu'elles n'ont pas des aspirations à cet égard mais parce que leurs conditions de travail ne s'accordent pas à l'idée qu'elles se font d'une carrière : « J'appelle pas ça une carrière, moi ! » Et ceci, en dépit de la définition très « prosaïque » que nous avons pris soin de donner de ce terme.

Quant aux obstacles liés à la culture et aux modes de gestion (cités respectivement par 31,6% et 68,4% des sujets) ils renvoient, pour les premiers, à des attitudes et valeurs qu'elles estiment inacceptables notamment : la compétition agressive, le mépris à l'égard des personnes, l'individualisme, l'obséquiosité ou l'allégeance inconditionnelle et, pour les secondes, à des pratiques qu'elles jugent tout aussi inacceptables ou nocives, telles que le favoritisme, la supervision incompétente ou tatillonne des subordonnées et subordonnés, l'utilisation inadéquate des ressources, le manque d'encouragement — sinon le découragement — de l'esprit d'initiative, etc.

Les obstacles liés à l'organisation du travail (cités par 53,2% des sujets) sont de plusieurs ordres : exigences abusives ou injustifiées de présence, exigences excessives de mobilité ou de disponibilité, horaires rigides, programmes de recyclage ou de formation insuffisants ou inadéquats, quand ils ne sont pas simplement inexistants, etc.

Les responsabilités domestiques qui font obstacle à la progression dans la carrière sont abordées (par 68,1% des sujets) avec beaucoup d'ambivalence. Les sujets hésitent à les traiter d'«obstacles», car ils représentent à leurs yeux de dimensions valorisées de leur existence et le terme « obstacle » leur semble être un vocable par trop négatif pour être associé sans problème à des personnes qui leur sont chères (conjoints mais surtout enfants) et auxquelles elles ont choisi d'accorder une place importante dans leur vie. Par contre, elles ne peuvent s'empêcher de reconnaître que ces responsabilités constituent « objectivement » des obstacles à leur carrière. Les tâches d'entretien ménager échappent à cette ambivalence et sont simplement reconnues comme un des obstacles qui affectent la quantité de temps ou d'énergie disponible pour le travail ou le perfectionnement professionnel.

En ce qui concerne le sexisme, il est le plus souvent nommé comme tel ou alors ce sont simplement les pratiques qui le révèlent qui sont décrites et dénoncées (par 55,3% des sujets).

Finalement, nous avons demandé aux sujets de nous faire part de leurs craintes — si elles en avaient — relatives à une éventuelle réalisation de leurs aspirations concernant la progression dans leur carrière. Certaines nous ont fait part de ces craintes sans que nous ayons à les solliciter. Elles sont de deux ordres : 44,7% ont exprimé des craintes se rapportant à leurs relations avec les autres (se retrouver seule, sans amis ou amies ; avoir à affronter la résistance ou les critiques du conjoint, des enfants ou de la parenté ; être incapables de se libérer d'une responsabilité assumée à l'égard d'une personne dépendante) et 70,2% disent craindre l'épuisement physique ou psychologique.

L'examen des moyens qu'elles utilisent ou comptent utiliser pour surmonter les obstacles auxquels elles font face vient confirmer, ainsi qu'on pourra le constater, le bien-fondé de ces craintes.

7. Les moyens utilisés pour surmonter les obstacles :

Comme on a pu le voir, la liste des obstacles évoqués par les travailleuses interviewées est longue. Ce qu'elles mettent en cause dans leurs propos ce sont, le plus souvent, des caractéristiques de leur milieu de travail et de leur univers familial, parfois aussi, mais dans l'ensemble moins fréquemment, leurs propres insuffisances. On s'attendrait, par conséquent, à ce que les moyens qu'elles mettent en œuvre pour surmonter ces obstacles visent, dans les mêmes proportions, à transformer des aspects de leur milieu de travail, de leur milieu familial ou d'elles-mêmes. Nous leur avons demandé de nous décrire les moyens qu'elles utilisent pour faire face aux divers obstacles dont elles nous avaient parlé, mais sans en rappeler la liste ni la nature. L'analyse de leurs réponses à cette demande et des informations qu'elles ont fournies spontanément sur ce sujet nous a réservé des surprises. Elle a permis de faire ressortir les catégories d'action décrites dans les paragraphes qui suivent, mais surtout elle a permis de constater que, parmi ces catégories, il y en a une dont la popularité surpasse de loin celle des autres. C'est par elle que nous commençons la présentation de l'analyse des moyens auxquels ont les sujets disent recourir.

a) L'action sur soi (91,5%)
Les résultats de l'analyse nous montrent que la cible privilégiée des actions entreprises par les travailleuses pour surmonter les obstacles de diverses natures auxquels elles se heurtent, c'est leur propre personne. Presque toutes les salariées (91,5%) interviewées sont engagées dans une forme ou une autre (quand ce n'est pas plusieurs à la fois) de perfectionnement d'elles-mêmes. Ceci est d'autant plus remarquable qu'elles sont beaucoup moins nombreuses à estimer qu'une part des problèmes qu'elles cherchent ainsi à résoudre sont liés à des déficiences chez elles.

Tout se passe comme si les autres instances identifiées comme sources d'obstacles à leur progression dans leur carrière constituaient à leurs yeux des cibles trop difficiles, voire même impossibles, à atteindre et qu'elles en étaient ainsi amenées à détourner d'elles leur énergie et leurs efforts pour les concentrer sur la cible la plus à leur portée : leur personne.

b) L'action sur le milieu de travail (40,4%)
La comparaison des pourcentages respectifs de sujets qui se sont dites aux prises avec des obstacles liés à leur milieu de travail ou à leur milieu familial, avec ceux des sujets qui cherchent à agir sur ces

mêmes milieux pour y induire des changements, vient appuyer l'hypothèse que nous venons d'avancer.

L'action sur le milieu du travail prend parfois une forme collective ; celle de la lutte syndicale, par exemple. Dans certains cas, cependant — lorsque les efforts de négociation collective ou individuelle semblent, pour diverses raisons, inutiles — les salariées se résolvent à signifier leur insatisfaction, au patron, par leurs actes. L'un de ceux-ci, le congé de maladie, comporte aussi le bénéfice secondaire de sortir l'employée pour un temps, tout limité soit-il, de la situation frustrante qu'elle vit au travail. Une salariée, particulièrement désespérée par ses conditions de travail, nous a même avoué que la perspective d'y échapper temporairement avait joué un rôle important dans sa décision d'accepter de subir une opération chirurgicale.

c) L'action sur le milieu familial (23,4%)

Les nombreuses responsabilités domestiques qu'elles ont à assumer ont été identifiées par un fort pourcentage des femmes interviewées (68,1%) comme des obstacles à leur progression dans leur carrière. Le pourcentage de celles qui disent tenter de modifier les choses sur ce plan est beaucoup plus modeste (23,6% de l'ensemble des sujets). Et les moyens qu'elles utilisent se résument à ceci : tenter de convaincre les membres de leur famille de la nécessité, ou du bien-fondé, d'un partage plus équitable du fardeau des tâches domestiques.

Les hypothèses susceptibles d'expliquer ce phénomène ne sauraient être simples. Trop de facteurs entrent ici en cause et s'en tenir à un seul relèverait d'un réductionnisme inacceptable. Aussi désirons-nous insister sur le fait que l'analyse qui va suivre ne constitue qu'une tentative d'explication partielle.

Nous voulons rappeler, pour commencer, les observations dont nous avons fait état plus haut, concernant la difficulté éprouvée par un grand nombre de femmes à parler de leur vie familiale en des termes qui leur semblent négatifs et à admettre, sans hésitation, que leurs responsabilités domestiques entravent leur progression dans leur carrière. Il nous faut maintenant rapporter une autre particularité que révèle l'analyse de leur discours sur ce sujet. Elle consiste en ceci : parmi les travailleuses qui ont un conjoint, beaucoup insistent sur le fait qu'elles ont choisi de combiner travail et famille, sur leur désir de protéger l'équilibre auquel elles tiennent entre ces deux sphères de leur existence et de préserver l'harmonie de leur vie familiale. Leur travail apparaît dans leur discours comme relevant du privilège accordé et non pas d'un droit et d'une nécessité reconnus. Que ceci traduise leurs propres convictions ou exclusivement celles de leur entourage auxquelles elles ne feraient que se plier, l'analyse n'a pas permis d'en décider avec certitude.

Il est compréhensible, dans ces conditions, qu'elles ne se sentent pas pleinement autorisées à exiger des membres de leur famille qu'ils assument avec elles les conséquences de ce qui est désigné comme « leur choix ». Elles semblent aussi se considérer comme les principales, sinon les seules responsables de l'harmonie familiale et de sa préservation et préfèrent, par conséquent, accepter un partage inégal des tâches plutôt que de risquer de mettre en danger cette harmonie.

Et pour pouvoir assumer ce partage inégal sans que leur carrière n'en souffre d'une manière excessive, il ne leur reste plus qu'un moyen : agir sur elles-mêmes. Cela signifie, selon le cas, « s'efforcer » de devenir « plus fortes », « plus organisée », « plus efficace » ; « s'exercer » à se montrer « plus souples », « plus patientes », « plus attentives » ; apprendre la relaxation, l'affirmation de soi, la maîtrise de soi, l'anglais, la comptabilité, l'informatique, le yoga, l'art de parler en public et celui, non pas de se faire, mais de conserver des amis et amies, quand on a très peu de temps à leur consacrer ; puis, par dessus tout, savoir « rester optimistes » et « pratiquer la pensée positive ».

Cette liste, non-exhaustive, des actions de perfectionnement de soi dans lesquelles se lancent les femmes, donne une idée des voies par lesquelles elles s'astreignent à passer pour contourner ou surmonter les obstacles à leur progression dans leur carrière. Certaines en empruntent une ou deux, d'autres s'engagent dans plusieurs à la fois, dépensant une énergie considérable pour se changer elles-mêmes, à défaut de pouvoir changer le milieu qui les opprime.

d) L'action sur la société dans son ensemble (6,4%)
Il y a peu de choses à dire ici de cette forme d'action sauf que, même si elle est utilisée par un nombre très restreint de sujets, elle est coinsidérée comme souhaitable et même désirable par plusieurs. Certaines avouent cependant n'avoir aucun goût pour l'engagement de type politique ou social et même s'en méfier (elles l'associent tantôt à « combines » et « recherche de prestige » et tantôt à « endoctrinement»).

Les raisons fournies spontanément par les autres pour expliquer leur absence d'engagement dans une forme d'action qu'elles jugent souhaitable sont de deux genres : les unes tiennent à elles — à leur lassitude à la fin d'une double journée de travail et à la pénurie chronique de temps dont elles souffrent — les autres relèvent des caractéristiques de l'objet à transformer, lequel semble trop grand, trop résistant et par conséquent trop long à entamer.

e) L'aide offerte par les membres du réseau social
Une des questions qui intéresse un nombre toujours croissant de

chercheuses et de chercheurs est celle de l'aide fournie par les
« mentors » à de jeunes collègues qu'ils ou elles prennent ainsi sous
leur tutelle pour faciliter leur progression. Nous étions intéressées à
savoir si les femmes interviewées bénéficiaient de cette forme de
parrainage ou de marrainage. Nous leur avons, à cette fin, posé la
question suivante : « Y a-t-il des éléments ou des personnes, liés à votre
travail, qui facilitent votre progression dans la carrière? » Les réponses
qu'elles y ont donné nous ont appris que 40,4% des salariées et 37,5%
des entrepreneures de notre échantillon estiment qu'elles bénéficient,
de la part de leur entourage, d'une forme ou d'une autre d'aide.

Cette aide consiste surtout, pour les salariées, en une écoute
sympathique et, à l'occasion, en conseils de la part de leurs amis et
amies ou de membres de leur famille (mère, sœur, enfant, conjoint).
Parfois aussi ce sont les collègues qui fournissent conseils ou
réconfort. Plus rarement, ce même genre de support psychologique
est offert par un patron ou une patronne. Quant au pourcentage de
celles qui obtiennent l'aide d'un ou une mentor pour progresser dans
leur carrière, il est vraiment minime (4,2% des sujets, à peine).

8. Les valeurs et les attitudes considérées comme importantes, ou les
dimensions valorisées par les sujets dans la vie professionnelle :

De façon souvent spontanée, mais aussi en réponse à une question
sur ce sujet, les salariées nous ont fait part de leurs valeurs et des
attitudes qu'elles considèrent comme importantes dans la vie professionnelle. Le tableau qui suit résume les résultats relatifs à ce thème :

TABLEAU 2
LES VALEURS ET ATTITUDES CONSIDÉRÉES COMME
IMPORTANTES DANS LE TRAVAIL

Valeur et attitudes	Fréquences relatives exprimées en %
Le respect pour les personnes	61,7
L'égalité des chances	46,8
L'élimination du sexisme	59,6
La compétence et l'intégrité	91,5
L'efficacité	83,0
L'intérêt porté à la tâche	100,0
Le sentiment d'accomplir une tâche utile (à la société ou à l'entreprise)	72,3
De bonnes relations interpersonnelles	93,6

Presque tous les sujets se sont aussi exprimées spontanément sur la place et la signification du travail dans leur vie. Ce qu'elles en disent présente un intérêt d'autant plus grand que la très grande majorité d'entre elles décrivent leurs conditions de travail en termes plutôt négatifs.

Toutefois, en dépit de leur insatisfaction à l'égard de bon nombres d'aspects de leur vie professionnelle et de leurs perspectives de progression dans leur carrière, 93,6% des salariées perçoivent le travail comme un élément important de leur développement personnel. Les raisons fournies spontanément à cet égard sont les suivantes : le salaire est un facteur indispensable au sentiment d'autonomie personnelle, le travail est le lieu et le moyen de l'intégration sociale, le travail donne la possibilité de mettre en pratique ses compétences et d'acquérir des connaissances ou des compétences nouvelles. Cette importance accordée à l'acquisition de connaissance ou de compétences nous a particulièrement frappée, car non seulement elle revient de façon insistante dans les propos des répondantes quand elles parlent des aspects frustrants de leur travail, des dimensions qu'elles valorisent ou de leurs aspirations, mais on la retrouve aussi, comme nous allons le voir, dans leur définition de la réussite professionnelle.

Mais avant d'en parler, il nous faut compléter cet aperçu des valeurs des sujets par l'analyse des réactions qu'elles ont eues devant l'énoncé des principaux points sur lesquels on considère traditionnellement que peut porter la progression dans la carrière, et de leurs réponses à une question qui leur demandait de parler « des choses avec lesquelles elles étaient en désaccord ou auxquelles elles attachaient de l'importance, de la valeur [s'agissant de leur vie professionnelle ou de leur progression dans la carrière] ». Parmi les dimensions et attitudes mises en cause dans le discours de plus de 50% des sujets, les suivantes nous semblent présenter un intérêt particulier :

TABLEAU 3
LES RÉACTIONS FACE AUX ATTITUDES ET
DIMENSIONS COMMUNÉMENT PRÉSENTES
DANS L'UNIVERS DU TRAVAIL

Attitudes et dimensions relevées	Positions des répondantes exprimées en %	
	acceptation	rejet
La compétition agressive (51,1%)	4,2	95,8
La soumission inconditionnelle à l'autorité (85,1%)	7,5	92,5
L'individualisme (83,0%)	5,1	94,9
L'interdit placé sur les émotions ou sur l'empiétement de la vie privée sur la vie professionnelle (61%)	24,1	75,9
La recherche du pouvoir décisionnel (91,5%)	100,0	0,0
Le pouvoir sur les individus (85,1%)	42,5	57,5

La mise en relation de ces diverses réponses, combinée à une analyse attentive des propos des répondantes sur ces questions, révèle qu'il existe une dimension de la vie professionnelle valorisée unanimement par la quasi totalité des sujets : le pouvoir décisionnel. Par contre, elles rejettent presque tout aussi unanimement la compétition agressive, l'autoritarisme et l'individualisme. Quant à l'exercice ou la recherche du pouvoir sur les individus elles sont plus de la moitié à le rejeter, et cette moitié n'a pas de mots assez forts pour exprimer son rejet. Le pouvoir sur les individus est perçu par elles comme étant un pouvoir essentiellement négatif, destiné à brimer les autres, à les priver de leur autonomie, un pouvoir exercé de façon dictatoriale, ou à tout le moins arbitraire, une force destructrice utilisée par les personnes qui en disposent pour satisfaire leur égo et humilier ou écraser leurs subordonnés et subordonnées.

Et il ne s'agit pas là de conceptions abstraites du pouvoir sur les individus. Les sujets qui nous en parlent décrivent des pratiques dont elles ont fait les frais et des personnes qu'elles ont eu tout le loisir de voir à l'œuvre. Certaines répondantes proposent en contrepoint le portrait d'un patron ou d'une directrice qui exerce le pouvoir sur les individus de façon bénéfique, comme elles aimeraient pouvoir le faire elles-mêmes, mais elles sont persuadées qu'il s'agit d'exceptions qui bénéficient de circonstances extraordinaires et qui, comme toutes les exceptions, confirment la règle. D'autres encore, affirment que les conditions dans lesquelles le pouvoir sur les individus est exercé (conditions qui en font toujours un pouvoir limité par des pouvoirs supérieurs et par une organisation ou une structure du travail contraignante, c'est-à-dire, en fin de compte, un semblant de pouvoir) le rendent fort peu attrayant à leurs yeux, puisqu'il ne réussit surtout qu'à isoler les personnes qui le détiennent des autres, sans leur donner réellement le moyen de contribuer à l'amélioration de leurs conditions de travail.

Cette différence entre les attitudes des répondantes relativement au pouvoir décisionnel, selon qu'il s'exerce ou non sur les individus — et la façon dont il s'exerce — pourrait être un élément important de compréhension de ce qui se présente souvent comme des propos contradictoires des femmes sur la recherche et l'exercice du pouvoir. Ce que rejettent, en fin de compte, les femmes que nous avons interviewées, c'est bien une certaine conception du pouvoir et certains contextes d'exercice du pouvoir et non point le pouvoir lui-même. Bien au contraire, non seulement elles le valorisent mais elles y aspirent et l'incluent dans leur définition de la réussite professionnelle.

9. La définition de la réussite professionnelle ou de la carrière :

Avant de passer à l'exposé des principaux éléments des définitions données par les travailleuses de la réussite de leur vie professionnelle (voir le tableau 4), je voudrais ajouter qu'à travers leurs réponses concernant leurs conditions de travail, les obstacles qui s'opposent à leur progression dans leur carrière ou les aspirations qui s'y rapportent, 97,9% des sujets ont mis en rapport spontanément, et souvent à maintes reprises, les divers secteurs de leur vie pour en préciser l'importance relative. Dans 80,4% des cas, ces sujets ont tenu à préciser qu'elles s'estiment incapables d'accorder une priorité absolue dans leur existence à la vie privée ou à la vie professionnelle, que les deux leur semblent tout aussi indispensables à leur épanouissement, et que ce qu'elles valorisent justement par-dessus tout c'est un juste équilibre entre la vie privée et la vie professionnelle.

TABLEAU 4
LA DÉFINITION DE LA RÉUSSITE PROFESSIONNELLE

Eléments importants de la réussite	Fréquences relatives exprimées en %
L'intérêt pour la tâche (en raison de son contenu ou du sentiment de son utilité)	95,7
L'augmentation des connaissances	83,0
Un bon ou un meilleur salaire	72,3
L'équilibre entre la vie professionnelle et la vie privée	66,0
L'amélioration du statut	63,8
L'obtention de plus de pouvoir décisionnel	55,3

La lecture du tableau qui précède permet de constater, une fois de plus, à quel point l'acquisition de connaissances, le salaire, l'intérêt pour la tâche, le pouvoir décisionnel et la sauvegarde de l'équilibre entre la vie privée et la vie professionnelle sont au centre des préoccupations des sujets.

En guise de conclusion, je voudrais souligner le fait que les résultats relatifs aux thèmes explorés dans cette recherche convergent tous dans le même sens : l'immense majorité des femmes interviewées sont très investies dans leur vie professionnelle ; en dépit de leurs nombreuses insatisfactions et des obstacles auxquelles elles disent se heurter, elles aspirent à progresser dans leur carrière, et au cœur de leurs aspirations, se place la question du pouvoir décisionnel, de l'acquisition de connaissances et d'un indispensable équilibre à construire et à maintenir entre leur vie privée et leur vie professionnelle. Elles se trouvent ainsi à reprendre à leur compte les affirmations de Freud sur la place de l'amour et du travail dans la vie. Il leur reste, maintenant, à tenter de transformer les milieux de travail pour qu'ils soient plus propices à cet équilibre, et plus conformes à leurs valeurs. Dans cette optique, leur insistance sur l'obtention du pouvoir décisionnel me semble être de bon augure.

Notes

1. Cette recherche, terminée en 1989, a été subventionnée par le Conseil de la Recherche en Sciences Humaines (CRSH), le BSR de l'Université Laval et le Conseil Québécois de la Recherche Sociale (CQRS). À tous ces organismes nous désirons exprimer nos remerciements.

Nos remerciements vont aussi aux nombreuses personnes qui ont collaboré à cette recherche, notamment : Hélène Lee-Gosselin, professeure en Sciences de l'Administration de l'Université Laval, et nos assistantes de recherche, Marthe Bolduc, Nicole Piché et Marie-Claude Gagnon. Mais surtout nous voulons dire toute notre gratitude aux femmes sans lesquelles cette recherche n'aurait pu être entreprise, toutes celles-là qui ont accepté de nous accorder des entrevues et de nous parler de leurs aspirations.

Références

Andrew, C., C. Coderre et A. Denis. « La recherche confrontée aux modèles pluriels de carrière des femmes-cadres », dans *Femmes : Images, Modèles* (Actes du colloque de l'ICREF), publication conjointe de l'ICREF et du GIERF, 1984.

Andrew, C., C. Coderre, A. Daviau et A. Denis. « Entre la liberté et les contraintes ; essai sur les trajectoires des gestionaires », dans *Tout savoir sur les femmes cadres d'ici*, sous la dir. de F. Harel Giasson et J. Robichaud, Montréal, H.E.C., 1988, p. 13-51.

Armstrong, P. et H. Armstrong. *Une majorité laborieuse : les femmes qui gagnent leur vie, mais à quel prix*, C.C.C.S.F., Ottawa, 1983.

——. *The Double Ghetto : Canadian Women and Their Segregated Work*, éd. rév., Toronto, McClelland and Stewart, 1984.

Aubert, N. *Le Pouvoir usurpé I ?* Paris, Éd. Robert Laffont, 1982.

Bardwick, J., et E. Douvan. « Ambivalence : The Socialization of Women », dans M. Gornick et B.K. Moran, *Women in Sexist Society*, New York, Basic Books, 1971, p. 225-241.

Baron, P. « Crise économique et counseling de carrière ; quelques réflexions », *Le Conseiller Canadien* 19, nos 3 et 4, 1985, p. 186-189.

Blishen, Bernard. « The Construction and Use of an Occupational Class Scale », dans B.R. Blishen, F. E. Jones, K.D. Naegele et J. Porter, réd., *Canadian Society ; Sociological Perspectives, rév. éd.*, Toronto, MacMillan of Canada, 1965, p. 449-458.

Bourbannais, Renée. « Travail salarié, famille et santé mentale. » *Santé Mentale au Québec* 10, no. 1, 1985, p. 64-73.

Chanlat, J-F. « Femmes cadres et santé », dans *Tout savoir sur les femmes cadres d'ici*, sous la dir. de F. Harel Giasson et J. Robichaud, Montréal, H.E.C., 1988, p. 75-98.

Conseil du Statut de la Femme (C.S.F.). *Pour les Qébécoises, égalité et indépendance*, Gouvernement du Québec, 1978.

Crealock, C. « The Influence of Fear of Success and Need for Achievement on the Vocational Aspirations of Male and Female High School Students », *Le Conseiller Canadien* 14, no. 1, 1979, p. 32-36.

David, Hélène. *Femmes et emploi : le défi de l'égalité*, Sillery, Presses de l'Université du Québec, 1986.

Denis, A. « Career Paths of Women in Management : The Challenge of Non Sexist Analysis », dans *Women and Work : Workshop Presentations*, Waterloo,

University of Waterloo, 1987, p. 42-46.

Descarries-Bélanger, F. *L'école rose et les cols roses*, Laval, Éd. Coopératives Albert St-Martin, 1980.

England, P. « The Sex Gap in Work and Wages. » *Society* 22, no. 5, 1985, p. 68-74.

Fahmy, P. « Egalité et dépendance ou l'impossible aspiration des adolescentes », dans *Femmes et politique*, ouvr. en coll, sous la direction de Y. Cohen, Montréal, Éd. du Jour, 1980.

——. « Socialisation des filles et problèmes d'orientation des femmes », *L'Orientation Professionnelle* 18, no.1, 1982, p. 41-50.

Gilligan, C. *Une si grande différence*, Paris, Flammarion, 1986.

Goulet, D. « Les problèmes relatifs à l'accessibilité des enseignantes du primaire au poste de directrice d'école, » thèse de maîtrise, Université Laval, 1982.

Grisé, J., et H. Lee-Gosselin. « Les femmes propriétaires-dirigeantes : mythes et réalités (première partie) », *PMO* 3, no. 1, 1987, p. 9.

——. « Les femmes propriétaires-dirigeantes : mythes et réalités (2ème partie) », *PMO* 3, no. 2, 1988, p. 10-17.

Herman, J.B., et K.K. Gyllstrom. « Working Men and Women : Inter- and Intra-Role Conflict », *Psychology of Women Quarterly* 1, no. 4, 1977, p. 319-333.

Huppert-Laufer, J. *La féminité neutralisée ? ; Les femmes cadres dans l'entreprise*, Paris, Flammarion, 1982.

Kanter, R. Moss. *Men and Women of the Corporation*, New York, Basic Books, 1977.

Kergoat, D. *Les femmes et le travail à temps partiel*, Paris, La Documentation Française, 1984.

Laufer, J. *Le sexe du travail*, Grenoble, Presses Universitaires de Grenoble, 1984.

Leith, N., et G. Fitzsimmons. « An Evaluation of the Vocational Readiness Package for Girls ; a Solution to One Problem », *Le Conseiller Canadien* 13, no. 1, 1978, p. 18-21.

Long-Laws, J. « The Bell Telephone System », dans Phyllis A. Wallace, réd., *Equal Employment Opportunity and the AT &T Case*, Cambridge, MIT Press, 1976.

——. « Work Motivation and Work Behavior of Women : New Perspectives », dans Julia A. Sherman et Florence L. Denmark, réd., *The Psychology of Women : Future Directions in Research, New York, Psychological Dimensions, 1978*.

Moscovici, S. *Psychologie des minorités actives*, Paris, P.U.F, 1979.

Paquette, Louise. *La situation socio-économique des femmes : faits et chiffres*, Gouvernement du Québec, Secrétariat à la condition féminine, Québec, 1989.

Plasse, M., et C. Simard. *Gérer au féminin*, Montréal, Agence d'Arc, 1989.

Richardson, M.S. « Occupational and Family Roles : A Neglected Intersection », *The Counseling Psychologist* 9, no. 4, 1981, p. 13-29.

Roberts, J.I. « Changing Roles of Women : Birth of a New Reality », *Women and*

Therapy 4, no.1, 1985, p. 41-52.

Ryff, C.D., et S. Mygdal. « Intimacy and Generativity : Self Perceived Transi-
tions », *Signs* 9, no. 3, 1984, p. 470-481.

Simard, C., et G. Tarrab. *Une Gestion au féminin ? Nouvelles réalités*, Montréal,
Vermette, 1986.

St-Onge, L. « Valeurs de travail d'étudiants universitaires orientés dans des
disciplines masculines, féminines et androgynes et perceptions associées
aux femmes de carrière », *Le Conseiller Canadien* 17, no. 4, 1983, p. 175.

Travail Canada. *Egalité des sexes sur le marché du travail : exposés d'une conférence
parrainée par le Bureau de la Main-d'œuvre féminine*, Toronto, 1982.

Veress, M., et Z. Veress. « L'orientation, aliénation ou désaliénation ? », *Revue
de Psychologie et des Sciences de l'Education* 17, 1972, p. 3-25.

TEACHING,
LEARNING,
RESEARCHING

ENSEIGNER,
APPRENDRE,
RECHERCHER

All of us for some period of our lives are involved in the work of teaching, learning and researching, whether in the formal setting of the classroom or in the so-called informal setting of the community. As feminist teachers and researchers, we struggle continuously with our location in this work. Our own schooling and training have taught us that teachers and researchers have power over us, and that when we become teachers and researchers we in turn have power over our students and the objects of our research, with the right to set agendas in the classroom and the research setting. As feminists, we reject these teachings of patriarchy. We are subversives in the academy. We search for ways to break down hierarchies by empowering our students to take control of their own learning, to co-operate in the work of creating new systems of meaning and action, rather than to compete for positions at the pinnacle of the hierarchy where they in turn can assume the right to control others. We seek ways of becoming co-researchers with people who become active subjects in the work rather than passive objects, who set their own questions and work to find answers to them, instead of answering our questions and allowing us, "the experts," to appropriate their knowledge for our ends.

In this work of feminist teaching and research, we learn as we go. As explorers in unmapped territory, we look to each other for advice, support and affirmation. Our store of provisions is growing: many wise women are sharing their experience and wisdom with us, writing it down so that we can use it again and again, to help us assess our own experience more critically and see more clearly the shape of this new terrain. The papers in this section contribute to this provisioning in significant ways.

Jaya Chauhan and Anne-Louise Brookes make concrete for us many of the features of feminist teaching just described. In the form of letters to each other about their classroom practice, the authors share their struggles to confront their own positioning in terms of race, class and gender. Chauhan, a black woman originally from Kenya, begins her classes by telling students of her own experiences of living as a black, poor woman in a world ruled by non-black, rich men, as a way of engaging her students in a dialogue about the social construction of reality and the plurality of truth and knowledge. Using a combination of novels, films and theoretical readings, Chauhan tries to build a nonthreatening space where students can explore what it means to be black or non-black, feminine or masculine, oppressed or powerful. This is not easy. In encouraging these young women and men to take risks, Chauhan also has to resist the elitist assumption, with which we have all been raised, that "teacher knows best." As a minority woman who has lived on the margins and seen racism, sexism and class oppression from the inside, she finds herself inadvertently taking a defensive position that she very much regrets. As she problematizes this position and works through its etiology and implications, readers are prompted to wonder how honest they are with themselves and their students in confronting their own positioning in society.

Brookes's focus in her response to Chauhan is the question of from what place she as a "white, able-bodied, middle-class, privileged, salaried, university teacher" can speak about racism. Brookes describes how, from this position of privilege, she had learned to think in a language which forced her constantly to categorize the world in binary terms — good/bad, rich/poor, white/black, male/female — in essence, "me and we" versus "the other." She was forty-three when she began seriously to question how her social history, and especially her understanding of racism, had been shaped by her experience as an abuse survivor. How had she learned to "not know"? With the support of a feminist community, Brookes came to see the interconnectedness of sexist, racist and class oppression, and began a search for ways of enabling her students to see this interconnectedness in their own lives. Brookes closes by describing the method with which she is now working, based on an approach developed by Sylvia Ashton-Warner, which aims to develop critical reading and writing skills that enable students to name their world, and read and write the realities of their lives.

Elizabeth Epperly's paper also deals with ways of enabling students to confront their own attitudes by means of reading and writing. Epperly's vehicle, however, is an existing text, Elizabeth Barrett Browning's novel-length poem *Aurora Leigh*. As she struggles against her "own internal, culturally supported silencers," Epperly feels a kinship with and admiration for Barrett Browning, who not only dared to claim a male preserve, the epic, as her own, but created in the person of Aurora a woman artist who claimed and demonstrated that she is the best champion of her own power and vision. Through a process of confronting students with their own assumptions about sexuality, gender and vocation, and having them compare their experiences with those of Aurora and the people with whom she shares her life, Epperly enables students to become participants in and even co-creators of the text. Aurora is no longer "the other" but their contemporary, someone they recognize as part of their own world. In true feminist fashion, through this process of pushing assumptions Epperly ends by questioning her own assumptions about private and public change, the effect of these assumptions on her classroom practice and their potential for enabling transformation of the self.

Moving from feminist teaching to its sister, feminist research, Evangelia Tastsoglou tells us of the struggle against the kind of silencing that the writing of a dissertation can impose. By "storying" her dissertation, Tastsoglou is able to trace for us, and for herself, the ways in which she was creating or "forging" herself in the process of writing her dissertation. For Tastsoglou, the story restores the link between herself as creator and her dissertation as her creation; it gives her back the voice that was silenced by the rigid discipline imposed by the thesis format. Perhaps most important, by sharing her story Tastsoglou hopes to empower other women, in particular other immigrant academic women like herself, with the knowledge that their stories are not theirs alone. For Tastsoglou's storying process has many layers: in reading and analyzing the novels of interwar Greece that formed the subject matter of her thesis, for example, she found herself taking on the personae of their heroines and living their lives with them, in the process "composing and improvising [her] own script." Writing her own script, pushing against the barriers of academic structure, Tastsoglou's storying of her thesis captures for us in microcosm the work that women everywhere do in composing their own lives.

Finally, Sharda Vaidyanath's paper offers us a deeply personal account of why and how she undertook a thesis that she hopes will make a difference to the lives of Hindu immigrant women in Canada. Her article opens with the stories of the marriages of three women who have been central in her life: her mother, her aunt and herself. These are stories of violence, in which the act of marriage erases these women's identities and renders the women subservient in the most total way imaginable to the wills and wishes of their husbands and families. Summarizing her dissertation, Vaidyanath exposes the supporting structure she finds for this power relationship in the Hindu scriptures concerning marriage, and outlines for us her own empirically based research indicating that first-generation Hindu women in Canada remain subject to the same oppressive ideology. Vaidyanath closes with some challenging comments on Canadian multicultural policy and legislation, pointing out how, by attempting to treat all traditions as worthy of support, it violates women's rights and contradicts the Charter of Rights and Freedoms. This is indeed a solemn reminder of the power of the forces with which women must contend in creating their lives, and which can emerge from feminist research that grows out of women's lived experience.

Teaching Racism: Our Different Classroom Experiences

Jaya Chauhan and Anne-Louise Brookes[1]

Ce document prend la forme des lettres échangées entre deux correspondantes dans laquelle nous faisons part, en tant qu'enseignantes non noire et noire, de nos réflexions sur les expériences que nous vivons en classe lorsque nous enseignons le même sujet, notamment le racisme, d'un point de vue féministe. Nous apportons avec nous en classe, en tant qu'enseignantes et étudiantes, la race, la classe, le sexe, l'hétérosexisme, les capacités et d'autres attributs qui nous sont propres. Nous croyons que notre situation particulière donne lieu à des expériences et perspectives différentes sur le racisme. Ainsi, faut-il nous poser le problème de nos multiples opinions sociales contradictoires si nous voulons apprendre à délaisser nos pratiques sociales discriminatoires. Comment nos positions asymétriques et la différence des privilèges dont nous jouissons nous permettent-elles « d'élever la voix » et de « rétorquer » ? La dynamique de la salle de classe peut perpétuer certains phénomènes de domination plutôt que de les renverser. Nos expériences nous indiquent la nécessité d'entériner la voix des marginalisés, une voix qui a trop longtemps été exclue de nos institutions sociales.

This paper takes the form of letters to each other in which we, as a non-black and a black woman teacher, reflect on our classroom experiences when teaching the same subject matter — racism — from a feminist perspective. We bring into the classroom as teachers and students our own race, class, gender, heterosexism, ableism and other positions. We believe that our positions give us different experiences of and perspectives on racism. Thus, our multiple and contradictory social positionings need to be problematized if we are to unlearn our discriminatory social practices. How do our asymmetrical positions of difference and privilege allow us to "speak out" and "talk back"? Classroom dynamics can perpetuate relations of domination rather than subvert them. Our experiences point to the need to validate voices from the margin, voices that for too long have been excluded from all social institutions.

September 15th, 1991

Dear Anne-Louise:

I am delighted by your suggestion that we write our paper in the form of a letter to each other. This breaks the traditional conventional style of writing an academic paper and demonstrates how we can do things differently, in ways that are comfortable for us. Coming from a background of working in science, where it was continuously drummed into me that there is a "right way" of writing an academic paper, I am also excited by not being bound to traditional academic forms. I feel a sense of freedom; if anything, this can only contribute to my writing. I am saddened by how traditional academic structures, particularly in science, often thwart creativity rather than nurture it, and I value your insights and struggles to work in alternative academic forms.

Anne-Louise, I want to take this opportunity to reflect on my teaching experiences this past year at St. Francis Xavier and, in particular, on my attempt to teach students about unlearning racism as a black woman/teacher from the diaspora. Elizabeth Ellsworth, in a paper forthcoming in *Radical Teacher*, writes of her "teaching to support unassimilated difference" as a white woman in terms of working together across difference without having to assimilate to a single, dominant definition of knowledge. I am inspired by her work and her commitment to unlearn racism and to find ways to interrupt it and other oppressive formations. Ellsworth writes that the content and structure of her course, "Using Media for Education About and Across Race, Class, Gender, and Other Differences," was informed by her desire to not "celebrate" cultural and social differences as "diversity," which leaves the mythical norm of dominant class, race, gender, sexual orientation, ethnicity and so on unchallenged. Rather, she wanted the course to provide an understanding of "how histories and struggles for cultural and social self-definition inform our senses of our own social and cultural identities, our classroom interactions with each other and the ways we construct knowledge through discussion and critique."[2] I agree with Ellsworth that pedagogies are situated and not generalizeable and that it is important to discuss how classroom discussions might be reframed, rather than to scrutinize the results of a particular, local instance of reframing. In this exchange between us, Anne-Louise, my hope is to learn to construct classes differently and to find support for my teaching, which is fraught with contradiction and struggle.

I will focus on the course "Sociology of Gender (310)," which I taught this past year. Marian McMahon (1991:25) has stated that "formal education espouses specific forms of rational thinking and pragmatic concepts and linear models of knowledge, and very specific, life-long learned, notions about what counts as knowledge and the world: a world that exists independent of the knower." To counter this, my intent in my teaching is to enable students to bring to the foreground the production of knowledge and to critique the organization of our society that leads to the production of models and notions like those McMahon outlines. Thus, I organized the course content and structure of Sociology 310 to reflect my understanding of the work of critical pedagogy from a feminist perspective.

I attempted to decentre the authority of the teacher in the classroom by using a *facilitating* mode rather than a *lecturing* mode. The subjective sphere is the means through which we make sense of ourselves to ourselves and the world. In the first class, therefore, I shared with the students my own struggle of living with gendered, classed and raced practices, a history that constitutes me as its subject in formation. And to quote you, Anne-Louise,

> *Given the vested and varied versions of reality which students and teachers bring to any learning situation, creative exchanges between students and teachers demand something important of everyone involved. They must bring to the exchange either the understanding of, or the willingness to consider, the view that all knowledge, what it is we "know" about our world, is socially constructed. (Brookes and Kelly, 1989:119)*

Furthermore, as Ursula Kelly (Brookes and Kelly, 1989:123–124) has said, "To acknowledge that meaning is always plural and always contested is to allow student and teacher to dialogue apart from the tyranny of absolute truth." Thus, the aim of liberatory education, as I understand it, is to develop critical consciousness and to get beneath the "taken-for-granteds" that differently benefit the interests of the dominant race, class, gender and sexual preferences.

In order to encourage class discussions, I used novels and films juxtaposed with so-called theoretical essays. Even so, I had great difficulty building a dialogue of trust and a safe but critical space where students could openly discuss how they, as young men and women, take up social practices defined as feminine and masculine. How do we as individuals come to understand the social relations of power, the intersections of race, class, gender and sexuality?

Much as I resist the elitist assumption that as a teacher I am always in a position to know better than students, as a minority woman who has lived on the margins of society and struggled to be heard, I have inadvertently taken this position when talking about racism in my classroom with predominantly non-black students. I see this as a defensive position which I think needs to be problematized.

Let me illustrate this with the example of the class in which we reviewed the film *Home Feeling — Struggle for a Community* (NFB 1983), a film in which black members of a community in Toronto speak in their own voices of their struggles with housing, employment and policing. They give examples of the blatant institutional racism they experience and of how their efforts to resist racist practices are thwarted by state agencies such as the police.

The Sociology 310 class, the overwhelming majority of whom were non-blacks from middle-class backgrounds, criticized the film for being biased and for exaggerating the racism endemic within our social institutions. A sizeable proportion of the class considered the police to be helpful rather than unnecessarily harassing individuals in the name of protecting the community. Many students, however, were discomforted that the police could walk into an apartment without a warrant and that the police were almost permanent fixtures in the subsidized social-housing project. I questioned the students' assumption that the police protect people and that the justice system considers all citizens equal regardless of race, gender, class and sexuality. This caused arguments over whose version was correct, mine or theirs. I recognized my relative privilege of being a black woman in academe, a salaried university teacher, who has learned to speak English with a British accent and can identify with the dominant culture, but racism was staring me in the face everywhere I looked. The students' positions of privilege did not allow them to recognize institutional racism and their own complicity in the history and dynamics of racism. I was only too well aware of the history of racism in Nova Scotia[3] and the failure of the state to address this, whereas my students clearly did not feel the gravity of racism as a social problem. Ultimately, I think that they were threatened by my challenging dominant social relations as they understood them.

How could I articulate the silencing and exclusion that I experienced at that moment, with the history of oppression weighing on my shoulders? I knew of cases in which, because of the racist practices of the police force, which is a vital arm of the capitalist state, individuals had been brutally killed or held in police cells charged with crimes they knew nothing about. Their only crime was their black skin. The pain and despair I experienced is eloquently summarized by Maria Lugones and Elizabeth Spelman (1983:576):

> *And yet, we have had to be in your world and learn its ways. We have to participate in it, make a living in it, live in it, be mistreated in it, be ignored in it, and rarely be appreciated in it. In learning to*

> *do these things or in learning to suffer them or in learning to enjoy what is to be enjoyed or in learning to understand your conception of us, we have had to learn your culture and thus your language and self-conceptions. But there is nothing that necessitates that you understand our world; understand, that is, not as an observer understands things, but as a participant, as someone who has a stake in them understands them. So your being ill at ease in our world lacks the features of our being ill at ease in yours precisely because you can leave and you can always tell yourselves that you will soon be out of there and because the wholeness of your selves is never touched by us, we have no tendency to remake you in our image.*

This heated discussion caused me much agitation and frustration. I looked for support from my male student from El Salvador, the only other visible minority present, but his voice was drowned by the rest of the class. I expressed anger at the social injustice that I was witnessing at that moment, which also represented my history. I felt despair and powerlessness. I recognize anger to be an emotion necessary to retaining self-respect in the face of systematic social discrimination. Nevertheless, I am discomforted that this class did not work smoothly, and that perhaps I incorrectly used the power accorded to me by my position to make a point and to make my voice heard. I was making the class responsible for the injustices of this world, perhaps without showing them how institutional racism works. It is also discomforting to me that such classes leave me feeling that I have a chip on my shoulder. In the words of one of my students, "This was supposed to be a course on gender relations; however, I feel as if I have completed a course on 'how to feel guilty for racism' or 'lighten up — blacks and women aren't the only ones that matter' or 'don't take everything personally.'"

Thus, Anne-Louise, I struggle to construct a classroom context that begins from where students are and makes possible a liberatory dialogue. Clearly, I cannot expect students to unlearn in a few classes the racism that is pervasive in our everyday practices and that they have learned systematically through the organization of our social institutions. I understand that, as individuals living in a society that (at worst) defines itself as multicultural, we are organized to think of those who do not identify with the dominant culture as the *other*. I wanted my students to think of our socially constructed differences as the place and historical legacy of oppression as well the place of resistance and definition of self.

Also, as one individual teacher, I cannot realistically expect to reach all of my students, especially when the teaching load is heavy. What I can hope is that other teachers are also taking up the issue of racism in the classroom. I am aware that despite our constructing safe but critical spaces in the classroom, we are not usually able to challenge the practices outside the classroom that also need to be transformed. In a society organized to benefit differently race, class, gender and sexuality, how might we learn to speak from the authority of our own self? I presume that this always involves contradiction and struggle, since, as teachers and students, we bring into the classroom our own race, class, gender, heterosexism and other positions. Ellsworth (1989:293) has argued that the "key assumptions, goals, and pedagogical practices fundamental to the literature on critical pedagogy — namely, 'empowerment,' 'student voice,' 'dialogue,' and even the term 'critical' — are repressive myths that perpetuate relations of domination." I agree with Ellsworth that we must grapple with the issues of trust, risk, and the operations of fear and desire around such issues of identity and politics in the classroom.

Anne Louise, as you know, I came out of many of my classes disillusioned, upset and angry, and I can only wonder if I would have had the courage to continue if I had not had your support. Through our dialogues, I felt my struggles to be legitimate and I felt comforted by your support of my struggle to teach in better ways, to consider alternative ways of thinking and being in this world. And often you gave me the words for what I was feeling but knew not how to say, words for which I have been searching for a long time. This looking to you for words is not surprising, given that English is a language I was not brought up with, but one that I learned very quickly at primary school in Kenya because we were severely punished by the school principal if she found us not speaking English. Anne-Louise, this year at Xavier, we shared several students; C.P. comes to my mind straight away. It is clear to me that my work was not lost on her, and that by being in your class also, she got a double dose of unlearning racism and other oppressive formations, and that there was a remarkable shift in her thinking. I can only wonder whether she would have got as much out of my class if she had not been in your class as well. C.P. is such an inspiration to me; students like her motivate me in my work.

I will end here for now and I look forward to your response, dear friend. I know you will agree that there is much work to be done with respect to transforming formal education and unlearning discriminatory practices. I think that we must remember what bell hooks (1989:116–117) has pointed out: "black people are not born into this world with innate understanding of racism and white supremacy." Thus, as I understand it, we must all take responsibility for challenging discriminatory practices and seek to transform the self and the world around us.

Thank you, Anne-Louise, for your support in my struggles. You give me much hope, and there is power in our resistance for change to occur.

Love and hope,
Jaya

October 15, 1991

Dear Jaya:

It was a joy to receive your letter. Your words, and the love with which you write them, prompt me to remember our hours of shared discussion about teaching practices. When we first discussed our interest in co-authoring a paper about racist practices and classroom pedagogy, I felt fear. From what place could I, a white, able-bodied, middle-class, privileged, salaried university teacher, speak about racism? The intent of my letter is to address this question as a response to concerns that you raise in your letter.

The history of oppression that weighs on your shoulders pains and angers me. From discussions with you I know that my experience of racism differs from yours. Unlike you, I observed and felt, rather than lived, the racism that you knew in your viewing of the film *Home Feeling*. Your letter reminds me, however, of the places where we do speak across our differing experiences of racism. Quoting bell hooks (1989:116–117), you remind me gently that "black people are not born into this world with an innate understanding of racism and white supremacy." Rather, as you point out, blacks and non-blacks are taught the practices of institutional racism from birth. In our differing ways, together we learn how to produce and reproduce relations of power and authority from the perspective of white supremacy. For most of my adult life, I did not know about institutional racism. I did not know, for example, that I had learned to think in a language that organizes reality in binary terms such as good and bad, rich and poor and white and black — abstract concepts that eventually worked to separate you from me and me from myself. I did not know the significance of learning to read from the perspective of white, male supremacy. I did not know the effects of learning to think of black as *other*. I did not know that I lived in a world which was organized to prevent me from knowing the interconnectedness of race, gender and class inequality. Not knowing, I learned that racism was a theory that had little to do with me. Your letter prompts me, yet again, to question why this is so.

I first began to question seriously my own understanding of racism at the age of forty-three, when I wrote for the first time about the way in which my social history was shaped by my experience as an abuse survivor. I did not, of course, write about this experience in a social vacuum. Rather, I wrote because I felt supported by a feminist community that enabled me temporarily to adopt a collective voice, while I worked to discover my own voice through the process of analyzing how abuse stole my authority to speak about key areas in my own social history. I struggled to know why I had not spoken about an experience that so profoundly affected me. This struggle to understand how I had come to think of my abuse as insignificant forced me ultimately to question how I had learned to not know. Aided by the work of Dorothy Smith (1987, 1990), I began to consider differently the interconnectedness of racism, sexism and classism. Specifically, I began to understand racist practices as socially organized rather than as singular aspects of discrimination against individuals, though they are, of course, experienced in this manner.

In a material way, this shift is manifested in my classroom practice. No longer, for example, do I debate with students "whether or not racist structures and practices" are operative in the classroom (Ellsworth, 1989:299). Instead, I begin each new class with a discussion about my assumption that I am racist, sexist and classist. This is so, I suggest, because of the way in which our society is organized. My work is to examine how and why this organization of inequality works. This approach enables students to work from a location of examination rather than from one of defence. It is a shift that enables us to examine together our shared experiences of institutional racism. As a teacher, this shift fuels my desire to alter the institutionalized social structures and practices that prevent non-blacks, blacks and people of colour from learning and knowing in critically informed ways about how racism is socially produced through institutional practices which we come to know as normal and natural.

In your letter, Jaya, you ask, "How can we transform formal education and unlearn discriminatory practices in order to make possible liberatory dialogue?" As a teacher, this question is of interest to me because I, like you, want to know how to effect social change in a classroom context. This change is not, of course, without basis in a social analysis of power. However, I do insist that it is a change that can occur at the level of teaching practices that are constructed consciously to create spaces within which students and teachers can learn to work in critically informed ways, rendering obsolete the context within which practices such as racism are first learned as acceptable ways of knowing.

As a teacher of sociology, I struggle daily with a problem which I think of as an illiteracy problem. I refer here to university students who are often able to read and write well, within the boundaries of mainstream practices, but who from my perspective are unable to read and write in critically informed ways. I suggest elsewhere (Brookes 1992) that this form of illiteracy is produced through specific kinds of schooling practices such as lecturing; little classroom dialogue; classrooms devoid of openly expressed struggle, emotion and feeling; few written assignments; and multiple-choice, easily graded, standardized examinations — practices that I suggest constitute violence to students and teachers because their use does not allow for the creation of an environment within which to examine how practices such as racism are lived and produced. In other words, it is my assumption that practices that structure learning in hierarchical and authoritative ways can work to impede the self-authority required to learn how to think in critically informed ways.

This is not a new idea. I borrow it from the creative work of Sylvia Ashton-Warner, who, in the late fifties, produced a "Creative Teaching Scheme" (*Teacher*, 1963) based on her work with Maori children whom she taught in rural New Zealand for over fifty years. This way of teaching first-time readers how to read and write is a method, notes Judith Robertson (1988), that is similar to the work of Paulo Freire (Freire, 1971; Shor and Freire, 1987), though Ashton-Warner's work emerged prior to Freire's now famous literacy work with Brazilians.

Ashton-Warner's teaching scheme is of interest to me as a basis from which to develop methods of teaching critical reading and writing skills to university students who often find it difficult to conceptualize practices such as racism, because the rote methods within which they are taught to read, write and think are antithetical to the development of creative, critical thinking skills. These same methods made it difficult for me to name my experience of abuse.

Ashton-Warner's teaching scheme involves both a philosophy of how people learn and a method of teaching people how to read and write. She assumes that "there is only one answer to destructiveness and that is creativity" (1963:93). In her opinion, children (like adults) are destructive when they are unable to name their world. Children, she theorizes, cannot make sense of their world because non-creative reading practices prevent them from learning how to read and write the realities of their lives. To address this lack, she devised a language program that she felt would empower Maori children to understand the conditions of their lives as lived in a dominant white culture at the same time as they learn to read and write. Maori children, she suggests, found it difficult to read and write because they were expected to read and write the dead language of white writers — a language imposed by the use of texts that had no relationship at all to their inner or outer worlds. In the courageous act of abandoning basic readers, Ashton-Warner devised her Creative Reading Scheme.

Two significant principles inform this scheme. One is the principle of harnessing communication: "Since I can't control it, I base my method on it." For this reason, children are taught to read in pairs. They teach each other all their work, so that "learning is so mixed up with relationship that it becomes part of it." The second principle is related to Ashton-Warner's observation that most children have a natural desire to make things. "I use this desire. I help them to read and write their own books. I don't speak often," she wrote (1963:93). Both principles are antithetical to authoritarian models of education.

Primary to this scheme is the assumption that key words provide access to the inner thoughts and experience of first time readers. In Ashton-Warner's opinion (1963:29), children have "two visions, the inner and the outer." Of the two, she writes, "the inner vision is brighter." It is this vision that she teaches children to name. Key words, she theorizes, are often words of violence, fear, love and sexuality, words generally not present in "nice, happy" readers. In her opinion, first words — key words — must mean something to a child, must have intense meaning and must be part of their being. "There's no occasion whatever for the early imposition of a dead reading, a dead vocabulary" (1963:84).

The process whereby students learn their key words is not complex. Each morning, individual students are to name and converse about a word of importance to her or him. These words, Ashton-Warner (1979:449) writes, "are tied to the heart and soul. One look and they belong to the child forever. No pictures can convey them. The picture is already deeply etched into the mind." Once the word is printed onto a card, the child returns to the group to share with another, and later with the larger group, a story about this word. At the end of these meetings, each child's word is deposited into a box to be retrieved the following day. Should a word not be immediately recognized by a child, the next day the word is discarded and the process begun anew. In time, children are constructing two-word phrases, small books with three-word phrases and full sentences and, finally, books with "stories about anything" (Ashton-Warner, 1979:449).

Teaching university students how to read and write in critically informed ways is, I imagine, as exciting as teaching young children how to read for the first time. Based on this assumption, I am developing ways of teaching that draw extensively on Ashton-Warner's scheme but are designed to help "second-time" readers and writers to discover and uncover the multitude of ways in which their knowledge has been socially organized to benefit differently race, sex, gender and class interests. My intent is to create a space within which learners can begin to question all authority. Ira Shor (Shor and Freire, 1987:28) refers to this form of relearning as a "desocializing process." It is a process, he suggests, that involves "learning the key themes and words from the consciousness of students," for the purpose of teaching students how to view their worlds as constructed and hence changeable. In effect, this method of learning is empowering in that it teaches learners how to critique rather than how to repeat.

Racist literacy, like empowerment and safety, is not something that we give to students. Rather, this way of knowing must be struggled into existence in classrooms in which struggle, expressions of joy, fear, rage and anger are perceived to be key to how learning occurs. Safety, empowerment and racial literacy occur when students believe that what they say and do is significant to themselves and to others. Such meanings are difficult to produce in classrooms organized by practices such as lecturing and multiple-choice, easily graded, standardized examinations. This is so, I think, because students learn only the words of the Other, the teacher and the authority. When I teach in this manner, I am teaching racism because I leave standing the institutions and practices that organize and reproduce racism. In my next letter, I will describe to you more specifically how I am adapting and implementing my version of Ashton-Warner's reading scheme. In anticipation, I await your response. Know, dear friend, how deeply I value your responses.

Love and solidarity,
Anne-Louise

Notes

1. Jaha Chauhan was employed by the university on a one-year contract and is not currently affiliated with it. Anne-Louise Brookes continues to teach there.
2. Personal communication, 1991.
3. See the poem *Nova Scotia Reality Song* and other poems that speak of racism in Nova Scotia in Woods (1990) and in the songs of the four-woman a capella group Four the Moment, whose words are published on pp. 346–352 in Miles and Finn (1982). See also Calliste (1989).

References

Ashton-Warner, Sylvia. *Teacher*. New York: Bantam, 1963.
— . *I Passed This Way*. New York: Alfred A. Knopf, 1979.

Brookes, Anne-Louise. "Teaching, Marginality and Voice: A Critical Pedagogy Not Critical Enough?" In *Canadian Perspectives on Critical Pedagogy*. Canadian Critical Pedagogy Network Occasional Monographs, No. 1. Edited by D. Henley and J. Young. Winnipeg: Manitoba Press, 1990.

— . *Feminist Pedagogy: An Autobiographical Approach*. Halifax: Fernwood Press, 1992.

Brookes, Anne-Louise, and Ursula A. Kelly. "Writing Pedagogy: A Dialogue of Hope." *Journal of Education* 171, no. 2 (1989): 117–131.

Calliste, A. "Canada's Immigration Policy and Domestics from the Caribbean: The Second Domestic Scheme." In *Race, Class, Gender: Bonds and Barriers*, Socialist Studies 5, 133–165. Edited by J. Vorst et al. Toronto: Between the Lines, 1989.

Ellsworth, Elizabeth. "Why Doesn't This Feel Empowering? Working Through the Repressive Myths of Critical Pedagogy." *Harvard Educational Review* 59 (1989): 296–324.

— . "Teaching to Support Unassimilated Difference." *Radical Teacher*. Forthcoming.

Freire, Paulo. *Pedagogy of the Oppressed*. New York: Herder and Herder, 1971.

hooks, bell. *Talking Back: Thinking Feminist — Thinking Black*. Toronto: Between the Lines, 1989.

Lugones, Maria C., and Elizabeth V. Spelman. "Have We Got a Theory for You! Feminist Theory, Cultural Imperialism and the Demand for Woman's Voice." *Hypatia* (1), published as a special issue of *Women's Studies International Forum* 6 (1983): 573–581.

McMahon, Marian. "Nursing Histories: Reviving Life in Abandoned Selves." Feminist Review 37 (1991): 23–37.

Miles, A.R., and G. Finn, eds. *Feminism in Canada: From Pressure to Politics*. Montreal: Black Rose, 1982.

National Film Board of Canada. *Home Feeling: A Struggle for a Community*, 1983.

Robertson, Judith. "Patterns of Resistance and Struggle: The Politics of Education in Virginia Woolf and Sylvia Ashton-Warner." An unpublished qualifying research paper for entry into the doctor of philosophy program at the Ontario Institute for Studies in Education, University of Toronto, 1988.

Shor, Ira, and Paulo Freire. "What is the 'Dialogical Method' of Teaching?" *Journal of Education* 169, no. 3 (1987): 11–31.

Smith, Dorothy. *The Everyday World as Problematic*. Toronto: University of Toronto Press, 1987.

— . *Texts, Facts, and Femininity: Exploring the Relations of Ruling*. London: Routledge and Kegan Paul, 1990.

Woods, D. *Native Song*. Lawrencetown Beach, NS: Pottersfield Press, 1990.

Confronting Gender and Sexuality in Barrett Browning's "Aurora Leigh"

Elizabeth R. Epperly

Le très long poème d'Elizabeth Barrett Browning, *Aurora Leigh*, invite lecteurs et lectrices à regarder en face leurs propres attitudes concernant le sexe, la sexualité et la vocation. Dans un cours d'anglais avec spécialisation de quatrième année sur la poésie victorienne, j'ai demandé aux étudiants et étudiantes de lire le poème/l'histoire de Barrett Browning concernant les luttes d'une femme poète au cours du milieu du XIXᵉ siècle en Angleterre. Cette histoire comporte une analyse des obstacles inhérents aux classes, à l'éducation des femmes, au rôle des femmes artistes et écrivaines, à la prostitution, au viol, à la maternité, aux privilèges des hommes et des femmes, au mariage et à l'amour. Les étudiant(e)s sont émerveillé(e)s de constater à la lecture du texte à quel point les questions soulevées par Barrett Browning sont appropriées encore aujourd'hui. Le texte lui-même met le lecteur/la lectrice en présence de ses idées préconçues et de ses préjugés et l'encourage à parler ouvertement de ses propres attitudes et valeurs.

Elizabeth Barrett Browning's novel-length poem *Aurora Leigh* invites students to confront their own attitudes about gender, sexuality and vocation. In a fourth-year honours English course on Victorian poetry, I asked students to read Barrett Browning's poem/story about the struggles of a woman poet in mid-nineteenth-century England. The story involves an analysis of class barriers, education for women, the role of women artists and writers, prostitution, rape, motherhood, male/female privilege, marriage and romance. When students engage with the story, they are amazed to find how appropriate Barrett Browning's questions are for today. The text itself confronts students' preconceptions and unexamined biases and encourages them to talk, in a safe but challenging way, about their own attitudes and values.

Introduction

In wrestling with the preparation of this paper, I hunted up Hélène Cixous's wonderful advice in "The Laugh of the Medusa". She says: "And why don't you write? Write! Writing is for you, you are for you; your body is yours, take it. I know why you haven't written. (And why I didn't write before the age of twenty-seven.) Because writing is at once too high, too great for you, it's reserved for the great — that is for 'great men'" (Cixous, 1986:227). I was reminded of these words because I find every act of writing a struggle against my own internal, culturally supported silencers, and because I wanted to suggest to you that Cixous's words tell us how great and how small a distance we have come since Elizabeth Barrett Browning published her radical epic-length novel-poem in 1857. According to Cora Kaplan (1986:113), Barrett Browning was breaking several "taboos" in her book: not only was she daring to write in the male preserve of epic, but she was claiming and demonstrating that a woman artist is the best champion of her own power and vision, defying the "great men" tradition in writing a first-person story about art and the necessity of writing. Helene Cixous's advice is still needed today; Barrett Browning's poem about a struggling woman poet is as relevant to us as it was to the mid-Victorians.

Last winter and this fall, I used Barrett Browning's 350-page poem *Aurora Leigh* as the centrepiece for a fourth-year honours English course in Victorian poetry. I could have chosen other long poems of the mid-Victorian period to raise questions about gender and vocation and class, such as Tennyson's *The Princess* or Coventry Patmore's *The Angel in the House*, both talking about women and marriage and the roles of men and women in contemporary society, but I chose Barrett Browning's because it is by a woman and because its publishing history parallels the history of the women's movement itself. It is also, in my view, richer and more compelling than any of the contemporary works. I wanted the class to consider Aurora Leigh's voice for itself but also within the context of its time, as part of the Woman Question debate that raged through Britain from 1830 to 1860 and beyond (Helsinger, Sheets and Veeder 1989). In other words, I used this text because I wanted students to understand something of the context for Victorian ideas, and I wanted them to see — perhaps with a shock — that the hot topics of 1857 are the stuff of their own lives. I use *Aurora Leigh* to urge students to confront their own ideas on gender, sexuality, art and love — the issues that find full play in Barrett Browning's text.

To clarify my adaptation of the militant position — confrontation through text and discussion — I will tell you about the class, about *Aurora Leigh* and about the kinds of questions we posed and generated.

The Class

In the winter of 1991, I had fifteen Victorian poetry students, eleven women and four men. Most of them were in honours English in their fourth or fifth year; only one (a woman) was in her second year and was taking an education rather than an arts degree. Most had a B average or better and were used to writing short and long papers. They were not noticeably comfortable talking in class (we sat in a circle every day), but they did engage with me and, in moments of great excitement, with each other. They were all far more comfortable writing their views than speaking them, and gave me the fullest response to Barrett Browning, and to points raised in class, in their term papers on *Aurora Leigh*. For this term paper, I had asked them to write about the poem as a poem and to consider some aspect of gender in Barrett Browning's re-creation of mid-Victorian life, urging them to read Marjorie Stone's article on gender in Tennyson and Barrett Browning as a starting place.

Aurora Leigh

Barrett Browning's poem was enormously popular in her own day. Despite disparaging remarks by critics, who feared the freedom of the heroine, the book sold well, going into thirteen editions in its first sixteen years of publication (Woolf, 1948:203). Conservatives were startled by the heroine's outspoken demands for equality and downright shocked by Barrett Browning's descriptions of prostitution, the life of the English poor and Marian Erle's abduction and rape. Liberal and radical readers found the book stimulating, powerful, sincere and believable. But after Barrett Browning's death, in 1861, her general reputation began to decline as that of her husband, Robert Browning, ascended. By the turn of the century, Barrett Browning had become best known for her series of love sonnets written for Robert Browning, including the famous "How do I love thee? Let me count the ways" that marks the sum total of most university students' knowledge of her, even today (Kaplan, 1986:112–114). Virginia Woolf's essay on *Aurora Leigh* started people thinking about the poem again. Although Woolf praises the energy and breadth of the work, she also says that it is "stimulating and boring, ungainly and eloquent, monstrous and exquisite, all by turns, it overwhelms and bewilders" (1948:208). Readers of Woolf seem to have discounted the praise and concentrated on the difficulties, and *Aurora Leigh* continued to be considered unreadable until second-wave feminists rediscovered it and heard in it the ardent voice of long-neglected genius (Cooper 1988:1–11). The inclusion of Barrett Browning's poem opens up discussions of the canon and is a perfect illustration of the way denigration by mainstream critics and the power of stereotypes and culturally preferred images of womanhood can bury even a successful and highly popular work.

Now, let me give you a quick outline of the shape and story of *Aurora Leigh*. The story is told in nine books, each dealing with some crucial stage in Aurora's development as woman and artist. The first five books are told in the past tense, as Aurora decides to write about her own life and fills us in on her past. The last four books are told as though the events are occurring immediately, with Aurora keeping a journal and catching us up to the moment. A twenty-seven-year-old *Aurora Leigh* decides to write about her life up to the present; a thirty-year-old Aurora ends the poem with us by her side.

Aurora was born in Italy to an Italian mother and an English father. When she is four, her mother dies; her mournful, scholarly father cares for her until he dies, when she is thirteen. She is shipped off to England, to be reared without dowry by a stern, unmarried aunt who believes in all the conventional patterns and images of womanhood. Outwardly, Aurora conforms to her aunt's rules, but secretly she discovers her father's books and learns to love poetry. She steals out of the house to walk and read as soon as it is light in the mornings. She consecrates herself to poetry and keeps a journal of poems and thoughts.

On her twentieth birthday, she is proposed to by her cousin, Romney Leigh, heir to the ancestral estates and a nearby neighbour who has visited her regularly over the past seven years. He has not read her poems and believes that women cannot write poetry because they do not know how to generalize about life and suffering. He believes them incapable of insight into large issues, squandering their sympathy on the particular rather than the universal. His dismissal of her poetry incenses Aurora. They debate. She ultimately refuses him, saying that he wants a helper for his philanthropic work rather than an equal with her own work to do. Romney goes on working at his charities and Aurora moves to London to struggle with making a living by her pen. After seven years of grueling work, she establishes some small fame as a poet and feeds herself by writing reviews and prose pieces.

Aurora finds out from a scheming Lady Waldemar that Romney plans to marry a working-class girl named Marian Erle, with whom he intends to share his charitable works. Lady Waldemar hopes to enlist Aurora against Marian, but Aurora spurns such base interference, and she visits and befriends Marian. On the wedding day, however, Marian does not show up; it turns out much later that she has been persuaded against the marriage by Lady Waldemar, who wants Romney for herself. Marian was told that she would be taken to Australia to begin a new life but instead she is drugged and shipped to Paris, turned over to a brothel and raped. She flees, half-mad, and then learns that she is pregnant. She lives in Paris, doing what work she can, feeling that she is living only because of her little son, on whom she dotes.

Meanwhile, Aurora and Romney have given up the search for Marian, and Aurora continues her writing. She is beginning to think that she has missed the best in life by not having love, and she wonders if she can continue to live such a lonely, isolated life. She hears that Romney is to marry Lady Waldemar, and in order to avoid their wedding and her own growing despair over what life means without love, she leaves England for Italy, stopping in Paris. There, she stumbles upon Marian Erle. She is horrified and humbled by Marian's story, and she adopts her and the baby and takes them with her to Italy. She hears that the poor for whom Romney laboured have burned down his ancestral hall and that he is ill; she assumes that he is married by this time.

One night, as she is watching Marian and her son from her balcony, in walks Romney. He offers to marry Marian Erle so that her son will have a father, but Marian refuses. Romney and Aurora again debate about women and art, but this time it is Romney who must convince Aurora that her poetry is powerful and that art is worth the commitment of love and self she has given to it. He has read her latest long poem, delivered to the publisher just before she left for Italy, which has become famous in England, and he has been converted to the greater truths that poetry can inspire. He sees that bread alone cannot convert or save people, and he has given up his old ways of trying to redress single-handedly the social inequities around him. It turns out that he is now blind and at first will not propose to Aurora because he does not want her to marry him out of pity. After many long pages of argument and persuasion, they agree to marry, and together they enjoy the sunrise, she describing to him, as only a poet can, the inspiring colours of the newly dawning world.

Yes, it is a romance.

Questions Generated

How did the text make students confront their own conceptions of gender and roles?

In giving you a plot summary of the story, I cannot give you a feel for Barrett Browning's passionate pronouncements on art. What you hear is the development of the love story between Aurora and Romney. But the love story itself works in the poem because Barrett Browning has Romney change positions. At first, he is anti-feminist and anti-art, and finally he is pro-feminist and pro-art. So the discussions about the love story and how believable it is naturally also address Romney's and Aurora's positions in relation to art and to the culture around them.

Before I talk about some of the questions we pursued, I should describe the role I assumed. While I expected the text to do the initial confronting, I had to ask students pointedly how a response to the text squared with their responses to their own culture. When we looked, for example, at Aurora's reaction to Marian's story about her abduction and rape, I got them to tell me how people respond to rape in our culture, then how *they* respond. I asked, "Why did Marian use metaphor rather than straight description in telling Aurora about the rape? Why did Barrett Browning use metaphor? How would we tell it differently? What kind of sympathy did Barrett Browning expect from readers of her time? What kind do we expect from each other?" With each question about the text and its assumptions, we followed with others about our assumptions. I could not and would not force all students to respond, but they heard each other and I trusted that the process of confrontation by text, followed by self-questioning, would continue to open up new readings for them.

I asked students to consider Aurora's models — male and female, literary and living — to see what choices she could have seen as the usual responses for women. We looked at Aurora's responses to her aunt, to her dead mother, to Marian Erle, to Lady Waldemar; I asked the students to consider Barrett Browning's own interest in George Sand (Aurore Dupin), the radical French author, celebrated for her sexually liberated books. Of course, students could (and did) name contemporary equivalents for all the forces on Aurora Leigh. Some were surprised at how modern Barrett Browning's ideas were, and some asked why we were still having these problems if women "back then" were saying what we are saying today. We tried to figure out how Barrett Browning shaped the story to create sympathy for Aurora for the potentially resisting reader of Barrett Browning's time, and we looked at why the book about art (book five) is at the centre of the poem.

The most interesting problems brought up in class and in the papers had to do with the crucial changes in the lives of Romney and Marian and Aurora. And this is where students ran up against themselves as readers of and as participants in the text. They thought that Romney's initial attitude to Aurora and her poetry was "silly," but they wondered if he really would have thought that her work was as great as he did at the end of the poem. This question alone involves all of the reader's assumptions about the power of art to change lives and shape consciousness. I pushed at the assumptions behind the assumptions. They thought that Marian Erle was right to keep and love her baby, but they seemed a little surprised that she did not choose to marry Romney at the end so that her son would be assured of a name and an income. It had not occurred to them that the same assumptions underlying the Victorian insistence on purity and marriage could be underlying their apparently practical views about economic security and public approval. They were surprised by the similarity between their supposedly liberated views and the supposedly stodgy Victorian view.

The biggest surprise for me had to do with their responses to Aurora's concern for Romney's approval. I thought that they would see this need as a normal part of the love story, but instead they grew impatient with Aurora's pining over one person's opinion when she apparently thought enough of herself to have given up marriage in the first place to pursue her poetry. Yet the people who objected to Aurora's dependence on Romney's good opinion were also, interestingly, the same people who thought Aurora would find true fulfillment in marriage and motherhood. We moved to the edge of exasperation in trying to uncover the grounding for these two apparently opposing views. I asked them to consider whether particulars are easy to disparage or dismiss, while the general cultural formula (marriage and motherhood as fulfillment) is still unquestionably powerful.

When we first started *Aurora Leigh*, I had the impression that many students thought it was an okay story about Victorian sentiments, but by the time we had worked on it for a couple of weeks, and they had begun to research and write about the poem, the attitude was distinctly different. Most of them, female and male, were enthusiastic about the debates suggested in the poem, and many had changed their views of both Romney and Aurora. It no doubt helped that a couple of the students in my class were also taking a critical-theory course at the time, and were looking at feminism and gender and different critical strategies for approaching texts. In any case, as they examined the text on their own, they were encouraged to see how the Victorian audience at whom Barrett Browning aimed *Aurora Leigh* looked very much like one in our own times. They even imagined videos and music that could deal with the scenes Barrett Browning described.

I am currently using *Aurora Leigh* with another section of the Victorian poetry course. This group is smaller and more reserved and

I am not sure how they will finally decide to deal with the personal challenges in the poem. So far, a few of them are most concerned that Romney is simply not good enough for Aurora. That judgment itself is but the first unravelling thread in the loose-weaving, and I am sure that in pulling it we will find other surprising tangles and strands.

Using a text to urge students to confront themselves works in two ways. Initially, when they are most tentative, they have the illusion of talking about something separate from themselves, some other time and some other people's stories; later, when they have engaged with the text and with themselves as readers of and readers within that text, they step into the depicted world and recognize it as their own. Best of all, with *Aurora Leigh* they see the power of what Helene Cixous advocates; they see in Aurora's life and hear in Barrett Browning's voice the passionate power of writing out the self.

Postscript

When my co-presenters and I got together to share rough drafts of our papers, I was amazed to find what happened to me when one or the other of them confronted me with my own text. Suddenly I saw this paper and my class in wholly new ways. I realized that for all my insistence on sharing thoughts and pursuing ideas openly in class, I really do believe — have always believed — that the transformative power of literature operates in private. That is not to say that discussions are not important, sometimes even vital, but that the real and continuing learning takes place between the awakened individual and the text she engages. I saw that my hopes for the classroom are pinned on two things: inspiring students to read the text with interest, and showing them how to question what they read in relationship to themselves and their culture. I wonder, now, having worked with *Aurora Leigh* and having written this paper, whether I should allow more time in class for discoveries — theirs and mine and ours — instead of assuming that we will bundle all the class's new material away to some safe and private place where each will go on to discover by herself what was only suggested in class. Have I helped to keep learning in the closet? I now wonder if my assumption that most of the transforming takes place out of class is actually keeping me from pushing students harder and demanding more truth and exposure of myself at the same time. Perhaps — I now see with wry surprise — I have always been too polite to show them the brutal but magnificent energy of a self changing.

References

Cixous, Hélène. "The Laugh of the Medusa." In *Feminist Literary Theory: A Reader*, 225–227. Edited by Mary Eagleton. Oxford: Basil Blackwell, 1986.

Cooper, Helen. *Elizabeth Barrett Browning, Woman & Artist*. Chapel Hill: University of North Carolina Press, 1988.

Helsinger, Elizabeth K., Robin Lauterbach Sheets and William Veeder, eds. *The Woman Question: Society and Literature in Britain and America 1837–1883*. 3 vols. Chicago: University of Chicago Press, 1989.

Kaplan, Cora. "*Aurora Leigh* and Other Poems." In *Feminist Literary Theory: A Reader*, 112–114. Edited by Mary Eagleton. Oxford: Basil Blackwell, 1986.

Stone, Marjorie. "Genre Subversion and Gender Inversion: The Princess and *Aurora Leigh*." *Victorian Poetry* 25 (1987): 101–127.

Woolf, Virginia. *The Common Reader*. 2nd series. London: Hogarth, 1948.

Forging a Self Through Writing a Doctoral Dissertation

Evangelia Tastsoglou

Ce document s'intéresse au processus de rédaction d'une thèse de doctorat comme moyen de se conscientiser davantage, de se « forger un soi ». Les rapports dialectiques entre le produit et le producteur sont expliqués (« raconter » la dissertation) d'après certains « paramètres de subjectivité » qui sont les notions de classe sociale, de sexe, de culture, d'immigration, de lieu physique et d'art. Les données utilisées sont excluvisement autobiographiques.

This paper focusses on the process of writing a doctoral dissertation as a means of expanding consciousness, of "forging a self." The dialectical relationships between the product and the producer are illuminated ("storying" the dissertation) along certain "parameters of subjectivity," which are social class, gender, culture, immigration, physical location and art. The data used are exclusively autobiographical.

Traveling in that early Time involved sailing the surface of the Subliminal Sea, Sensing its depths, while not being overtly conscious of the contents of those depths, at least not to a sustained degree. (Daly, 1990:xxviii)

Prolegomena

In 1990, I was awarded the degree of doctor of philosophy with a dissertation entitled "Social Class, Ideology, and the Novel in Interwar Greece (1922–1940)." In this paper, I reconstruct the story of the dissertation, which is at the same time the story of my own consciousness expansion, increasing self-awareness and process of self-building. This kind of storytelling is important for me personally; it is my uncensored "voice," which the formal dissertation process, with its narrow focus, discipline, rigidity and deadlines, denied me. Ex-doctoral students often feel that finishing their dissertation marks their "entrance into Logos." The dissertation itself has been a silencing and alienating experience for me so far, because there has been no room in it for me to narrate the story of its process, which is far more important for me in an existential way than the concrete end-product, as well as a part of it, with its ramifications extending well into the future. Organizing the experience of the process into a story — that is, restoring in words the continuum between the product and its creator — is a way of empowering myself, of reclaiming and re-appropriating my silenced voice.

Reflecting on the self and understanding the world in which we live are closely interconnected. As Mary Catherine Bateson argues, "composing" our lives is our central metaphor for thinking about the world, making it a friendlier and more intelligible place to live: "Storytelling is fundamental to the human search for meaning, whether we tell tales of the creation of the earth or of our own early choices" (Bateson, 1989:34). As a result, the possibilities of future directions appear clearer in the forefront: "The past empowers the present, and the groping footsteps leading to this present mark the pathways to the future" (Bateson, 1989:34).

But this kind of storytelling about women's lives in particular may be important to other women as well. My experience, though the circumstances may have been unique, was not unique in itself but common to many an immigrant academic woman in North America. It is another empowering experience to realize, even in retrospect, that one has never been, nor will be, alone. The personal is political, and knowing "herstory" will liberate us from the illusion, isolation and powerlessness of the belief that our lives are only our individual stories.[1]

The dissertation project came to occupy most of my time, and at its peak moments, I was certain that I was living in a new dimension of the world that appeared familiar but in fact was not. I was making amazing connections among things apparently unrelated, or certainly not related in such a way before. This dimension was a new layer of meaning in my reality. It involved a radical shift in my world view, encompassing thought, feeling, will and even sensation. There was a structural change in the way I saw myself and my relationships; my physical state of health was directly affected. Suddenly everything acquired a new meaning; thoughts were felt and feelings were both thought out and linked to the senses. The experience is referred to in the literature as a perspective transformation (Mezirow, 1978), a change in world view (Osborne, 1985) or a vertical shift in consciousness (Weiser, 1987). What at the time seemed uncomfortable and even devastating, made even worse by my own personal circumstances as an immigrant woman in Canada, I now know is a not uncommon experience in graduate school, especially among researchers doing qualitative and heuristic research (Douglas and Moustakas, 1985).

I will attempt to make explicit one more of the above-mentioned connections here, by locating myself in relation to the project, by tracing the link between the dissertation and its author's concrete location at the cross-section of her social class, gender, ethnic origin and life experience as a Greek immigrant in Canada. John Weiser (1987:100) calls such work:

> *the horizontal dimension of growth of consciousness the piece by piece concretizing of a frame of meaning [or] filling in the gaps within an unchallenged larger frame of meaning ... This process occurs in small shifts of insight, of confirming hunches and hypotheses, of adding additional detail so that again our reality becomes an unquestioned given.*

I will relate here how I ended up choosing a particular topic, given who I was as an individual, and what the consequences of the choice have been so far, in terms of altering the stories that I have been telling myself and my very sense of identity, by expanding my consciousness, by building bridges among neglected and forgotten fragments of myself and by integration. Such a project I call "storying" the dissertation.

Social Class, Gender, Culture, Immigration, Physical Location and Art: The Parameters of Subjectivity

When I started the dissertation research, I was trying to understand the complex relationship of literature and art to society, and especially to social classes. How do individual works of art relate to the social class of their makers? Is art a unique product of human experience, creativity and mind, in which social factors play a minimal role or no role at all? Are there common elements in the fiction of a people who grew up in the same generation, culture and socio-economic class? How do the diverse experiences of human beings, and their unique ways of synthesizing them, get moulded by structures and become creatively transformed into individual literary projects?

In the initial stages of the study, I constructed a theoretical framework for a sociological analysis of Greek interwar literature and a better understanding of the complex relationship between literature and society. The framework combined a critical revision of Lucien Goldmann's genetic structuralism with Sartre's psycho-biographical approach to literature, as well as the poststructuralist problematic. The historical research focussed on the relationship between social class, ideology and literary production in interwar Greece (1922–1940). The hypothesis was that class ideology and the ideology of a writer-member of the class, as expressed in fiction, are "structurally homologous" — that is, similar in origin and development on a structural level. All other social factors and unique individual experiences in a writer's biography, although crucial in understanding the literary work, were but a mere fleshing out of the skeleton of universality that social class provided (Sartre, 1949). At the time, I was oblivious to the dynamics of gender and the differentiations it introduces into the experience of social class.

When I started the social-class and literature project, I saw it as the culmination of another preparatory research project on the concepts of structure and superstructure in the Marxist discourse of social change. I had been struggling for years in my academic work with the concepts of structure and human agency, the notions of an objective, limiting, real, external world versus a subject: creative, thinking, capable of and willing to overcome its confining structures and to effect changes. Where exactly had been the limits? How was social change to come about? As a result of structural factors, of inevitable economic/technological developments in the society's foundation (or structure), of the forces of production "outgrowing" and inevitably conflicting with the relations of production? Or as a result of consciously changed decisions, ideological and organizational practices by human agents, conditioned by structural developments? I tended to agree with the second, dialectical interpretation of the Marxian scheme (the "Western" or "Praxis" Marxism),[2] but I had further questions. If structure and culture affect each other dialectically, can their circularity be broken by an altered human practice? What triggers such a change in the human practices of a society and how does change occur? Out of these questions had come a long research paper, entitled "On Dialectical and Historical Materialism: Marxist Theories of Social Change," in which I researched the above questions in the classical Marxist literature, on both an epistemological and a historical level.

The academic questions reflected similar, agonizing, personal concerns. How much control did I have over my fate at all? How had I found myself in the position of an immigrant in North America? In the position of a sociology student after having studied law in another country? In a language that was not my mother tongue, in a mode of thinking which, although exciting, had been alien to me so far?[3] Had I indeed made an informed decision when I emigrated, rebelling against my family and against surroundings that I perceived as utterly oppressive, in alliance with a male partner in a joint graduate and life project? Or was I merely drifting along, swept by the traditional roles and expectations of a patriarchal society, rebelling on one level and really submitting on another by merely replacing one structural limitation by another? Sometimes I felt like someone who has virtually created her reality at every given moment. At other moments, I could also see myself as merely succumbing to outside sources of pressure, "going with the flow."

Questions of class started to arise in my American graduate school. It took me more than a year to come to grips with the sociological perspective, to make the transition from a legal, positivistic frame of mind, a world of facts and truths, to a questioning of old truths, a searching behind the façade. In that new mode of existing I was a participant, along with other people, in situations that entailed rights and obligations over which I had no choice and no control. I started realizing the overwhelming effect of my membership in these structured situations on all the decisions I had ever made. I turned first to social class, which I saw as most important. I realized that I had been so strongly discouraged from going into medical school because my parents' social class and education did not allow them to understand and support my aspirations. I became a Marxist in the United States, which is an oxymoron in itself.

The academic-personal questions of the time were phrased in the language and problematic of social class. I had always been painfully aware of the limitations of my gender, as at every given moment I had been reminded and even admonished by family that I should limit my intellectual curiosity and curb my restlessness because, after all, I was "only a woman." The advice was to conserve energy for raising a family in the future. This family argument was couched in the same *fact*: a woman doctor was supposed to either faint at the sight of blood, if she were a *real* woman, or be totally unattractive, unlovable, childless and lonely, if she insisted on being successful (read: masculine). Culture and the educational system conveyed similar messages. In senior high school, I was awarded a prize by the city I was living in for an essay on the importance of eliminating illiteracy among women, in which my basic argument, much applauded by the all-male committee, was that it was important for women to be able to read and write, so that they could become better mothers.

For many other women of my age and class and in the context of a post-dictatorship political climate in Greece, gender was constructed in a most constricting way. Out of a graduating high-school class of forty women in a classical-studies curriculum, five women made it to university, two of them made it to graduate school in Europe and the United States, and one has insisted, in difficult moments purely on instinctual grounds, on not going back to a familiar, comfortable, leisurely, middle-class modus vivendi, in which women are feminine and know their place in the world.

Nevertheless, even for those of us who went to university, the gender-limit theory was the taken-for-granted assumption permeating our entire lives and informing all of our choices. The bitter realization of limitations, even in the best of circumstances, remained private, compartmentalized knowledge, not integrated with the rest of ourselves, and certainly not translated into conscious political practice. I used to think of myself at the university and in graduate school as competing fairly with my classmates for academic excellence. Academia was the free market of individuals struggling under conditions of equality to achieve intellectual enrichment. I could observe the effects of class and gender inequalities on academic achievement, but these effects I thought of as consequences of a natural order of things.[4] I thought of gender and class as personal limitations of the same order as other subjective experiences of an individual life.

> *Of Greece's nearly ten million people, one in ten is illiterate, and since many families still consider educating girls a waste of time, two-thirds of the illiterate population are women. At age fifteen, less than two-thirds of Greek girls are still in school, compared to nine out of ten in most other countries in the European Community. (Anderson, 1991:34)*

Then, in the process of writing my dissertation, I was forced to pay attention to the fact that in the stories, characters, values, ideas and themes of women writers, their social class, ideology and gendered subjectivity were interconnected. I found out that their class experience and ideology were different from that of the male writers of the same class and generation. The bourgeois women writers' world vision was mediated by their own experiences as bourgeois women. My structural homology hypothesis was not confirmed in their case. The inevitable next step was to see that what I had initially thought of as class ideology in the case of male writers was a masculine class ideology, shaped by unquestioned patriarchal values and structures of the hegemonic bourgeoisie.

> *There is a difference here between men and women writers: the latter's problematic still revolves around current social problems, as they perceive them through their gender experience ... Despite their class limitations which blurred considerably the image of their social reality and set the limits of their gender consciousness, they were able to register their protest against the social conditions that hindered woman's realization in both the individual and social realms. The gender inequality they experienced helped them overcome their class barriers and identify with the oppressed and*

exploited. Thus, they identified the source of the "evil" they experienced in the social system and not in some inherent limitations of man (and woman), and they worked, individually and collectively, in real life and in fiction, to redress it. (Tastsoglou, 1990:382)

"I have always come to life after coming to books," wrote Jorge Luis Borges (quoted in Oates, 1990:214), describing poetically but accurately my experience from then on. The dissertation process awakened me to the social construction of gender and its overwhelming effect on individual social reality and perception of the world. One more connection between the project and myself became suddenly clear: not only was I a subject, determined to a large extent by my social-class experience, but I was also a female subject, greatly affected by the social construction of her sex. I could have, and have had, some input in the shaping of my life insofar as I could manipulate these structures, utilizing and synthesizing them in a way that was best for me.

As a graduate student in sociology in the United States since 1981, and as a landed immigrant in Canada since 1986, I finally acknowledged on a practical level, as well, that not everyone in this world was Greek and that I had my own distinct historical roots and a rich cultural heritage. I was defined as a Greek, and I came to live the definition consciously. Coming to terms with my new self-awareness meant that I had to know and understand as much as I could of that cultural heritage. The topic of my doctoral dissertation reflected a yearning to seek my roots, a joyous homecoming and a new understanding of the old and the familiar.

But there was more to uncover in my choice of topic. For years, as I was travelling back and forth in the summer months, I had been experiencing an awesome and troubling split between my North American self and my old self, left behind in Greece. Every time I went back, as I was crossing the physical and cultural boundary, I would become what I had been before; I would continue living in that space as if I had never left. In the midst of changing physical and human surroundings, my family would conspire with me to confirm the delusion. I would become enmeshed in a torrent of released emotions. As tension was mounting and the sad realization was creeping in that a whole world, my past, idealized by necessity, was lost, I would usually leave and arrive in North America not knowing who I was any more, exhausted and in fragments. It would take me a while to shift my weight toward my North American self/present. As I was contemplating my return, the intellectual and emotional parts of myself turned into polarities with a basic geographical, cultural, language and relationship identification.[5] Each part was fighting to survive against the other, and the need for some resolution of the conflict and for peace was becoming increasingly urgent. My choice of topic, therefore, reflected one more painful attempt to reconcile the cognitive part of myself, well nourished in North America, with what Greece had come to symbolize for me in North America — emotions, family, the past, separation and wounds, but also the sun and the joy of life — by opting to deal academically with the latter.

The culmination of that struggle in the final stages of the dissertation proved that there was no stable way of reconciling the fragments by choosing one over the other; the outcome of the choice shifted with the direction of the physical dislocation. With a decreasing range of solutions, and still unwilling to pack up and leave, I tried next to create connections between the fragments, across physical space. I tried to strip geographical space of its symbolic meaning and open up communication between mind and feelings, by creating emotional ties in Canada, in the hope that I could feel that the new space was home. When I started working in the Wife Assault Program in the Greek community, I was ready for the experience of connecting with the abused Greek immigrant women, as well as with the other workers there. Despite my own privileged position, I soon realized I had more in common with them than I had with my women friends of my own class and educational background in Greece. I realized that the new category "ethnicity," in the context of immigration, broke down and made irrelevant the class distinctions of our country of origin in the new environment. I was needed here, and I was a part of a large sisterhood, which was my family.

Finally, the factor that I believe facilitated the vertical shift of consciousness in the dissertation stage was my reading and analysis of the literature. Art has the effect of reaching depths of emotion whose energy alone can bring about self-transformations. The initial "sensing of the depth of the subliminal sea" (Daly, 1990:xxviii) was possible because of my immersion in literature. I had always thoroughly enjoyed fiction and have had the sense of living multiple lives through it. However, while reading and feeling it deeply for my research, I took on the personae of its heroines, and even rehearsed parts of their lives, as I was composing and improvising my own script.

My research and life journey in North America have been "full of adventure, full of discovery," but also stormy and with occasionally frightening encounters with "Laistrygonians, Cyclops, and wild Poseidon."[6] Every time I go back to the times of trial, with the intention of making sense of the adventure, of cleaning house and healing, I discover something new that was present there all along and that might have helped me through, had I been able to detect it earlier. It seems that although a record is kept somewhere in the subconscious mind, we can really see something only when we are ready for it. As we acquire language, theory, feminism and political participation, we invest it with meaning and reinforce it, which is the next step toward transformational change, a never-ending process.

> *There is no end to that which, not understood, may yet be*
> *noted and hoarded in the imagination, in the yolk of one's*
> *being, so to speak, there to undergo its (quite animal)*
> *growth,*
> *dividing blindly,*
> *twitching, packed with will,*
> *searching in its own tissue*
> *for the structure*
> *in which it may wake.*
> (Kinsella, 1973:11)

Notes

1. Hannah Arendt says (quoted in Heilbrun, 1988:71), "If we do not know our own history, we are doomed to live it as though it were our private life."
2. This is the interpretation on which Lucien Goldmann based his theory of genetic structuralism.
3. I remember vividly the discussion with my advisor about one of the first research papers that I wrote on Greek rural women. Being a lawyer, I quickly came up with an impressive array of laws regulating work, family, property issues and so forth, from the point of view of rural women. I was quite pleased with myself and expected at least a good word on it. Instead, this woman kept asking me, when I reported back to her the results of my search, "Yes, so this is what the law says. But what is the situation in reality?" I did not have a clue what she was talking about. What could she possibly mean by reality?
4. With an eerie feeling, I had watched all my female cousins getting engaged at the ages of fifteen and sixteen, and getting married and dropping out of school a year later. I had breathed a deep sigh of relief when I was over the critical age and not yet afflicted.
5. Mezirow's (1978) notion of "subpersonalities" may be one way of conceptualizing this "split." The "resolution" of the conflict then consists in the subpersonalities "joining into a more unified and integrated identification" (Weiser, 1987:106).
6. The Greek-Alexandrine poet C. P. Cavafy (1984:29) describes the journey to "Ithaka" (whence the verses in the text) and gives advice to the traveller: "Keep Ithaka always in your mind. / Arriving there is what you're destined for. / But don't hurry the journey at all. Better if it lasts for years, / so you're

old by the time you reach the island, / wealthy with all you've gained on the way, / not expecting Ithaka to make you rich. / Ithaka gave you the marvellous journey. / Without her you wouldn't have set out. / She has nothing left to give you now."

References

Anderson, Doris. *The Unfinished Revolution*. Toronto: Doubleday, 1991.

Arato, Andrew, and Paul Breines. *The Young Lukacs and the Origins of Western Marxism*. New York: Seabury, 1979.

Avineri, Schlomo. *The Social and Political Thought of Karl Marx*. Cambridge: Cambridge University Press, 1968.

Bateson, Mary Catherine. *Composing a Life*. New York: The Atlantic Monthly Press, 1989.

Cavafy, C. P. "Ithaka." In *Collected Poems*, 29. Translated by E. Keeley and P. Sherrard. London: Chatto and Windus, 1990.

Daly, Mary. *Gyn/Ecology: The Metaethics of Radical Feminism*. Boston: Beacon Press, 1990.

Douglas, B. G., and C. Moustakas. "Heuristic Inquiry: The Internal Search to Know." *Journal of Humanistic Psychology* 25 (1985): 39–55. Eagleton, Terry. *Literary Theory*. Minneapolis: University of Minnesota Press, 1985.

Feenberg, Andrew. *Lukacs, Marx and the Sources of Critical Theory*. Totowa, NJ: Rowman and Littlefield, 1981.

Goldmann, Lucien. *Towards a Sociology of the Novel*. England: Tavistock, 1975.

— . *Method in the Sociology of Literature*. Oxford: Blackwell, 1981.

Heilbrun, Carolyn G. *Writing a Woman's Life*. New York: Norton and Company, 1988.

Kinsella, Thomas. "Hen Woman." In *Notes from the Land of the Dead and Other Poems*, 9–12. New York: Knopf, 1973.

Lukacs, Georg. *History and Class Consciousness*. Cambridge: MIT Press, 1979.

Mezirow, J. "Perspective Transformation." Adult Education 28 (1978): 100–110.

Oates, Joyce Carol. "Literature as Pleasure, Pleasure as Literature." In *Women's Voices: Visions and Perspectives*, 214–221. Edited by Pat C. Hoy II, Esther H. Schor and Robert Diyanni. New York: McGraw-Hill, 1990.

Osborne, J. "Learning as a Change in World View." *Canadian Psychology* 26 (1985): 195–206.

Sartre, Jean-Paul. *Literature and Existentialism*. Secaucus, NJ: Citadel, 1949.

— . *Search for a Method*. New York: Vintage Books, 1968.

Smith, Sidonie. *A Poetics of Women's Autobiography*. Bloomington, IN: Indiana University Press, 1987.

Spelman, Elizabeth V. *Inessential Woman*. Boston: Beacon, 1988.

Vitti, Mario. *The Thirties' Generation*. Athens: Ermis, 1987.

Waugh, Patricia. *Feminine Fictions: Revisiting the Postmodern*. London and New

York: Routledge, 1989.

Weiser, John. "Learning from the Perspective of Growth of Consciousness." In *Appreciating Adults Learning: From the Learners' Perspective*, 99–111. Edited by David Boud and Virginia Griffin. London: Kogan Page, 1987.

Williams, R. "Base and Superstructure in Marxist Cultural Theory." *New Left Review* 82 (December 1973): 3–16.

Setting the Record Straight: Hindu Concepts of Marriage in the Canadian Context

Sharda Vaidyanath

De par son expérience personnelle quérie dans trois mariages hindous, soit comme témoin ou soit comme participante, l'auteure en est venue à choisir comme sujet de recherche la confrontation des concepts du mariage hindou et des concepts occidentaux en contexte canadien. Ce document est un résumé des résultats de recherches concernant la place des femmes dans le mariage et dans la famille telle que prescrite par les écritures sacrées hindoues, les torts causés aux femmes par ces prescriptions, jusqu'à quel point elles continuent de s'appliquer au mariage des couples hindous dits « de première génération » canadienne et, finalement, les répercussions que certaines législations et politiques canadiennes en matière de multiculturalisme et des droits de la personne peuvent avoir sur ces femmes.

Personal experience as either witness to or participant in three Hindu marriages has led the author to an academic study of Hindu concepts of marriage and family and how they intersect with Western concepts in the Canadian context. This paper presents in summary form the results of research on the place of women in marriage and family prescribed by Hindu scriptures, the damage done to women by those prescriptions, the extent to which they continue to apply to Hindu marriage among first-generation Canadians and some implications for Canadian policy and legislation in the areas of multiculturalism and human rights.

To my mother Meenakshi, whose life and death
inspire all my work.

My father stigmatized my mother, along with other relatives, for being an orphan, for her "ordinary" background and for giving birth to four daughters, one a year. Simply stated, as a wife to my father she was a bad omen "dumped" on him by a callous father and family members. My mother often recalled with a sense of humour that on her wedding day, all the female members of my father's family had a "crying party." In fulfilling her role as a wife, although I think the term "slave" is more appropriate, my mother suffered every conceivable hardship spanning the more than forty years of her marriage. It was the manner in which my Goddess-worshipping father treated my mother for most of her life, my mother's continuous acceptance of that treatment and, above all, her belief that there was no viable alternative either to her relationship with my father or to the manner in which she interacted with him as his wife that made marriage an intriguing subject for my undergraduate and graduate theses.

My uncle, a wealthy, high-profile philanthropist, died of a stroke at age fifty while vacationing with his family in South India. To me, the most unforgettable impression of that death was the drastic change in that family's economic status, which took effect a month after my uncle's death. I believe that the experience of widowhood in India is far more complex and difficult than it is in the West, mainly because of its extraordinarily negative religious and cultural connotations. My aunt dressed like a widow, making her more visible as one. Her right to participate in religious and social events was snatched away by the stigma of widowhood. Finally, even the psychological burden of caring for five children on her own was no argument for remarriage. Like the vast majority of Hindu women in such situations, she was condemned to live the rest of her life as a single woman, a widow.

The manner in which my marriage was settled is a classic example of the differential treatment and rights of single women and men in Hindu families. As the woman whose marriage was being considered, I was a nonparticipant in any of the discussions that took place (except for the one word "yes," which was strictly a formality). In essence, despite all my accomplishments I was a "child" whose destiny was the business of men. The shock of being ignored in decisions critical to my future, the humiliation of having to eavesdrop to inform myself of developments in arranging my marriage, and especially the daily terror I felt wondering about the outcome of every bit of communication between the two families and my husband-to-be, left me weighing eighty-four pounds at age twenty-three.

In these three stories of Hindu marriage — that of my parents, which ended with the death of my mother in April, 1988, in Montreal; that of my aunt, who was widowed in her thirties in 1959; and finally my own, which is ongoing — lie the origins of my academic interest in the institution of marriage. These stories are excerpts from the autobiographical introduction to my M.A. thesis in Canadian studies, titled "The Intersection of Concepts of Marriage in Canada: A Study of the Influence of Western Ideologies of Marriage on First Generation Hindus" (Vaidyanath, 1990).

Our experiences within marriage provide examples of marital abuse, the trauma of widowhood and the absence of rights and freedoms for Hindu women in marriage. My witnessing of these marriages, and my own experiences of marriage, have profoundly shaped my radical feminist/rejectionist approach to the Hindu concept of marriage, initially through my discovery of the parallels between scriptural prescriptions for women's roles in Hindu marriage and family life and the subordinate, "wifely" roles of women in my family. Subsequently, I explored the radical feminist literature, drawing ideas from Kate Millet, Shulamith Firestone and Christine Delphy, but I also went beyond their work to suggest that women's experience *as women* is based on more than biological reality; it is a cultural and historical reality that can be changed. I then went on to explore Western ideologies of marriage, with a special emphasis on marriage in Canada. As a final link between my feminist approach to Hindu marriage and my Canadian research, I undertook a study of the influence of Western ideologies of marriage on first-generation Hindus in Canada.

The Hindu arranged marriage must be understood within the concept of *dharma*, a comprehensive religious and moral code on which Hindu society is based. According to this code, the spiritual progression of the Hindu married male is more important than is his material prosperity. The system of *asrama*, or the stages of life, channels and structures the spiritual progression of the Hindu male. *Vivaha*, or marriage, grants him entry into stage two in this progression, the *grhastha*, or householder, stage, which allows him to experience or fulfil the human values of *artha*, wealth, and *kama*, sensual pleasure. The married male is now required to pay off the three debts, or *rnas*, that he owes to the sages, his ancestors and the gods. This allows him a transition into stages three and four, *Vanaprastha*, the forest dweller, and *Samnyasa*, he who renounces the material world for moksa, or spiritual salvation, which is unity with *Brahman*, an otherworldly realm of pure blissful consciousness.

Dharma negates ideas of "self" or "individualism." Male–female relationships within marriage and family are depersonalized to focus on service and sacrifice for the sake of familial and social well-being. As for woman, *dharma* does not grant her a separate identity. Marriage represents the fulfilment of religious duty by the father, who must transfer guardianship of his daughter to the husband. The idea of a woman's giving consent to marriage is incompatible with *dharma*. The Hindu woman is admitted into the "householder" stage as a child bride. Her core function is to give birth to a male, critical for the sustenance of Hindu religious, familial and cultural traditions. The desire for a child is expressed as *putrakama*, the desire for a male child. The fulfilment of reproduction of the male species occurs within elaborate and complex behavioural codes for women. These codes are articulated as *stri-dharma*, a concept which enshrines the total surrender of female sexuality and reproduction to the male ritualistic role in the family, and includes qualities such as self-effacement, sacrifice, modesty and chastity. A particular expression of *stri-dharma* is *pativ-ratya*, devotion to one's husband under all circumstances, including widowhood. For example, Hindu scriptures prescribe that "though destitute of virtue, or seeking pleasure [elsewhere], or devoid of good qualities, [yet] a husband must be constantly worshipped as a god by a faithful wife." Furthermore, "if a wife obeys her husband, she will for that [reason alone] be exalted in heaven." Finally, "she must never even mention the name of another man after her husband has died" (Bühler, 1969:196).

In the theoretical chapter of my thesis (Vaidyanath, 1990:75–117), I raise several concerns about this system of arranged marriage, which I describe as a "breeding program" to ensure the birth of males while systematically eliminating the female of the species. It is also a fundamental means of sustaining the caste system. In sum, my argument for consistency between ideological and scriptural injunction and centuries of cruelty toward women (such as *sati* — the burning of widows on the husband's funeral pyre — or the use of amniocentesis to determine the sex of the fetus so that if it is female it can be aborted) forms the basis for my rejection of the Hindu concept of marriage.

The final portion of my thesis explores the extent to which Western ideologies of marriage have influenced first-generation Hindus in Canada. A survey of research on this issue indicates that first-generation Hindus in Canada maintain both the impersonal attitude to marriage and the differences in attitudes, requirements and moral standards for Hindu males and females within marriage that are prescribed by Hindu scriptures. This is borne out in my own research, which involved a comparison of advertisements for marriage partners in twelve Indian papers published in 1987 and 1988 with advertisements in twelve issues of the Canadian edition of *India Abroad* published during the same period. My hypothesis, that the concept of marriage of first-generation Hindus in Canada for the most part will *not* be influenced by Western ideologies of marriage, is supported by this analysis and comparison. Compared with the Indian advertisements, the Canadian ads continue to reflect many of the sex-role expectations, prejudices and discriminatory practices against women that characterize traditions of Hindu arranged marriage. Some interesting differences emerge as well, however. In Canada siblings frequently substitute for parents in obtaining marriage partners, and there is greater flexibility in terms of caste restrictions and remarriage in Canadian ads compared with those in Indian papers.

In general, however, my theoretical and empirical explorations suggest that Hindu women in Canada continue to be strongly discouraged from exploring and experiencing the alternative life styles available to them in Canada. More importantly, this generally uncompromising Hindu attitude, which sustains traditional models in marriage and family, has the very poignant consequence of effectively insulating the continuing abuse of women from public admission and scrutiny. Finally, my cross-cultural study challenges Canada's Multiculturalism Act (C-93) in its assumption that the various "cultures" it admits into the political process do not conflict in ideologies and value. It exposes the Act as naive, ill-informed and in error. We have as yet failed to recognize and grapple with the fact that this Act is in profound contradiction to the Canadian Charter of Rights and Freedoms. While the Act exists essentially to protect and promote the cultural and political rights of ethnic minorities, it also needs to state that ethnic groups have political obligations, namely, to evaluate critically their cultural heritages in terms of the Charter, and to consider issues concerning Canadian unity in the face of conflicting heritages and values. I believe that the elimination of "culture" from political dialogue and a separation of "race" and "culture" could provide a basis for solutions. I offer my work, which grows out of and informs my life experiences, as a contribution to this evaluation and to the struggle for furthering women's human rights.

References

Bühler, Georg, trans. *The Laws of Manu*. New York: Dover Publications, 1969.

Vaidyanath, Sharda. "The Intersection of Concepts of Marriage in Canada: A Study of the Influence of Western Ideologies of Marriage on First Generation Hindus." M.A. thesis, Carleton University, 1990.

LIVING AND WORKING IN COMMUNITIES

VIVRE ET TRAVAILLER DANS NOS COMMUNAUTÉS

In the preceding sections, we have joined with women as they struggle to define themselves in a diversity of contexts. In this section, we follow the struggle for definition to the yet more public sphere of the workplace and the community. Again, we are presented with an amazing diversity of contexts: the Philippines, the so-called free-trade zones around the globe, Quebec communities. But within this diversity there are recurring themes, as the authors speak of women's fight to define themselves and their communities in their own way and their refusal to accept others' definitions, even when those "others" are well-intentioned feminist researchers. They also refuse to have these definitions reduced to one dimension, insisting that at the same time as they are women they are also community organizers and skilled and knowledgeable workers and designers, capable of learning whatever new skills are required in order to maintain themselves and their families. This struggle for holism — to hold all the pieces of their lives together, to meet the demands of all their jobs, paid and unpaid, visible and invisible, public and domestic — is no joyful crusade. The "bread" of the feminist anthem is hard enough for most of the world's women to come by. Whatever "roses" come their way tend to do so by dint of collective action — in other words, more work.

These contradictions in women's lives are not confined to women living in underdeveloped countries or regions, however. In affluent countries, where roses are more plentiful, the struggle takes on somewhat different forms. Feminist academics, who, as we have already seen, act in the world from a position of relative privilege, may be too quick to appropriate the struggles of all the world's women as their own, without being aware enough of the power they exercise simply by being what they are. This is one of the several challenges Colette St-Hilaire throws out to us in her account of what is like to be "woman, white and 'Canadian'" in the Philippines. As a Québécoise who at home is engaged in a power struggle over nationalist identity, St-Hilaire found herself identified by the Filipina women with whom she had come to study and work as a "Canadian" and, what is worse, as a representative of the Canadian power structure as embodied in CIDA (the Canadian International Development Agency). This realization forced St-Hilaire to rethink her reasons for being in the Philippines and, on a deeper level, to explore the Canadian discourse on development. St-Hilaire enables us to see the ways in which the so-called development process continues to serve the interests of the power structure that made the process necessary in the first place. Her closing argument is for feminists to preserve the diversity of the world's women by choosing coalitions of action over alliances that presuppose a worldwide unity and identity of women.

Lynn Bueckert's work points to a coalition that women in the North and South should be making. Bueckert's article details how advances in telecommunications technology now make it possible for North American businesses to have much of their routine office work done offshore at cut-rate prices. Why such savings? Because the women who sit at these offshore terminals work for 75 cents U.S. an hour, many of them for six or even seven days a week, for as many weeks per year as possible. Their work is monitored and paced electronically and leaves them exposed to all the health hazards associated with working long hours in front of video display terminals. The terms of the "structural adjustment" imposed by agencies like the World Bank ensure that women have few opportunities open to them for jobs that enable them to support their families at even a minimal level, and guarantee that there will be a continuing supply of workers to supply this "growth industry." Canadian women's welfare is inextricably linked with that of their sisters offshore: the more jobs that are sent offshore, the fewer jobs will be available to Canadian women, the lower the likelihood of their achieving gains in pay and working conditions and the faster their rate of impoverishment.

The paper that closes this section also deals with women in communities, but from a more theoretical perspective. Denyse Côté challenges us to consider where women fit within the development of paradigms of community development. She concludes that both neo-conservative and neo-liberal positions maintain a discourse that is limited to the public sphere and excludes any consideration of the domestic or private sphere, which is left to women. This will not do, Côté argues. Given the ways in which the gendered nature of our political and economic structures limit women's access to social resources, it is essential that theorists and practitioners of community development revisit their notions of what constitutes adequate concept and practice, to ensure that these explicitly include both the formal and informal contributions women make to the development of their communities.

This image crystallizes the aspirations of women in the DIWATA programme brought to us by St-Hilaire, as well as the work that links the welfare of Canadian working women to that of their sisters doing office work offshore, and brings this section on women working in communities to a powerful and forward-looking conclusion.

Femme, blanche et "Canadian" aux Philippines. Une réflexion sur nos pratiques féministes de développement

Colette St-Hilaire[1]

In Manilla in 1989, even as Canada was intensifying its efforts to establish its program for the "integration of women in development," a debate was raging among women's groups there over the possible consequences of this foreign intervention on the autonomy of their movement. The following article problematizes the Canadian feminist role in the Philippines through a study of the SHIELD and DIWATA projects of the Canadian International Development Agency (CIDA). It suggests the need to reflect on our discourses on women and development, on the institutions and projects that embody these discourses and on their effects on women in the Philippines. It calls for a rethinking of the concept of global feminism and an analysis of its institutionalization in the gender and development approach. To avoid the trap of essentialism, to avoid imposing a feminism of the North on the rest of the world, we must begin to attend to questions of identity, diversity and difference as sources of resistance.

À Manille, en 1989, alors que le Canada redoublait d'efforts pour mettre en œuvre son programme d'«intégration des femmes au développement», le débat faisait rage au sein des groupes de femmes, où l'on redoutait les conséquences de cette intervention étrangère sur l'autonomie du mouvement. L'article qui suit problématise la présence féministe *Canadian* aux Philippines à travers l'étude des projets SHIELD et DIWATA de l'Agence canadienne de développement international (ACDI). Il nous propose de réfléchir aux discours que nous tenons sur les femmes et le développement, aux institutions et aux projets qui actualisent ces discours, et à leur effet sur les femmes des Philippines. Il nous invite à repenser le concept de féminisme mondial et à analyser son institutionnalisation dans l'approche genre et développement. Pour éviter le gouffre de l'essentialisme, pour ne pas imposer à travers le monde un féminisme qui vient du Nord, il importe de faire place à l'identité, à la diversité et à la différence, sources de résistance.

En septembre 1989, je débarquais à Manille dans le but d'y effectuer une recherche sur le rapport femmes-hommes dans la paysannerie. Ce projet faisait suite à plusieurs années de travail dans les réseaux de solidarité et s'était élaboré à l'occasion de nombreux contacts avec des groupes de femmes des Philippines. L'arrivée d'une *Canadian* en un sens tombait à point. L'Agence canadienne pour le développement international (ACDI) venait en effet de proposer 3,5 millions de dollars aux groupes de femmes, dans le cadre de son programme de développement des ressources humaines. Le centre de recherche qui avait accepté de m'accueillir et l'organisation féministe avec laquelle je comptais faire ma recherche appartenaient tous deux à une coalition formée à l'issue d'une consultation commandée par l'ACDI. Les débats faisaient rage dans le mouvement des femmes devant la perspective de dépendre de l'aide étrangère. Des tensions existaient déjà entre les groupes et l'intervention du Canada les avaient exacerbées : Qui allait négocier avec l'ACDI ? Qui allait administrer les fonds ? Qui allait en bénéficier ? Qui allait profiter des contacts au Canada ? Je me suis vue interpellée, consultée — pour ne pas dire coincée — du seul fait de ma citoyenneté. En même temps, j'essayais d'organiser ma recherche. Et les choses n'avançaient guère : là où j'avais envisagé un projet de recherche féministe, des femmes pressentaient une intervention étrangère dans leur mouvement. Nos rapports étaient marqués par la présence de l'ACDI : nous nagions toutes avec difficulté dans cette mer canadienne d'intégration des femmes au développement (IFD).

J'ai commencé à m'interroger : d'où m'est venue cette idée que je pourrais faire une recherche aux Philippines ? D'où sort cette *Canadian* que je ne connais pas ? Québécoise et féministe, je découvrais mon appartenance au discours canadien du développement, à ce dispositif de pouvoir qui met en branle une armée d'institutions, d'experts, de projets, de bourses de recherche, de millions, un dispositif qui commence même à s'exprimer au féminin. J'ai abandonné mon projet initial et décidé de tourner mon regard vers nos pratiques, vers la présence féministe canadienne aux Philippines.

Ces dernières années, le Canada s'est taillé une bonne réputation aux Philippines en matière d'intégration des femmes au développement. L'ACDI a en effet inauguré son volet femmes en 1987, en affectant une coordonnatrice à temps complet à la tâche. En 1989, l'ACDI lançait le projet mentionné ci-haut, maintenant connu sous le nom de DIWATA. Cela dit, avec un budget total de 5 millions de dollars, le volet IFD ne représente que 3% du programme canadien aux Philippines. Mais cette marginalité ne doit pas nous empêcher d'analyser les rapports sociaux qui se mettent en place au nom de l'IFD. Si le développement s'est bel et bien édifié sur l'invisibilité des femmes, il me semble qu'il commence à miser plutôt sur leur mobilisation. En ce sens, le problème qui m'intéresse est moins celui de l'oubli des femmes dans le développement, que celui de leur production comme catégorie de la pensée (femmes du Tiers-Monde …), celui de leur rattachement à des lieux de pouvoir (section IFD de l'ACDI …), celui de leur transformation en cibles des pratiques du développement (bénéficiaires de ceci ou de cela …), bref celui de leur inscription dans les structures sociales, en particulier dans l'État, par le biais de leur mobilisation dans le développement. Je soutiens que, malgré leur marginalité, les discours et les pratiques d'IFD annoncent une tendance, celle da la gestion sociale des femmes, et qu'il est important de l'analyser parce qu'elle suppose la mise en place de nouveaux rapports de pouvoir au sein desquels des femmes du Nord, et jusqu'à un certain point des femmes du Sud, occupent une position privilégiée. Cette tendance émerge aussi maintenant dans la mise en œuvre de l'approche genre et développement (GED), nous renvoyant à la critique de nos pratiques féministes les plus chères.

Le projet SHIELD et la gestion sociale des femmes

Le projet SHIELD (*Sustained Health Improvement through Expanded Local Development*)[2], un projet intégré de développement communautaire financé par l'ACDI, me permettra d'illustrer ce que peut signifier la gestion sociale des femmes. SHIELD s'étend à une centaine de villages de Mindanao aux Philippines et bénéficie d'une subvention de 3,5 millions de dollars de l'ACDI, à laquelle s'ajoute un montant de 1 million de dollars destiné à l'Université de Calgary pour l'administration du projet. En plus d'être un programme d'éducation en matière de santé, SHIELD comporte un important volet d'organisation communautaire et des activités créatrices de revenus.

Dans le jargon de l'ACDI, SHIELD appartient à la catégorie II, c'est-à-dire qu'il est ouvert aux participants des deux sexes, mais qu'on y encourage particulièrement la participation des femmes et qu'on prévoit qu'elles seront les premières à bénéficier du projet. Les statistiques disponibles confirment que les femmes participent activement à SHIELD. La quasi totalité des bénévoles de la santé qui constituent le noyau de départ de SHIELD sont des femmes ; les femmes dominent aussi largement dans les cercles de qualité, la structure de base du projet, et constituent la majorité des bénéficiaires du crédit accordé par SHIELD.

La participation des femmes dans SHIELD est toutefois bien contrôlée : elles n'interviennent qu'après n'aient été définies de façon minutieuse les tâches de planification, de mise en œuvre, de surveillance et d'évaluation du projet. SHIELD est un discours scientifique et spécialisé et il obéit aux règles du discours : il faut pour le parler appartenir aux institutions qui le portent et détenir les qualifications de la profession. Lire le texte de SHIELD, c'est comme lire le Code civil ou le Code criminel : des centaines de pages de procédures vous submergent. Des exemples ? Vous trouverez dans SHIELD un cadre logique comprenant la liste des objectifs, les activités prévues, les résultats quantitatifs attendus, les moyens de vérification et les conditions requises à chaque étape ; un échéancier prévoyant les activités et les objectifs de chaque trimestre pendant cinq ans, un calendrier de remise des rapports, une grille d'évaluation, etc. Des technocrates, pris d'une peur incontrôlable de la nouveauté, ont tout prévu jusque dans les moindres détails, normalisant tous les comportements, structurant l'ensemble des activités du projet, définissant d'avance la nature et l'ampleur des résultats.

Permettez-moi d'illustrer comment fonctionne concrètement cet appareillage destiné à gérer les femmes dans le développement. À l'entrée de chaque village, on trouve un grand tableau (il doit bien faire dix pieds de hauteur et dix pieds de largeur) sur lequel chaque famille participant au projet est représentée à l'aide d'un dessin de maisonnette. Au bas de chaque maisonnette, des couleurs vives étalent aux yeux de tous le bilan de santé de la famille. Ce bilan est réalisé à partir de six indicateurs : nutrition, vaccination, eau potable, installations sanitaires, santé maternelle et planning familial. Une colonne rouge indique qu'il y a danger : les enfants de telle famille ne grandissent pas ; tel autre ménage ne pratique pas la planification des naissances ; un autre n'a pas d'installations sanitaires.

Ces tableaux mesurent essentiellement le travail domestique des femmes et leur fécondité. Les mauvaises mères y sont pointées du doigt, celles qui ne nourrissent pas bien leurs enfants, celles qui n'ont pas fait installer les toilettes. Et les tableaux ne sont qu'une des nombreuses procédures de contrôle : il y a encore les visites à domicile des bénévoles de la santé, les fiches de croissance des enfants, les fiches de santé familiale, les visites du personnel de SHIELD et j'en passe. Les techniques disciplinaires de SHIELD constituent un véritable bio-pouvoir, pour reprendre un thème développé par le philosophe français Michel Foucault, un pouvoir qui s'exerce à partir des corps qu'on scrute, qu'on mesure, qu'on contrôle.

Ces procédures ne sont pas les seules mesures utilisées dans SHIELD. Il y aurait tout un chapitre à écrire sur la mobilisation des femmes dans des « cercles de qualité de vie », la structure de base du projet, dont la fonction consiste essentiellement à créer chez la paysanne philippine l'identité qui lui permettra de se mobiliser dans les projets de développement qu'on a conçus pour elle. Au terme du processus, la femme paysanne n'a pas gagné d'autonomie ; elle est cependant devenue plus facilement *administrable*, mieux adaptée au développement.

Le projet DIWATA : à l'intersection de la résistance et de la gestion des femmes

Le projet DIWATA propose une version un peu différente du discours canadien du développement. DIWATA est un mécanisme de financement destiné à soutenir des projets féministes innovateurs : sessions de formation sur les rapports femmes-hommes, publications et réseaux féministes, etc. (DIWATA, 1990:3). Le pouvoir, dans DIWATA, est en grande partie entre les mains des femmes élues par leurs réseaux pour administrer le projet. DIWATA s'est engagé à accorder une attention particulière aux femmes travailleuses, aux femmes des communautés culturelles, aux femmes paysannes et aux femmes engagées dans le secteur informel. DIWATA constitue une concrétisation de l'approche GED. En ce sens, le projet vise moins l'intégration des femmes au développement que la féminisation du développement.

Mais la résistance féministe n'épuise pas ce que DIWATA représente. Pour accéder au financement de l'ACDI, il a fallu que DIWATA entre à son tour dans *l'ordre du discours*. Ainsi, après que les femmes du Groupe des Dix eussent passé des mois à consulter leurs membres et à formuler leurs objectifs de développement, la machine de l'ACDI s'est chargée de tout absorber, réécrire, normaliser. Aujourd'hui, DIWATA parle la langue de l'intégration des femmes au développement : on y cause description de projet, stratégie, cadre logique, plan de surveillance, de révision et d'évaluation, conformément au manuel déjà utilisé dans SHIELD. La contribution des femmes est ainsi inscrite dans des grilles qui reconstruisent la réalité par le texte, modifiant d'autant les pratiques qui viendront s'y articuler au cours de la mise en oeuvre du projet.

On pourrait croire que l'acceptation des termes de l'ACDI n'est qu'une tactique qui demeurera sans effet sur le travail de DIWATA. Ce serait sous-estimer le rôle du discours : lorsqu'elles auront passé des heures à formuler des objectifs et à remplir des rapports selon des catégories qui leur sont étrangères, les femmes engagées dans DIWATA devront encore mettre les bouchées doubles pour échapper à la pensée bureaucratique et retrouver leurs mots et leurs projets. En fait, DIWATA se situe à une intersection où les intérêts et les discours

sont multiples et contradictoires. Par la diversité des organisations qu'il mobilise, par ses objectifs et ses activités, le projet
DIWATA est avant-gardiste et contribue en pratique à la construction d'une société féministe, démocratique et pluraliste ; par son
rattachement aux institutions de développement, DIWATA
s'articule à un dispositif de pouvoir. DIWATA ouvre un espace de
lutte où s'affrontent diverses définitions du développement, d'où
émergent de multiples femmes, à la fois gestionnaires du sous-
développement au féminin et agentes de féminisation du
développement. À ce jour, la voix de DIWATA apporte une note
agréablement discordante dans le discours du développement.
Mais pour combien de temps ? Le discours et les pratiques de
l'orientation GED ne risquent-elles pas de se substituer à l'IFD pour
assurer la gestion des femmes?

Les premiers rapports d'activités de DIWATA laissent perplexes.
On y apprend que le manuel d'opération de DIWATA sera révisé
pour être conforme à l'entente signée avec l'ACDI ; qu'à l'image de
l'ACDI, le secrétariat de DIWATA exigera des rapports trimestriels
des groupes ayant bénéficié de son appui financier (DIWATA, 1991:1-
2). DIWATA a d'ailleurs été invité par l'ACDI à professionnaliser son
travail et, pour ce faire, à centraliser certaines opérations. En avril
1991, la direction de DIWATA a donc embauché une firme privée,
Pacific Pioneers Information and Research Inc., pour informatiser
tout son système d'évaluation et de surveillance des projets, son
système de rapport et sa gestion ainsi que pour former le personnel
de DIWATA en regard à l'accomplissement de ces nouvelles tâches
(DIWATA, 1991). Bref, la consolidation de DIWATA, comme centre
administratif, laisse présager son enracinement dans le dispositif de
pouvoir du développement.

Bon nombre de chercheures commencent à redouter cette institutionnalisation de l'approche GED. Le fait que la Banque mondiale se l'approprie — et c'est ce qui est en train de se produire
comme en témoigne une session de formation organisée par cette
Banque à Washington en novembre 1991 — inquiète. L'approche
GED risque en effet de s'articuler aux programmes d'ajustement
structurel, accroissant leur efficacité par une connaissance plus
raffinée des besoins des femmes. L'apparition récente de manuels
pour l'utilisation de l'approche GED dans les projets de
développement est aussi un peu troublante3. En même temps qu'ils
témoignent d'une volonté féministe de défendre les intérêts des
femmes dans le développement, ces manuels mettent sur le marché,
à partir des ONG (organisation non gouvernementale) du Nord et à
grands renforts de financement, des discours et des procédures qui

vont orienter les pratiques féministes de développement au Sud. Le danger est d'autant plus réel que les ONG et les organisations de femmes des pays du Sud tendent, par elles-mêmes, à se tranformer en conduits grâce auxquels le développement peut étendre sa portée à de nouvelles clientèles et de nouveaux problèmes. En effet, là où les coûts deviennent trop élevés, là où la machine gouvernementale ne passe pas, on appelle les ONG et les groupes de femmes à la rescousse : elles prennent le relais de l'État, s'ajustent à son discours et se constituent en pôle privé de la gestion sociale des femmes.

En utilisant le concept de discours pour parler de SHIELD et de DIWATA, j'ai voulu montrer que ce qui se dit en matière de femmes et de développement est socialement organisé, contrôlé, réglé ; qu'en ce domaine, il se dit beaucoup de choses, mais pas n'importe quoi, et ne parle pas qui veut. Le discours du développement est traversé de rapports de pouvoir et « l'intégration des femmes au développement » n'y échappe pas. S'intéresser au discours ne signifie pas nier la matérialité des choses, oublier que des femmes souffrent du développement dans leur corps et dans leur esprit. Au contraire, le discours du développement s'articule à une structure économique, politique et sociale, s'actualise dans des institutions et structure des pratiques dont les effets sont réels et concrets. Il assujettit les femmes, c'est-à-dire qu'il contribue à en faire des sujets sexuels qui iront occuper une position subordonnée dans les rapports hommes-femmes. Le discours du développement s'articule à tous les autres rapports de pouvoir, structurant notamment les rapports entre le Nord et le Sud, et entre les classes.

Faut-il déserter le développement et le féminisme ?

Si l'on juge par les pratiques de l'ACDI aux Philippines, la question de l'autonomie des femmes dans le développement est loin d'être réglée. Si l'échec de l'IFD était déjà clair pour plusieurs, l'approche GED nous promettait des lendemains qui chantent. Des indices nous permettent maintenant de penser qu'il n'en sera rien. Quelles sont alors les implications stratégiques de cette analyse ? Devrions-nous déserter le féminisme et le développement ? Sommes-nous irrémédiablement condamnées à la corruption du pouvoir ?

Certaines militantes insistent pour restaurer à l'approche GED son intégrité originale. L'approche serait bonne, seule sa mise en œuvre serait en cause. Au nom des intérêts communs des femmes, au nom de leurs luttes exemplaires, on insiste sur leur capacité de formuler un projet féministe mondial et sur leur potentiel comme agentes de changement social.

Cette approche me paraît néanmoins problématique. Elle suppose que l'expérience des femmes — davantage que d'autres expériences — constitue la base à partir de laquelle il est possible de construire un savoir et d'élaborer une stratégie globale de lutte et de changement social. On en déduit que ce savoir et cette stratégie seront d'autant plus justes qu'ils auront réussi à intégrer tous les aspects de l'expérience des femmes : classe, race, préférence sexuelle, capacité physique, âge et autres. Les femmes les plus pauvres et les plus opprimées occupent ici une position privilégiée : succédant à la classe ouvrière au titre de sujet historique, elles incarnent le sujet politique d'un féminisme qui prétend intégrer toutes les luttes. Or, toute tentative de définir un tel projet global risque d'imposer une vision limitée des femmes et de faire du féminisme un nouvel universalisme totalisant. Restaurer l'intégrité de l'approche GED ne permet pas d'échapper à ce danger : l'approche GED porte en elle la tentation très forte de la vérité féministe, et donc du dogmatisme.

Mon expérience des Philippines m'a fait réaliser de façon bien concrète et bien personnelle jusqu'à quel point le monde des femmes et du développement est fragmenté et formé d'intérêts contradictoires, jusqu'à quel point l'expérience des femmes est diversifiée et jusqu'à quel point nous occupons, chacune d'entre nous, des positions qui nous mettent en relation de pouvoir avec d'autres femmes. Mais cette prise de conscience fait peur.

C'est pourquoi, aujourd'hui, les appels à l'unité par-delà la diversité se font de plus en plus pressants. Par exemple, le Centre international MATCH situé à Ottawa et spécialisé dans la coopération entre les femmes du Canada et du Tiers-Monde, hisse l'étendard du féminisme mondial, pour reprendre la formule-choc publiée en première page d'un bulletin de MATCH. Dans une publication que je lisais récemment, *Bridges of Power. Women Multicultural Alliances for Social Change* (Albrecht et Brewer, 1990), des auteures importantes, Charlotte Bunch par exemple, nous invitent aussi à dépasser les coalitions créées sur la base d'intérêts temporairement convergents pour aller vers l'établissement d'alliances plus fondamentales. La reconnaissance de la différence, nous dit-on, ne doit pas empêcher l'unité. De la même façon, partout où je vais depuis un certain temps, on parle de mondialisation : mondialisation des échanges, interdépendance des problèmes, convergences des luttes. Pour combattre la mondialisation, il faut développer l'unité. J'ai entendu ce discours dans le réseau Action-Canada, dans le réseau de solidarité avec les Philippines, dans le réseau femmes et développement.

Cette approche, il me semble, comporte certains dangers. Le retour en force de l'objectif d'unité nous ramène trop souvent à l'élimination des différences. Je vous cite deux exemples qui ont suscité chez moi des interrogations quant à la pertinence de cet appel à l'unité dans la diversité.

L'hiver dernier, j'ai accompagné la présidente d'Amihan, l'association des femmes paysannes des Philippines, à l'occasion d'une tournée canadienne. Nous avons rencontré plusieurs groupes de femmes et très souvent on lui disait : « C'est la même chose ici! ». C'était tellement « la même chose ici » que l'expérience particulière de Loretta, une paysanne de cinquante-trois ans de Mindanao aux Philippines, en a été presque oubliée, dissoute dans la nôtre. Parce que nous étions convaincues que « c'était la même chose », nous n'avons pas écouté ce que Loretta avait à dire sur la militarisation, nous avons peu réagi au fait que sa tête soit mise à prix dans son village, au fait qu'elle et son mari soient maintenant forcés de vivre à Manille, une grande capitale dont ils ne parlent même pas la langue.

Un problème similaire s'est présenté lors de l'assemblée canadienne annuelle du Programme philippino-canadien pour le développement des ressources humaines, un programme financé par l'ACDI et réunissant des organismes de coopération internationale, des groupes de solidarité et des mouvements sociaux au Canada. En compagnie d'invités et d'invitées des Philippines, nous avons parlé de mondialisation et d'unité pendant trois jours. Nous avons comparé nos problèmes et partagé nos acquis à travers des ateliers sur les questions autochtones et paysannes, les problèmes de l'environnement et de la pauvreté urbaine, et les luttes des femmes. Au moment de l'élection du comité de coordination, des femmes appartenant aux diverses communautés philippines du Canada sont venues proposer que leur groupe national élise séparément ses propres représentants et représentantes au comité de direction du programme. L'assemblée s'est soudainement retrouvée en état de choc : après trois jours d'échanges fructueux sur nos points d'unité, pouvait-on accepter un tel manque de confiance envers l'assemblée ? N'allait-on pas ainsi détruire l'unité nécessaire à la lutte ? N'allait-on pas à l'encontre d'un principe fondamental de la démocratie, à savoir la souveraineté de l'assemblée générale et l'égalité des membres de cette assemblée?

C'est qu'à force de parler de mondialisation et d'unité, nous en avions oublié les différences. Nous avions oublié que dans cette assemblée, il y avait des hommes et des femmes ; des Blancs et des personnes de couleur ; des membres de diverses nationalités, tous et toutes inscrits dans des rapports de pouvoir complexes que les appels à l'unité ne peuvent pas annihiler.

La question a fini par m'obséder : pourquoi sommes-nous portées et portés à oublier la différence dès que nous recommençons à parler d'unité ? Pourquoi dans cette tentative de saisir les problèmes à un niveau global, finissons-nous par réduire les problèmes à un seul, par absorber l'*Autre* dans le *Même* I ? Malgré notre reconnaissance de la diversité, nous demeurons attachées et attachés à cette idée que derrière nos différences, nous sommes des personnes ; qu'à titre de personnes humaines, nous partageons une identité fondamentale commune, nous sommes douées de raison et de conscience, nous sommes égales. C'est ce sujet humain universel que nous avons imaginé participant à l'assemblée générale du programme de l'ACDI auquel je viens de faire référence. C'est ce sujet universel qui conférait à l'assemblée générale sa souveraineté et qui permettait de supposer que les femmes et les hommes de la communauté philippine s'y percevraient égales et égaux aux autres personnes et n'auraient donc pas besoin de tenir une élection séparée.

Mais pourquoi alors les femmes de la communauté philippine ont-elles insisté ? Ma réponse, c'est que ce sujet universel, stable, unifié, n'existe pas. Les sujets présents à l'assemblée générale sont des sujets situés, contextuels. Ils et elles sont inscrits, définis même, par des rapports de pouvoir complexes et changeants. Même si nous décrétons leur égalité et leur unité, elle ne se réalise pas pour autant. Ce qui ne veut pas dire que toute unité soit impossible. La pratique démontre souvent le contraire. Mais peut-être devrions-nous penser autrement cette articulation de la diversité et de l'unité. Je pose la question : pour lutter, pour résister aux multiples formes de domination, avons-nous toujours besoin de partager une vision globale ? Avons-nous besoin d'une unité à priori et d'alliances fondamentales ? Pour être radicales, avons-nous besoin d'une stratégie qui prétende embrasser toutes les causes?

J'ose répondre non. Parce que poser l'unité comme objectif et l'alliance fondamentale comme stratégie ouvre la porte à l'affirmation d'une identité fondamentale commune. Poser l'unité des femmes du monde entier comme objectif stratégique suppose que nous reconnaissions en chacune de nous ce fond commun d'identité, ce sujet-femme qui s'élève au-delà des différences, que nous pouvons représenter politiquement sous la bannière d'un féminisme mondial. Et définir ce sujet féminin, c'est encore exclure car, inévitablement, des femmes refuseront de s'y reconnaître. Notre prétention à les représenter ne sera plus qu'une absorption de leur lutte dans la nôtre.

En ce sens, toute tentative de définir un sujet politique stable et une alliance fondamentale que le féminisme mondial représenterait au-delà des différences me semble vouée à l'échec. Ce sujet politique n'existe pas : il n'y a pas de *femme* au-delà *des femmes* ; elle n'existe pas cette militante universelle capable de saisir toutes les oppressions et de s'unir à toutes les opprimées.

Nous sommes forcées de construire des coalitions plutôt que des alliances si nous voulons préserver la richesse de la diversité. La coalition, au lieu de poser à priori les termes de l'unité fondamentale, travaille à reconnaître les différences comme les convergences. Ces convergences existent, et à certains moments elles sont si grandes que les luttes séparées peuvent créer un effet global et résulter en de grands bouleversements politiques. Mais nous ne saurions les poser à priori. Les femmes de la communauté philippine auraient eu moins de difficultés à se faire représenter sur le comité de direction (je signale que l'assemblée a fini par accepter leur position après un débat difficile) si l'assemblée avait reconnu les différences qui la marquaient et les rapports de pouvoir inscrits dans ces différences.

On m'objectera que la différence comporte elle aussi ses problèmes. L'écrivaine Hélène Cixous a écrit de très belles pages sur ce qu'elle appelle le paradoxe de l'altérité, cette définition de l'*Autre* comme différent, pour mieux le dominer et le ramener sous l'empire du *Propre* ou du *Même*. Si nous voulons préserver la richesse de la diversité, nous devons concevoir la différence autrement que dans cette logique d'appropriation binaire. La différence que je célèbre est moins une différence qu'une multiplicité ; elle implique que les identités sont précaires, instables et changeantes et que la représentation politique de ces identités s'apparente davantage à la mobilité de la guérilla qu'à la stratégie totalisante d'une lutte qui prétendrait défendre toutes les causes.

Pour conclure, mon expérience des Philippines m'amène à suggérer en quelque sorte un féminisme sans femme pré-définie. Des féminismes plutôt, avec des femmes toujours en train de se définir, au gré des rapports de pouvoir dans lesquelles elles interviennent. Dans ces féminismes, il n'y a rien de surprenant à ce que je sois une féministe québécoise à Montréal et une chercheuse *Canadian* blanche à Manille. Je suis tantôt l'une, tantôt l'autre. Mon expérience de la diversité m'amène aussi à proposer une stratégie de coalitions qui mettrait un bémol sur le discours de l'unité mais qui multiplierait les occasions locales de résistance. L'articulation des actions locales au contexte général se présenterait alors comme l'effet plutôt que comme l'objectif de nos luttes.

Notes

1. Mon travail a bénéficié de l'aide financière du Centre de recherches pour le développement international (CRDI) et du Conseil en sciences humaines du Canada (CRSH).

2. L'étude de SHIELD s'est faite avec l'autorisation des responsables du projet ; elle aurait été impossible sans l'aide des membres du personnel du Women Studies and Research Centre et du Community-Based Health Services de Davao City à Mindanao.

3. Voir à ce sujet le manuel publié conjointement par le Conseil canadien pour la coopération internationale (CCCI), l'Association québécoise des organismes de coopération internationale (AQOCI) et le Centre international MATCH, intitulé *Un autre genre de développement : un guide pratique sur les rapports femmes-hommes dans le développement*, Ottawa, CCCI, 1991.

Références

Albrecht, Lisa and Rose M. Brewer. *Bridges of Power. Women Multicultural Alliances for Social Change*, Philadelphia, New Society Publishers, 1990.

Butler, Judith. *Gender Trouble. Feminism and Subversion of Identity*, New York, Routledge, 1990.

Cixous, Hélène. *La jeune née* (en collaboration avec Catherine Clément), Paris, UGE, collection 10/12, 1975.

— . *Entre l'écriture*, Paris, Des femmes, 1986.

DIWATA Inc. *The Diwata Project. The Philippines. Management Plan (draft)*, Manille, février 1990.

— . *Semi Annual Report*, 1 avril à 30 septembre 1991.

Escobar, Arturo. « Power and Visibility : The Invention and Management of Development in the Third World », thèse de doctorat, University of California, 1987.

Foucault, Michel. *L'ordre du discours*, Paris, Gallimard, 1971.

— . *Histoire de la sexualité, 1. La volonté de savoir*, Paris, Gallimard, 1976.

MATCH International. « Avec ses nouveaux programmes, MATCH hisse l'étendard du féminisme mondial », dans *Bulletin MATCH*. Ottawa, hiver 1990, p. 1, 3, 4.

Mueller, Adèle. « The Bureaucratization of Feminist Knowledge : The Case of Women in Development », dans *Documentation pour le recherche féministe* 15, no. 1, p. 36-38, Ontario Institute for Studies in Education,1986.

SHIELD. *SHIELD Project*, 1988.

— . *Group Formation Manual*, 1988.

The Impact of Off-shore Office Work On Women Workers Globally and Locally

Lynn Bueckert

La restructuration de l'économie mondiale a entraîné la prolifération des zones de commerce libre et a donné lieu à une nouvelle répartition internationale du travail. Jusqu'à récemment, la réattribution du travail dans les pays du Tiers-Monde s'était fait ressentir davantage dans le secteur manufacturier ; cependant, l'évolution des télécommunications et des technologies informatiques ont favorisé l'exportation du travail de bureau à l'étranger. Ce document examine le travail de bureau fait en Jamaïque et les défis que ce travail pose aux travailleuses de l'hémisphère nord et de l'hémisphère sud qui luttent quotidiennent pour leur survie économique.

The restructuring of the world economy has brought about a proliferation of free-trade zones and the emergence of a new international division of labour. Until recently, the relocation of work to the Third World was most significant in the manufacturing sector; however, developments in telecommunications and computer technologies have made it possible for office work to be sent off-shore. This paper examines off-shore office work in Jamaica and the challenges it holds for women workers in the South and the North in their daily struggle for economic survival.

Introduction

Since the early seventies, the capitalist agenda of governments and transnational corporations has brought about the proliferation of free-trade zones and the emergence of a new international division of labour. A free-trade zone is a geographically designated area of land reserved specifically for multinationals to set up their off-shore, or "run-away," operations. It is also an area where companies are guaranteed cheap labour and are free from taxes for ten to twenty years, foreign-exchange controls, laws concerning workers' rights and health-and-safety regulations and, often, trade-union organizing. Since the mid-seventies, free-trade zones have been set up at a rapid rate. In 1975, there were thirty-one zones in eighteen countries; in 1986, there were five hundred in seventy countries (Watson, 1988). Most free-trade zones are situated in Third World countries. The zones employ over three million workers, of which 85 to 90 per cent are women (Mitter, 1986).

As we know from the Canada-U.S.-Mexico free-trade negotiations, the concept of free trade and free-trade zones is not about to be abandoned in the very near future. In July of 1990, U.S. President George Bush announced his government's sweeping vision of a western-hemisphere free-trade zone : "We must shift the focus of our economic interaction towards a new economic partnership ... We look forward to the day when ... the Americas ... are equal partners in a free trade zone stretching from the port of Anchorage to Tierra del Fuego" (Bilski et al., 1990:22).

Until recently, the relocation of work to the Third World and the new international division of labour was most prominent in the manufacturing sector, particularly in the textile and electronics industries; however, developments in telecommunications and computer technologies have made it possible for office work to be sent off-shore as well. This paper is about off-shore office work and the challenge it holds for women workers in the South and the North in their daily struggle for economic survival.

Off-Shore Office Work

Dear Mr. Jones,[1]

I wish to introduce you to the advantages your company will profit by setting up a data processing/keystroke operation in St. Lucia. These include:

- *Wage rates that are one-fifth of U.S. wages*
- *A willing and able English speaking work force*
- *High degree of accuracy*
- *Daily air service to and from the U.S.*
- *Good turnaround time*
- *Modern telephone system*
- *Dependable electricity*
- *Fully digital earth station for transmission of data both ways by satellite*

It may interest you to know that the foremost printing establishment in the United States, and some data processing service companies have recently opened data processing/keystroke operations in the Caribbean.

Yours sincerely,
Patrick Sylvester
Director
St. Lucia National Development Corporation

This is an actual letter sent to a small publishing company in Vancouver by the St. Lucia National Development Corporation. Unfortunately, it is not one of a kind; rather, it represents the thousands, and perhaps millions, of similar letters that are sent out continuously by Third World government agencies such as the Barbados Industrial Development Corporation, Jampro (Jamaica's economic-development agency) and the like to solicit off-shore office work from Canada, the United States, Britain, West Germany, France and Italy, to be done by women workers in the Third World.

Recently, I learned of two examples of office work being sent off-shore from Canada.[2] The 10–16 October 1991 issue of *NOW*, a Toronto newsmagazine, revealed that Confederation Life, Canada's fifteenth-largest financial institution, is exporting data-processing jobs from its Canadian office to an office in Barbados. Confederation Life's customers include Domtar, Bell Canada and the Canadian Imperial Bank of Commerce. One of its major customers is the government of Ontario, which holds the health-insurance policy for its sixty-nine thousand civil servants with Confederation Life (Cooley, 1991).

I discovered the second example by leafing through the Vancouver Yellow Pages. I stumbled upon a data-processing company in Coquitlam, a suburb of Vancouver, which advertises itself as "professional experts in off-shore data-processing." A telephone call to the company revealed that it brokers work for Canadian firms to Peru. The actual paperwork is sent to Peru by air, and the data are returned to the customer inputted onto a magnetic tape. The workers, predominantly women, are paid $70 to $100 (Canadian) per week; as the company's owner said, "You can hire ten women to data process in Peru for what it would cost you to hire one woman in Canada."[3]

Exporting office work is not, in itself, a new phenomenon. The practice has been silently and invisibly under way for the past twenty years and has only sporadically come to public attention. For instance, in 1981, during a clerical workers' strike at the Insurance Corporation of British Columbia (ICBC), it became public knowledge that ICBC was breaking the strike by sending data-entry work to the Philippines to be processed by clerical workers in Manila (Hansen, 1985). In 1985, American Airlines closed its data-processing centre in Tulsa, Oklahoma, and hired four hundred women in Barbados to process flight coupons (Mitter, 1986:138). In both of these situations, the companies transported the data off-shore by air. For many corporations that otherwise would have considered using such a service, this method was much too time-consuming.

The advancement of computer and telecommunications technologies has now made it possible for data to be turned around in hours rather than days and at a cheaper rate, making it much more lucrative for companies to send their work off-shore. Consequently, the long-speculated trend of run-away offices has become intensively realized over the last several years. For wages one third to one twentieth of those paid to workers in Canada or the United States, an overall cost reduction of 50 per cent, and substantially increased profit margins, corporations can get their office work done in the country of their choice. The list of countries with off-shore facilities has expanded over the years and includes the Philippines, Korea, India, China, Taiwan, Barbados, Jamaica, St. Lucia, St. Kitts, the Dominican Republic, Haiti, the Bahamas, Mexico, Ireland, Peru, Singapore, Malaysia, Sri Lanka and Grenada (James, 1987; Lohr, 1988; Meyers, 1986). The most recent addition to the list is the Commonwealth of Independent States, which will begin operating data-communications services in 1992 in the city of Nakhodka and on the island of Sakhalin, both of which are free economic zones in the far east of Russia.[4]

The country to which a company decides to send office work depends somewhat on the nature of the job. According to Norm Bodek, who brokers office work from Los Angeles, "If it's a short job requiring quick turn around I take it to St. Kitts. A longer job with bibliographic text goes to China and jobs requiring a lot of people go to India" (Meyers, 1986:30).

The work that is sent off-shore is not limited to keypunching or coding, as was once thought. Rather, it spans the entire spectrum of activities carried out in an office, including data processing, telemarketing, automated mapping and computer-aided design (CAD), keypunching, word processing, typesetting, hotel, car and airline reservations, computer programming and software development[5] — that is, work that tends to be extremely labour intensive.

Companies that use off-shore office services tend to be very secretive about their practice. Therefore, it is difficult to determine exactly who is exporting office work. There is much speculation on the part of workers and unions that all of the major insurance companies, banks, airline companies, publishing houses, hotels, car-rental companies and government departments employ this option at least some of the time; however, to date there is no evidence to what extent this is actually the case. Some of the companies that are known to send work off-shore are American Airlines, Boeing, New York Life, Confederation Life, Random House, McGraw-Hill Inc., Mead Data Central and All America Cables and Radio, a subsidiary of RCA of the United States (James, 1987; Lohr, 1988; Meyers, 1986).

The relocation of work to the Third World, or, as it is referred to in economic circles, the export-promotion economic-development strategy, is touted by the World Bank, the IMF, multinational companies and government leaders as *the* economic blueprint that will improve and stabilize debt-ridden Third World economies. A gender and development analysis of the relocation of work, however, recognizes the political nature of economic-development theory and reveals the capitalist, imperialist and patriarchal agenda of the export-promotion development strategy (Antrobus, 1989; Sen and Grown, 1987; Young, 1988). Gender and development theory takes a holistic approach to economic theory and analyzes the social, economic and political consequences of economic policies; hence, it poses critical questions. Why are companies relocating their operations? Who is working in off-shore factories or offices? What are the conditions of their work? Does the relocation of work improve or lower the standard of living in the South and the North? Does it remove or entrench poverty in the South and in the North? By answering these questions, a global feminist analysis exposes those who benefit and those who lose as a result of off-shore work (Antrobus, 1989; Sen and Grown, 1987; Young, 1988).

Let us look at the situation in Jamaica, for example. In 1987, the Jamaican government, with financial assistance from Teleport International, of the U.S., and Nippon Telephone and Telegraph International and C. Itoh & Co., of Japan, established a "digiport" in Montego Bay (James, 1987). The Jamaica Digiport International is situated in the Montego Bay Free Zone and offers voice, video and data communications between North America and users in the free zone. Data can be transmitted at the rate of thirty typewritten pages per second and at a much cheaper rate than previously available data communications. In addition to data-entry and word-processing services, the digiport handles telephone calls made on "800" toll-free lines (James, 1987). Thus, car-rental reservations or hotel and airline reservations made in the United States or Canada may well be processed through a clerical worker in Montego Bay.

The digiport is set up with state-of-the-art technology and is the only facility of its kind outside the industrialized countries, giving Jamaica a competitive edge within the off-shore office industry around the world (Hicks, 1989). According to Edward Seaga, the prime minister of Jamaica at the time the digiport was developed, this facility, along with the provisions of the Caribbean Basin Initiative (a Caribbean-U.S. trade agreement signed in 1983) would boost Jamaica's nascent off-shore data-entry industry and would enable it to expand to employ twenty thousand clerical workers by 1990 (James, 1987). More recently, the present prime minister of Jamaica, Michael Manley, and his government announced in their five-year plan that the off-shore office industry was one of the five main industries that would be groomed to boost the ailing Jamaican economy.[6]

There are currently approximately thirty companies that employ four to five thousand workers in the off-shore office industry in Jamaica;[7] 99 per cent of the workers are women; 98 per cent are between the ages of eighteen and twenty-five; for the majority, it is their first job experience (Barnes, 1989). Some of the firms are physically located in the free-trade zones in Montego Bay or in Kingston, while others are not. The Montego Bay Free Zone is like a large industrial park that is surrounded by a seven-foot-high cement wall. All workers employed in the zone must pass through the gate, which is monitored by a zone security guard, must produce company employment identification and must sign in and out as they come to and leave work.[8]

The company I observed in the zone has approximately 150 women working per shift and runs three shifts per day (Hicks, 1989). The women all work in one large room that houses rows and rows of computers. The room is glaringly lit with fluorescent lights and has a factory-like appearance. The women do not talk to each other during work; they work.

For the most part, the workers do the same task all day, every day. The data processors input batches of mailing lists, subscription lists, survey statistics and litigation petitions. Often their work is extremely confidential (Hicks, 1989). Their work is also paced and electronically monitored. That is, they are expected to produce a certain quota every day, and the computer calculates the number of keystrokes they make per hour and their error rate.

The teleport/digiport operators' work entails taking calls from people who wish to make car, hotel or airline reservations, as well as making calls to customers to solicit their business. The work is very fast, as the operators are expected to spend a minimum time per call.

They are also electronically monitored: the computer tracks the number of minutes the operator has spent on a call and the number of calls taken per hour (Hicks, 1989). The operator job requires good listening skills, concentration, precision, knowledge of world geography, a pleasant personality and speed.

The women working in off-shore office work are sometimes paid hourly, but very often they are paid piece rate: a low base rate per hour and an additional number of cents per call made or taken or per keystroke inputted into the computer (Hicks, 1989). This method of pay places additional stress and pressure on an already high-demand and low-control method of work.

The women officially work a forty-hour week and average $3.00 Jamaican (75 cents U.S.) an hour, or $520.00 Jamaican ($130 U.S.) a month. Many of the women work six or even seven days a week for as many weeks per year as possible. According to Michael Hicks, CEO of a data-entry company in the Montego Bay Free Zone, they do this to earn money to buy "extras" for the house or for themselves; however, when one compares their average wage with the ever-escalating cost of living in Jamaica, it becomes clear why they "choose" to work overtime. It is out of absolute necessity. A budget drawn up by a garment worker in Kingston and published in the article "A Free Zone Wage: 'Lawd Only Know How Mi Manage,'" in *Sistren* (1988:11), indicated that bare necessities cost her $456.00 a month. This budget allowed only for the bare minimum amount of food, and nothing for health insurance, clothes and personal items.

Low rates of pay, piece-rate method of pay, monitored and paced work and working in front of a computer all day every day with few breaks exposes the women in off-shore office work to a variety of health hazards. The well-documented health risks associated with working on computers for long periods of time are stress, musculoskeletal injuries, eye strain and fatigue and radiation exposure; however, as in Canada and the United States, these hazards are ignored by the off-shore office companies set up in Jamaica (Barnes, 1989).

An examination of the impact of off-shore office work on women workers' lives must take into account the high unemployment rate in Jamaica (40 per cent for women in 1987); the assurances offered to multinational corporations by the Jamaican government to keep wages low and productivity high; and the severe structural-adjustment programmes the IMF and the World Bank have forced the Jamaican government to implement in return for financial aid. The usual structural-adjustment formula requires the government to devalue its currency, eliminate food subsidies and severely cut back public spending.

Devaluation of the Jamaican currency and elimination of food subsidies have significantly increased the cost of living in Jamaica over the last ten years. The prices of food, housing and transportation have all increased, while wages have intentionally been kept low. In 1989, 36 per cent of the Jamaican population lived at or below the poverty line and 70 per cent consumed a below-average amount.[9] In addition, cutbacks in public spending have reduced the number of jobs in the public sector, which are female-dominated occupations, and have eliminated any possibilities for employment in this area. Off-shore office work may have created employment; however, the conditions under which the industry was established have decreased the number of jobs available in other areas. The cutbacks have particularly affected the services available in education and health care. For instance, children attend school only half days because of a shortage of schools: half go to school in the morning and half in the afternoon. Reductions in the number of beds and nurses limit the care available; thus, the sick and the elderly often must be cared for in the home. Caring for children, the sick and the elderly is considered a woman's responsibility. Cutbacks in education and in health care therefore increase women's workload in the home and the stress in their lives as they attempt to juggle their numerous responsibilities in their productive and reproductive roles. Thus, off-shore office work in Jamaica has also decreased the number of jobs available in other areas, escalated the general cost of living and made life an even greater struggle for survival.

Implications for Canadian Women

What are the implications of off-shore office work for women in Canada? The first, obvious answer is loss of jobs. As has already been mentioned, it is very difficult to know the extent to which this is occurring in Canada. Therefore, it is also difficult to predict the number of jobs that have been lost or not created as a result of the off-shore office trend. Second, the practice and threat of companies moving office work off-shore clearly undermines women office workers' strategies for organizing unions, lobbying for the implementation of health-and-safety regulations and pay equity legislation, and utilizing contract language that is already in place. A prime example of this is the VDT (video display terminal) legislation passed in Suffolk County, New York State, in 1989. Many of the corporations operating in the county at the time were against the legislation and threatened to pull their operations out of the jurisdiction if the legislation passed. The legislation did pass. However, rather than leaving, the corporations appealed the legislation and it was overturned.[10]

A third implication of off-shore work for Canadian women workers is potential poverty. Just like women in Jamaica, women in Canada are struggling to make ends meet. Our federal government has negotiated a free-trade agreement with the United States and has implemented its own structural-adjustment program to fight the federal deficit. As a result, we have borne the brunt of a decrease in wages, an increase in the cost of living, free trade, privatization and the erosion of jobs in the public sector and a decline in dollars for training, education, health care and social assistance.

Clearly, it is imperative that women in the North and the South join together in our struggle for survival. This process has already begun, particularly among women in the South. For example, a women's organization in Mexico, *Mujer a Mujer* (Woman to Woman), has established links with women in unions and women's groups in the Caribbean, Latin America, the U.S. and Canada and sponsored a global-strategies school in Mexico in February, 1992. The school brought together women from each of those areas to develop strategies and a plan of action to offset the negative impact of the continental integration we are presently experiencing. It is an historic and challenging moment for workers around the world and one in which women are forging the way for a better life.

Notes

1. The name of the person to whom the letter was addressed has been changed for confidentiality reasons.
2. The information available on off-shore office work tends to cite examples of American companies relocating office work. To date, few Canadian companies engaging in exporting office jobs have been named.
3. Telephone conversation with a company representative on 5 November 1991.
4. See "Russian Zones to Get Telecom," *The Vancouver Sun*, 5 November 1991, p. D10.
5. See "Jamaica — Your Information Services Location," *JAMPRO Jamaica's Economic Development Agency*, 1990.
6. "JAMPRO's Major Targets," *Daily Gleaner*, 2 June 1990, p. 11.
7. See "Jamaica: Your Information Services Location," 1990.
8. This description is based on my observation of the Montego Bay Free Zone in May, 1989.
9. "Below Average Consumption for 70% of Jamaicans," *Daily Gleaner*, 3 June 1990, p. 30A.
10. See "Employers Try to Pull Plug on VDT Law," *AFL-CIO News*, 30 July 1988, p. 3.

References

Antrobus, Peggy. "Women and Development: An Alternative Analysis." *Development 1* (1989): 26–28.

Barnes, Corienne. "Data Entry Demands." *Sistren* 11, no. 3 (1989): 18–23.

"Below Average Consumption for 70% of Jamaicans." *Daily Gleaner*, 3 June 1990.

Bilski, Andrew, Hilary Mackenzie, Dan Burke and Lucy Conger. "United the Americas: Bush Proposes a Hemispheric Free Trade Zone." *Maclean's*, 9 July 1990: 22.

Cooley, Glen. "Secret Secretaries: Insurance Company Farms out Ontario Government Health Claims to Low-paid Workers in Barbados." *NOW*, 10–16 October 1991: 10–11.

"A Free Zone Wage: 'Lawd Only Know How Mi Manage.'" *Sistren* 10, nos. 2 & 3 (1988): 11.

Hansen, Ken. "Insurance Corporation of British Columbia Case Study." British Columbia Federation of Labour Tehcnologies Impact Research Fund Project, unpublished paper, October, 1985.

Hicks, Michael. Interview with Chief Executive Officer, DataBay Ltd., Montego Bay Free Zone, Jamaica, 25 May 1989.

James, Canute. "Data Processing: Marriage of Convenience." *South* (August 1987): 41–43.

— . "The Instant Offshore Office." *Businessweek*, 15 March 1982: 136E.

Lohr, Steve. "The Global Office." *The Vancouver Sun*, 29 October 1988: B9.

Meyers, Edith. "A New Ball Game: Increasing Efficient Technologies are Making Offshore Data Entry Look More Attractive." *Datamation* (11 August 1986): 26–30.

Mitter, Swasti. *Common Fate Common Bond: Women in the Global Economy.* London: Pluto Press Limited, 1986.

Sen, Gita, and Caren Grown. *Development, Crises, and Alternative Visions. Third World Women's Perspectives.* New York: Monthly Review Press, 1987.

Watson, Noel. "Evaluating the Net Economic Benefits of Free Trade Zones in Theory and Practice: Applied to the Kingston Export Free Zone in Jamaica." Ph.D. diss., Simon Fraser University, 1988.

Young, Kate. "Women in Development: A Retrospective Glance into the Future." *Worldscape* 2, no. 1 (Spring 1988): 1–4.

Le développement communautaire : l'évolution des paradigmes en regard des rapports sociaux de sexe

Denyse Côté

This paper is a reflection on community development and gender. Energies that are devoted specifically to women's issues (aside from women's groups) often have been perceived as residual energies — efforts that are *additional to* or *apart from* those directly related to the survival of community groups or projects. Do the new paradigms in community development include women's issues?

Ce texte se veut une réflexion sur le développement communautaire et son rapport aux femmes. La répartition de toutes les ressources dans une société est médiatisée par les rapports entre les sexes. L'action communautaire n'y échappe pas. Les énergies consacrées à la question des femmes (en situation de mixité) ont souvent été perçues comme des énergies résiduelles, *en sus* ou *à part* des efforts consacrés à la survie des groupes ou des projets communautaires. Les nouveaux paradigmes en développement communautaire incluent-ils la question des femmes ?

Nous sommes témoins à l'heure actuelle au Québec d'un réaménagement de l'échiquier administratif et politique qui accorde au *communautaire* une légitimité nouvelle. À la désinstitutionnalisation mise en place il y a quelques années se conjugue depuis peu une politique de déconcentration des services sociaux et du développement régional. Nous assistons ainsi à l'émergence d'une association entre partenaires inégaux : les groupes communautaires d'une part, et le pouvoir politique, économique et administratif (institutions, déci- deurs locaux) d'autre part. S'il reconnaît la présence et l'utilité du *communautaire* et des groupes communautaires, ce nouveau partenariat ne semble pas entraîner un réaménagement du pouvoir décisionnel ou du financement en faveur des groupes communautaires.

Plusieurs pratiques communautaires de femmes ont été invisibilisées par des processus de légitimation et de professionalisation du *communautaire*. Malgré la présence d'une majorité de femmes dans les organisations populaires (Institut canadien des adultes, 1985), les contours du *communautaire* sont maintenant définis de façon à exclure les contributions informelles des femmes, et de façon à exercer des contrôles accrus sur leur bénévolat. Ce texte a pour objet de situer certains paradigmes du développement communautaire en regard des pratiques communautaires des femmes. Nous poserons les paramètres d'une réflexion qu'il est essentiel d'entreprendre dans la conjoncture actuelle.

Jusqu'aux années 80, le *communautaire* était un domaine d'action réservé aux groupes communautaires. L'expérience des garderies populaires en est un exemple : la Loi des services de garde, établie au Québec en 1978, a peu à peu institutionnalisé l'action communautaire des femmes autour de leurs besoins de garde. Par ailleurs, dans l'esprit de la réforme des services de santé et des services sociaux (Côté, 1990), les organismes de maintien à domicile gèrent de plus en plus le bénévolat orienté vers le soin des personnes âgées. Le militantisme et la créativité sociale des femmes s'institutionnalisent tranquillement. Parallèlement, la désinstitutionnalisation des services sociaux s'accompagne de l'émergence de modes d'intervention axés sur les *réseaux naturels*. Ceux-ci gagnent en visibilité (ils sont reconnus dans le discours) mais perdent en pratique (les soins autrefois donnés par les services de santé et les services sociaux doivent maintenant être dispensés gratuitement par les familles, autrement dit par les femmes, principales dispensatrices de soins dans les familles). Dans un contexte de partenariat qui se développe souvent de façon inégalitaire (Bourque & Panet-Raymond, 1991), la réforme du ministre Côté (services de santé et services sociaux) et la réforme du ministre Picotte (développement régional) s'appuient respectivement sur des modes de gestion régionaux des services sociaux et sur une répartition budgétaire du développement régional. Cette déconcentration administrative s'accompagne d'un intérêt renouvelé pour le développement des communautés locales. C'est pourquoi il nous semble important de se questionner sur le sens du développement communautaire, sur son sens pour les femmes en cette période de réaménagement néo-libéral de l'échiquier politique et économique. Dans un premier temps, nous aborderons l'étymologie des termes constitutifs du développement communautaire.

La communauté

Le concept de *communauté* ressemble à celui de *famille* : il réfère aussi bien à un groupe humain qu'aux interactions entre les membres de ce groupe. D'ailleurs, les concepts de *communauté* et de *famille* recèlent tous deux d'une forte composante normative et symbolique. Ceux-ci risquent souvent d'englober les femmes dans leur définition sans distinguer leurs apports spécifiques.

La communauté, « un groupe social dont les membres vivent ensemble ou (...) ont des intérêts communs » (Petit Robert, 1992:345), renvoie aussi bien à une communauté religieuse, à une communauté de biens entre époux, à une communauté nationale ou à une communauté locale. Les communautés humaines sont multiples et variées. Si les membres d'une communauté partagent des intérêts communs, *tous* leurs intérêts ne sont pas communs pour autant. Ainsi, certains intérêts des habitants d'un quartier peuvent être communs (l'embellissement ou la survie économique du quartier par exemple) et certains autres intérêts peuvent être divergents (l'élection d'un nouvel échevin par exemple).

Le concept de communauté réfère en outre à la notion de *ce qui est commun* (Petit Robert, 1992:345) ; il souligne l'affinité commune, l'accord, l'*unité*, l'*unanimité*. Il est fréquent de confondre ces deux définitions de la *communauté* : celle se référant à l'unanimité et celle se référant à un groupe d'individus partageant certains intérêts. Une telle confusion est très courante et mène à des distortions en développement communautaire. À notre sens, c'est la définition se référant à un groupe d'individus qui partagent *certains* intérêts communs qui doit être retenue.

Cela dit, une communauté n'est pas un agrégat d'individus : elle suscite un sentiment d'appartenance, de loyauté. Le concept de *communauté* est difficile à appréhender, mais son potentiel se réflète dans les sentiments d'appartenance et de loyauté qu'il suscite (Gadamer, 1981). Derrière les flambeaux brandis en défense de la communauté, tout comme ceux brandis en défense du foyer, se cachent cependant deux réalités. D'abord, celle d'une *communauté* qui permet aux individus de survivre (en temps de pénurie, la communauté resserre les rangs). Et celle que l'on a tendance à oublier, celle des énergies humaines nécessaires à son entretien (énergies bénévoles, réseaux de voisinages, de contacts, d'échange de services ... de femmes).

L'organisation communautaire est une professionnalisation des modes d'organisation propres à une communauté. Il s'agit d'une méthodologie d'intervention d'une communauté sur ses problèmes, ou encore, d'une méthodologie d'intervention *auprès* d'une communauté lorsque l'organisateur ou l'organisatrice provient de l'extérieur de la communauté. En organisation communautaire, la communauté est le lieu et la source de l'action, l'objectif final de l'intervention ainsi que sa méthodologie d'action. Traditionnelle-ment, l'organisateur ou l'organisatrice se réfère à la notion de communauté locale, c'est-à-dire à une communauté géographiquement délimitée. Cependant, depuis plus de quinze ans la notion de communauté s'est fragmentée et a été associée à celle de communauté de problèmes ou de caractéristiques, d'intérêts ou de droits : les femmes, les personnes handicapées, les minorités visibles forment des communautés même s'ils ne partagent pas une aire géographique résidentielle.

La communauté locale sera vue différemment selon le courant de pensée en organisation communautaire : elle sera fonctionnelle ou non-fonctionnelle, source de démocratie, ou potentiel revendicateur. L'approche classique du *community development* américain, que nous pouvons associer au conservatisme démocratique et à l'école fonctionnaliste, adjoint le concept de communauté à la notion d'harmonie des rapports sociaux à l'intérieur d'une localité géographiquement délimitée. Ainsi, la cohésion (réelle ou imaginaire) de la communauté villageoise d'antan est vue comme un idéal à atteindre ; les rapports sociaux en milieu urbain sont souvent vus comme dysfonctionnels et comme les résultats négatifs de l'industrialisation et de l'urbanisation. L'organisation com-munautaire a alors pour objet la création d'une communauté fonctionnelle et moderne.

L'école libérale en organisation communautaire perçoit la communauté locale comme le véhicule de rapports sociaux égalitaires : c'est dans la communauté locale que les rapports sociaux hiérarchiques produits par les sociétés technocratiques peuvent être contrebalancés, rapportés à l'échelle humaine, à l'échelle locale. L'organisation communautaire a alors pour objet la création d'une dynamique de concertation des forces en présence pour le mieux-être d'une collectivité locale.

En développement économique communautaire, la communauté est souvent définie comme partenaire dans la recherche d'une qualité de vie. La notion de réseaux naturels et de qualité de vie prend la place de la taylorisation et du processus bureaucratico-institutionnel d'antan (Lockhart, 1987:396). Une telle définition se situe, croyons-nous, à l'enseigne de l'école libérale bien que ce ne soit pas ici la notion de démocratie sur laquelle on insiste, mais plutôt celle d'une responsabilité partagée des différents agents sociaux dans l'atteinte d'un mieux-vivre collectif.

Enfin, l'approche radicale perçoit la communauté comme le cadre et le ferment d'actions revendicatives. Ces actions se concentrent dans des quartiers populaires, ou autour de mouvement d'appropriation des ressources par les laissés-pour-compte d'une situation. Les femmes et la défense de leurs droits se situent à cet enseigne.

Le développement

Le concept de *développement* se réfère, dans son sens propre, à la *croissance*, à l'*épanouissement* : c'est un concept à forte composante philosophique et symbolique, mais qui demeure de nature socio-politique et économique. La pratique socio-historique du développement en est une de changement planifié. On se réfère alors, par exemple, à des actions concertées initiées par une organisation ou un gouvernement du Premier-Monde vers une région, une localité d'un pays du Tiers-Monde.

Issu de l'ère Truman aux États-Unis, le développement international a pris son essor dans les années 60 et 70. L'investissement économique y était direct (reconstruction d'infrastructures) et accompagné d'une stratégie politique qui sera le fondement de la guerre froide en Europe occidentale (dont la création de l'OTAN en 1949). Une stratégie semblable fut rapidement envisagée par les anciennes puissances coloniales, par les États-Unis en particulier, lorsque les colonies africaines et asiatiques commencèrent à revendiquer et à obtenir leur indépendance. La paix sociale fut alors achetée au Tiers-Monde par le biais de promesses de développement et d'investissements dans des projets de développement. Il s'agissait de maintenir certains pays dans le giron d'une des deux idéologies rivales. L'URSS procéda à ses propres projets de développement avec les pays du Tiers-Monde qui étaient dans son orbite.

Ce développement s'est longtemps limité à la construction d'infrastructures (barrages hydro-électriques, routes, etc.) (Rahman, 1991:18-19). L'idée sous-jacente était à l'effet qu'un faible développement économique entraînait une propension à l'autoritarisme politique. Même si l'hypothèse du développement conjoint de la démocratie et de la richesse économique se trouve vérifiée en Occident, de nombreux États d'Amérique latine et d'Asie témoignent d'un développement différent, où l'autoritarisme bureaucratique s'ajuste parfaitement à une rapide croissance économique (Thifault, 1992).

Cette vision de la centralité du développement économique calqué sur les modèles européen et américain a freiné systématiquement l'évolution d'alternatives autochtones pour l'expression sociale des peuples (Rahman, 1991). Cependant depuis le début des années 80, les conceptions occidentalocentristes et hiérarchiques d'un développement basé sur la construction d'infrastructures ont perdu de l'influence, à cause du constat d'échec de ce type développement. À sa place, un développement endogène, conçu par et de concert avec les populations concernées, a été proposé et fait maintenant l'unanimité au niveau du discours. Le développement endogène propose une construction de soi et de l'autre basé sur des rapports non-hiérarchiques et sur un partage des connaissances entre le Nord et le Sud (Rahman, 1991:18-19).

Simultanément au Québec, la notion de développement régional a été employée pour désigner le développement des régions périphériques en rapport avec celui des grands centres urbains (Montréal et Québec). En outre, la notion de développement local a pris de l'ampleur, dans les grands centres urbains, suite à la récession des années 80. Les mouvements sociaux urbains avaient adopté, dans les années 60, une vision autodynamique du capital. Selon cette vision, les décideurs politiques et économiques étaient les seuls gestionnaires de l'économie. Ils planifiaient un changement sur lequel la population concernée n'a aucune emprise (Hamel, 1991). Celle-ci ne pouvait que protester ou revendiquer, mais ne participait pas au processus de planificaton. Parallèlement au constat de faillite du développement international géré par le haut, un courant réclamant le développement endogène, c'est-à-dire une pratique de concertation, s'est développée au Québec. Ces pratiques se sont développées graduellement depuis le Bureau d'aménagement de l'est du Québec (BAEQ) jusqu'aux Sommets économiques, et aux réformes actuelles.

L'action de développement met en jeu des décisions d'allocation des ressources prises dans un contexte précis et appliquées selon des modalités précises. Elle vise l'épanouissement d'une collectivité. Mais elle se doit de reconnaître que la réalité et la valeur symbolique font deux. En effet, la communauté visée est composée de plusieurs forces sociales, et le changement visé peut facilement favoriser certains intérêts plutôt que d'autres et « ... servent rarement les intérêts de tous en même temps » (Anadon et al., 1990).

Le développement communautaire

La définition de l'organisation communautaire ne sera jamais statique, puisqu'elle évolue selon l'idéologie et les pratiques du moment. Dans certains cas, en CLSC par exemple, cette méthodologie d'intervention ne répond plus à ses finalités propres. Ainsi, l'organisation communautaire y est souvent perçue comme un outil et un moyen de résolution de problèmes : on ne lui reconnaît aucune spécificité.

L'organisation communautaire est une méthodologie d'intervention qui privilégie la prise en charge collective par une communauté de ses

problèmes et des solutions à y apporter. Cette méthodologie d'intervention comporte plusieurs types de pratiques qui se situeraient, sur un continuum, entre les pratiques intégratrices et la contestation politique (tableau 1), (Doré, 1985).

Rothman a identifié en 1979 trois grands modèles de pratique en organisation communautaire : la planification sociale, le développement communautaire et l'action socio-politique. Le premier modèle, celui de planification sociale, correspond aux visées du développement décrites plus haut, celles d'un changement social planifié. On peut l'associer au paradigme d'intégration. L'action socio-politique correspond aux visées revendicatrices des communautés ou groupes sociaux laissés-pour-compte et qui cherchent une reconnaissance et l'attribution de ressources. Entre ces deux pôles se situe le développement communautaire. Il s'agit d'un modèle qui prône le changement par l'implication du plus grand nombre de personnes possible au niveau local. On peut l'associer au paradigme intégrationniste en organisation communautaire (Doré, 1985). La définition que donne l'ONU du développement communautaire se situe clairement dans ce paradigme (ONU, 1965:30 :

> L'expression *développement communautaire* est entrée dans la langue internationale pour désigner l'ensemble des procédés par lesquels les habitants d'un pays unissent leurs efforts à ceux des pouvoirs publics en vue d'améliorer la situation économique, sociale et culturelle des collectivités, d'associer ces collectivités à la vie de la nation et de leur permettre de contribuer sans réserve aux progrès de leur pays.

Mais comme toute action est tributaire de ses finalités et des acteurs qui y sont impliqués, le développement communautaire ne se limite pas au paradigme intégrationniste. Il est aussi le fait d'expériences autonomistes (non-associées aux autorités) et peut même devenir un point de jonction entre la planification sociale (réservée aux autorités compétentes) et l'action socio-politique (réservée aux groupes sans pouvoir). Le cas du développement économique est un exemple de ceci.

Le troisième modèle, celui de l'action communautaire autonome, se situe au pôle de la politisation et de l'appropriation en organisation communautaire (tableau 1). Son but est de travailler avec les sans-pouvoir et les démunis pour leur permettre de se réapproprier des moyens d'agir sur leurs conditions de vie. Se distinguant clairement du modèle médical ou thérapeutique en intervention communautaire, l'action communautaire autonome s'identifie à la façon dont les gens s'organisent et s'impliquent dans le cadre d'un processus social dont ils conservent l'entière initiative. Elle s'associe donc aux besoins et aux priorités exprimés par ceux-là même qui enclenchent un processus d'action communautaire. Elle se distingue des finalités institutionnelles et fonctionnelles d'une intervention communautaire commandée par un organisme étranger à la communauté où elle se réalise (Coalition des organismes communautaires du Québec,1988). Elle privilégie l'action socio-politique, modèle d'intervention qui vise la redistribution du pouvoir, des ressources sociales ainsi que la prise de décision à la base (Rothman, 1979).

Le développement communautaire en contexte néo-libéral

La portée du développement communautaire varie selon les cas. On retrouve en effet des cas de développement communautaire s'inscrivant dans la tradition critique des mouvements sociaux urbains, et d'autres qui héritent de la tradition libérale (Hamel, 1991)[1]. Jusqu'à tout récemment, les groupes constitutifs de ces mouvements sociaux urbains considéraient que le développement n'était pas leur affaire, mais l'affaire des corporations. S'adressant aux régions ou aux quartiers urbains les plus pauvres (Duncan, 1986:18), le développement économique est maintenant vu par les mouvements sociaux urbains comme une nouvelle expérience d'action collective pour la création d'emploi, le relèvement de l'employabilité et la revitalisation du cadre urbain (Duncan, 1986:162).

La tendance libérale en développement s'occupe moins des effets pervers de cette approche en termes de marginalisation sociale, d'appauvrissement et d'exclusion des travailleurs et travailleuses des secteurs de pointe (Hamel, 1991:156-157). Elle se fonde sur l'idée de l'investissement de tous les secteurs d'une communauté dans un projet de développement centré sur une localité restreinte. L'investissement dont la communauté assume alors la responsabilité se définit en termes affectifs, en termes de loyauté, et en termes de mobilisation autour du projet de développement. Ce modèle de développement veut se substituer au modèle de développement propre aux grandes corporations. Il introduit le concept de contrat social fondé sur la reconnaissance du bien commun et de la satisfaction des besoins individuels. Il se base sur les énergies communautaires, mise sur le potentiel et les ressources d'une communauté et fonde son action sur une notion de progrès qu'on oppose facilement à la tradition vue comme statique (Lockhart, 1987:397-398).

La conception du développement et de la communauté y est cependant orientée non pas vers les intérêts des démunis, mais plutôt vers les besoins propres au développement économique d'une région ou d'une localité. La frontière entre les différents courants de pensée et d'action est parfois difficile à saisir. En effet, les termes et objectifs se confondent mais, en développement économique local, le *small* est toujours *beautiful*. Les stratégies libérales, conservatrices et populaires en développement économique communautaire sont pourtant fort différentes. Ces stratégies s'insèrent dans un contexte de la libéralisation des échanges économiques. L'agenda néo-libéral a une portée à la fois globale et locale, macrocosmique et microcosmique. Au libre-échange, à la libre circulation des forces économiques se conjuguent des réformes fiscales favorisant la création d'une *richesse productive*. La compétitivité y est érigée au rang d'idéologie (Petralla, 1991:1). L'agenda néo-libéral prône le désengagement gouvernemental au profit des initiatives locales ainsi qu'une prise en charge limitée des problèmes sociaux par l'État. Cette responsabilité de répondre aux besoins sociaux est remise aux mains de la *communauté*, sans qu'il y ait à cet effet transfert de budgets ou d'investissements professionnels correspondants. Ceci change radicalement les termes de référence du développement communautaire (Lockhart, 1987:398). Et c'est en ce sens que le développement économique communautaire se trouve à la croisée des chemins. L'intérêt que les autorités portent au développement communautaire concerne surtout l'élaboration de politiques néo-libérales : c'est le développement de l'économie formelle qui les intéresse.

Le développement communautaire relève donc à la fois de politiques néo-libérales et d'un mouvement de développement socialement conscient. Dans les deux cas, l'apport de la communauté est central. Cependant, les finalités et les stratégies du développement diffèrent. Ce sont les paradigmes de l'intégration et l'appropriation (Doré, 1985) qui se rencontrent dans une mouvance de développement économique.

Le développement communautaire et les rapports sociaux de sexe

La question des rapports sociaux de sexe s'imbrique au sein d'un processus de développement — comme dans tout autre aspect de la vie sociale, politique et économique. En effet, ces rapports y demeurent un des fondements de la subordination réelle ou potentielle des femmes et, à ce titre, doivent être envisagées explicitement (Elson et Pearson, 1981:152). En effet, une action de changement (planifié ou non-planifié), au sein d'une communauté, aura une portée variable sur les rapports hommes-femmes. Une telle action, tout en rencontrant les objectifs visés:

- pourra avoir comme effet d'intensifier les formes existantes de domination des hommes sur les femmes;

- pourra servir à déconstruire les formes existantes de domination des hommes sur les femmes;

- pourra servir à reconstituer de nouvelles formes de domination sexuelle (Elson et Pearson, 1981:157).

La question du rapport des femmes au développement et, plus largement, les effets des programmes de changement planifié sur les femmes ont été abordées dans la littérature et dans la pratique du développement international. Elles n'ont été abordées que marginalement en développement régional et en développement communautaire.

Le développement communautaire renvoie aux paliers locaux de décision. Il a été dit que ce n'était pas la nature du travail domestique qui en diminuait la valeur mais plutôt le fait qu'il soit rattaché à la maison et accompli par des femmes (Delphy, 1978). En effet, ce qui est associé au domaine d'activités et de responsabilités féminines ne semble pas relever du domaine communautaire mais plutôt des rapports informels de voisinage. De plus, les rapports entre la communauté et la famille — domaine de prédilection des femmes et articulation nécessaire à toute communauté — sont absents du domaine municipal lequel est souvent plutôt préoccupé par les infrastructures politiques et économiques. Pourtant, certaines politologues féministes avaient prédit, au début des années 80, l'accession des femmes à la politique par le biais du municipal parce que cette sphère d'intervention était plus proche de leurs champs d'activités et de leurs responsabilités familiales. Ceci nous porte à croire que la politique municipale, toute comme le développement communautaire est, dans sa configuration, étrangère à plusieurs préoccupations et activités des femmes (Andrew, 1992).

La répartition des ressources dans une société est médiatisée par les rapports entre les classes sociales, les races et les sexes. Le développement communautaire n'y échappe pas. La contribution des femmes au développement de leur communauté est teintée par la quotidienneté : quotidienneté de la famille ou de la communauté. Il s'agit du rôle qu'on leur réserve et de la place qu'on leur assigne. Certaines femmes contesteront cette assignation, d'autres s'y modèleront, mais toutes devront agir en fonction d'elle.

Les femmes assument le soin des autres : ces activités sont la source de la double (et souvent triple) journée de travail : le maternage, le soin aux autres, la préparation de la nourriture font encore partie de la vie communautaire et sont dévolus, dans la majorité des cas, aux femmes.

Les femmes ont acquis cette connaissance du maternage et du soin des autres par le biais d'un long processus d'apprentissage. Même si ces tâches qui leur sont attribuées ne sont pas partie prenante d'un contrat de mariage, d'une offre d'emploi ou d'un projet de développement communautaire, elles sont souvent exigées des femmes, là où elles se retrouvent. Prendre soin des enfants, aller aux rencontres parents-professeurs, s'occuper du pique-nique communautaire, des scouts ou des Jeannettes, des besoins de logement d'une voisine sont autant d'activités communautaires familières aux mères de familles, qu'elles soient ou non en emploi.

Comment qualifier ces activités ? Font-elles partie du travail familial ou du travail communautaire ? Qu'en est-il des liens émotifs créés par ce travail, sur lequel est basée toute entreprise de développement économique local ? S'agit-il d'un travail de développement communautaire ? Une conception féministe du développement communautaire ne devrait-elle pas d'intégrer ce rapport entre la famille et la communauté, entre le travail familial et communautaire ?

Les femmes font fonctionner les réseaux informels au travers desquels s'effectue un partage des ressources et la gestion de la vie quotidienne. Les investissements familiaux et communautaires de cet ordre permettent aux membres d'une famille de survivre, aux membres d'un voisinage de se connaître, à une communauté de tisser des liens et éventuellement de survivre en temps de crise ou de catastrophe. Ces processus constituent une activité de travail, de gestion, de mise en place, de changement d'une communauté et constituent aussi à ce titre une action de développement communautaire. Mais il ne s'agit pas de changement planifié. Il s'agit plutôt d'un travail de mise en place de réseaux. Ces investissements communautaires des femmes sont souvent l'extension de leurs investissements familiaux ou de l'accent qu'elles mettent sur le service à autrui. C'est justement à partir de l'exercice de responsabilités familiales que plusieurs femmes se sont faites les instigatrices de nouveaux services, du changement de telle ou telle réglementation, de l'adoption de telle ou telle loi. C'est à partir de leurs activités familiales et communautaires qu'elles ont pu identifier un problème et imaginer une solution collective à ce problème. Poser un diagnostic social au niveau familial et communautaire et entreprendre bénévolement les actions qui s'en suivent restent l'apanage des femmes.

Une des marques de reconnaissance des activités communautaires reste le financement. Par le biais du financement, une initiative communautaire devient légitime et passe par la même occasion de l'informel au formel. Toutefois, aucun salaire rétroactif n'est prévu pour le long bénévolat qui aura permis l'obtention d'un tel financement : ce bénévolat souvent assumé par des femmes demeure informel.

Lorsque les autorités priorisent ce service nouvellement financé, on assiste souvent à un processus de professionalisation : ceci en l'éloigne encore plus de ses origines bénévoles tout en lui assurant qu'une intégration partielle au réseau des services sociaux. En effet, il y a de fortes chances que ce service demeure associé au réseau communautaire sans pour autant que ce réseau voit son financement augmenté en conséquence. Qui plus est, les femmes qui y travaillent se verront souvent reconnaître leurs compétences au prix d'une démarche de requalification dont elles doivent habituellement assumer les frais.

Les nouvelles politiques de désinstitutionnalisation et de déconcentration ont pour effet de modeler la contribution communautaire des femmes. En dehors des groupes constitués de façon formelle, la contribution des femmes à la communauté s'évapore dans le magma de ces *réseaux naturels*, sur lesquels s'appuient pourtant les services sociaux. Ce qui avait été reconnu comme du travail actif redevient du ressort de l'informel et de l'invisibilité suite aux restrictions budgétaires des services sociaux. Tout un pan de l'investissement communautaire des femmes est ainsi oublié. Dorénavant, le service à autrui, pourtant l'apanage de l'action sociale et familiale des femmes, relève des aires considérées comme non-essentielles en temps de récession, au moment même où les besoins des individus, des familles et des communautés se font de plus en plus criants. La contribution informelle des femmes au soin des autres est invisibilisée au moment même où l'on prône l'importance des réseaux naturels (Guberman, Maheux et Maillé, 1991).

Il est souvent dit dans un projet que tous doivent collaborer à un même objectif. Autrement, comment sera-t-il possible d'atteindre un objectif de développement pour une communaué, d'appropriation pour certains groupes démunis (Guberman, Maheux et Maillé, 1991:398) ? Dans ce contexte, la question des rapports entre les sexes a souvent été vue comme divisant les énergies d'un groupe ou d'une communauté.

Le premier argument en faveur de l'inclusion des femmes au niveau du développement communautaire relève de la justice sociale : comment exclure ou oublier les spécificités de 50 pourcent d'une population ? Les femmes ont toutes fait l'expérience d'une division sexuelle limitant leur accès aux ressources sociales à la maison, au travail et dans leur communauté. Socialisées à répondre aux besoins des autres, souvent même avant de répondre à leurs propres besoins, elles auront tendance à revendiquer pour leur communauté avant même de revendiquer pour elles en tant que femmes. Nous croyons que la participation des femmes aux projets de développement communautaire devrait sous tendre une reconnaissance publique ainsi qu'une récompense de leurs contributions informelles à la communauté puisque les projets de développement communautaire ont en général comme but la qualité de vie de la communauté concernée.

Il est faux de croire que c'est le développement de l'économie formelle qui va, à lui seul, améliorer les conditions de vie d'une communauté. Au contraire, les réseaux informels sont centraux à tout projet de développement communautaire et relèvent en grande partie du travail communautaire invisible des femmes. L'histoire recèle d'exemples où quelques hommes ont mis sur pied des projets de développement économique dont ils ont bénéficié exclusivement. De telles stratégies, invisibilisant la contribution des femmes, n'ont certes pas eu pour conséquence l'amélioration de la situation des femmes concernées.

Le changement que suscite un projet de développement communautaire donne lieu à la négociation de nouveaux rapports dans lesquels les femmes ne sont pas nécessairement gagnantes. Les femmes doivent donc toujours être vigilantes puisque dans la majorité des cas, les structures institutionnelles — mettant de l'avant les projets de développement — n'ont pas de politique explicite d'inclusion des femmes. Le fait que le changement planifié soit fait au niveau communautaire n'est pas garant de démocratie, c'est-à-dire, de l'inclusion des femmes à tous les niveaux.

D'autre part, les mouvements sociaux orientés sur les questions de classes sociales ont été bénéfiques pour les pauvres, dont la majorité sont des femmes. Ils ont eu une majorité de femmes comme membres. Cependant, l'intégration des femmes à la problématique de classes n'a pas toujours été harmonieuse.

Enfin, le déplacement des centres décisionnels vers la communauté locale comporte le désavantage certain de disperser les forces d'intervention : les décisions sont prises à de multiples endroits. L'intervention des groupes de femmes ne peut plus être centralisée puisque l'initiative vient de chaque communauté ; dans chacun des cas, on doit argumenter l'inclusion d'une problématique femmes.

Conclusion

Les énergies consacrées à la question des femmes (en dehors des groupes de femmes) ont souvent été perçues comme des énergies résiduelles qui devaient être dépensées *en sus* des efforts consacrés à la survie des groupes et des projets. C'est une triste réalité qu'il ne serait pas nécessaire de perpétuer si la question des femmes était intégrée à tous les niveaux.

Si l'on admet que la division sexuelle limite l'accès des femmes aux ressources sociales, il est essentiel de revoir le concept et les pratiques du développement communautaire pour que ceux-ci incluent explicitement les contributions formelles et informelles des femmes. Les thèses néo-libérales du développement communautaire constituent un tout qui exclue le domestique mais laisse les femmes implicitement en charge de celui-ci. Sans prendre en compte ces éléments, un projet de développement communautaire ne peut tendre à éliminer la discrimination à l'égard des femmes.

TABLEAU 1
PARADIGMES EN ORGANISATION COMMUNAUTAIRE

intégration	pratique visant le renforcement des collectivités autour de leaders et de projets reliés aux structures et pouvoirs en place
pression	pratiques visant un nouveau rapport de force en faveur d'intérêts immédiats de collectivités dominées
appropriation	pratiques visant le développement d'entreprises ou de projets économiques contrôlés par les consommateurs de produits et services
politisation	pratiques tentant de relier les actions collectives à la transformation de structures politiques

À partir de Doré (1985).

TABLEAU 2
DANS QUELLE MESURE LE PARTAGE DU POUVOIR EST-IL EFFECTUÉ DANS UNE COMMUNAUTÉ ?

- qui détermine les priorités?

- quelle définition de la communauté est privilégiée?

- qui contrôle (a une influence prépondérante sur) les processus décisionnels?

- quelles sont les normes qui sous-tendent le processus (ex : compétitivité des marchés)?

- où sont situées les femmes dans la structure décisionnelle et administrative?

- quelle est la place faite à l'économie informelle : aux initiatives informelles dans la communauté au travail au noir, aux préoccupations liées à la vie privée, à la famille?

Nota : Le tableau 3 reprend certaines questions à soulever au sujet de programmes de développement communautaire.

TABLEAU 3
PARADIGME DES RAPPORTS SOCIAUX DE SEXE EN RAPPORT AVEC TROIS NIVEAUX EN ORGANISATION COMMUNAUTAIRE DE DORÉ (1985)

Niveaux en organisation communautaire	Paradigme *femmes*
1. Pratiques sociales	**1. Pratiques sociales**
L'organisation communautaire constitue une intervention auprès des collectivités dans le but de susciter leur mobilisation et leur. insertion dans un processus de changement social	Les pratiques des femmes sont-elles inclues dans ce champ par la définition *traditionnelle* de l'organisation communautaire ? -pratiques familiales ; - pratiques de voisinage; - initiatives communautaires informelles non-recensées; -initiatives communautaires informelles non subventionnées.

2. Méthodologie d'intervention
L'organisation communautaire constitue aussi une professionnalisation au sein des écoles de travail social, et ce, malgré la dissociation traditionnelle entre le terrain et la tradition professionnelle.

2. Méthodologie d'intervention
Comment les pratiques des femmes sont-elles inclues dans le processus de professionnalisation des pratiques, ou dans le rapport entre le terrain et la tradition professionnelle?
- visibilité des femmes en organisation communautaire;
- visibilité et crédibilité des champs de pratique informels des femmes en organisation communautaire;
- inclusion ou exclusion des femmes comme professionnelles de l'organisation communautaire;
- interprétation féministe des pratiques professionnelles en organisation communautaire.

3. Modèle normatif d'intervention
L'organisation communautaire est une pratique codifiée par rapport à laquelle il est possible de se situer
- soit pour répéter cette pratique;
- soit pour s'en démarquer;
- soit pour définir sa propre pratique.

3. Modèle normatif d'intervention
Dans quelle mesure la pratique de l'organisation communautaire met de l'avant une idéologie et des principes d'action basés sur la transformation des rapports de domination hommes-femmes?

Colonne de gauche portant sur les niveaux en organisation communautaire à partir de Doré (1985).

Note

1. Plusieurs organismes en développement économique ont vu le jour. Les CDE prônent un développement économique traditionnel. Les CDC (Corporations de développement communautaire) prônent le partenariat économique et un développement à mandat socio-économique. Enfin, les CDEC prônent un développement économique alternatif coopératif. Les CDC et les CDEC sont de nouvelles formes de développement des communautés locales. L'une est axée sur le social et l'autre sur le développement de l'employabilité. Elles interviennent selon un territoire, une culture, et avec des acteurs locaux pour planifier un développement local de leur communauté.

Références

Anadon, Marta et al. *Vers un développement rose*, note de recherche no. 10, Groupe de recherche et d'intervention régionales, Université du Québec à

Chicoutimi, 1990.

Andrew, Caroline. « Women and the Welfare State », *Revue canadienne de science politique* 17, no. 4 (1984), p. 667-685.

— . *Le développement local.* Exposé à la table d'expertes sur le thème du développement régional convoquée par le Conseil du statut de la femme, Québec, 20 novembre 1992.

Bourque, Denis, et Jean Panet-Raymond. *Partenariat ou paternariat ?* Montréal, école de service sociale, 1991.

Christiansen-Ruffman, Linda. « Women in Community Development : A Comparison of Two Regional Communities in Atlantic Canada », présentation à l'International Sociological Association, 1978.

Coalition des organismes communautaires du Québec. *Pour la reconnaissance de l'action communautaire autonome* : document de base, mai 1988.

Cox, Fred, et Charles Garvin. « A History of Community Organizing Since the Civil War with Special Reference to Oppressed Communities », dans Fred M. Cox, John L. Erlich, Jack Rothman et John E. Tropman, réd., *Strategies of Community Organization*, Itaska, Peacock Publications, 1979, p. 45-75.

Côté, Marc Yvan. *Une réforme axée sur le citoyen*, Québec, Ministère de la Santé et des Services sociaux, 1990.

Delphy, Christine. « Travail ménager, travail domestique », dans André Michel, réd., Les femmes dans la société marchande, Paris, Presses universitaires de France, 1978.

Doré, Gérald. « L'organisation communautaire : définition et paradigme », *Service social* 34, nos 2 et 3 (1985) : 210-230.

Duncan, N. « An Economic Development Strategy », *Social Policy* 16, no. 4, (1986) : 4 et seq.

Elson, Diane, et Ruth Pearson. « The Subordination of Women and the Inte nationalization of Factory Production, » dans Kate Young, Carol Wolkowitz et Roslyn McCullagh, réd., *Of Marriage and the Market : Women's Subordination in an International Perspective.* Londres, CSE Books, 1981.

Fournier, Louis. *Solidarité Inc.*, Montréal, Québec-Amérique, 1991.

Gadamer, Hans Georg. *The Heritage of Hegel. Reason and the Age of Science*, Cambridge, MIT Press, 1981.

Guberman, Nancy, Pierre Maheux et Chantal Maillé. *Et si l'amour ne suffisait plus l ?* Montréal, Remue-Ménage, 1991.

Hamel, Pierre. *Action collective et démocratie locale*, Montréal, Presses de l'Université de Montréal, 1991.

Institut canadien d'éducation des adultes. *Les femmes dans les groupes populaires*, Montréal, ICEA, 1985.

Lockhart, A. « Community-based Development and Conventional Economics in the Canadian North », dans E.M. Bennett, réd., *Social Intervention : Theory and Practice*, Lewiston, Edwin Mellen Press, 1987, p. 393-414.

Panet-Raymond, Jean. « La place des femmes dans les organisations populaires : évolution et perspectives », *Interventions* n° 61 (1984) : 36-41.

Petit Robert Dictionnaire de la langue française, 1992.

Petralla, Ricardo. « L'évangile de la compétitivité. » *Le Monde diplomatique* (septembre 1991), p. 1.

Rahman, Anisur. « Towards an Alternative Development Paradigm », *IFDA Dossier* (avril-juin 1991) : 18-19.

Rose, Stephen. « Reflections on Community Organization Theory », *Community Organization for the 1980's,* Social Development Issues 5 nos 2-3 (été-automne 1981) : 180-194.

Rothman, Jack. « Three Models of Community Organization Theory », dans Fred Cox, John Erlich, Jack Rothman et John Tropman, Strategies of Community Organization, Itaska : Peacock Publications, 1979, p.25-44.

Thifault, R. « Démocratie, où es-tu ? Droits de l'homme, élections libres et pluripartisme suffisent-ils à définir le régime démocratique? » *Le Devoir,* 27 mars 1992, p. B8.

Warren, Roland. *The Community in America,* Chicago, Rand McNally, 1972.

Wilson, Elizabeth. « Women in the Community », dans Marjorie Mayo, réd., *Women in the Community,* chapitre 1, Londres, Routledge and Keagan Paul, 1977.

— . *Women in the Welfare State,* Londres, Tavistock Publications, 1977.

Conclusion

Conclusion

Looking Back and Looking Forward

In the closing paper, Glenda Simms dares to say it: we will not achieve any kind of global vision until we come to grips with our local reality, with our own race and class positions. This has been a thread running through the papers in this book. We have seen how some of us emerged from the centuries of conquest and settlement as privileged and kin to the powerful, while many more of us — the "others" — emerged displaced and dispossessed. In this harsh light, claims to sisterhood appear empty, hollow and even oppressive, since they ignore or, worse, deny the reality that dispossessed women live every day. One of the most painful aspects of this reality is the extent to which the words we use to justify the exclusion of these "others" from our discourse and our action, on any terms other than ours, are the same words that men have used and continue to use in excluding women from the halls of political, economic and intellectual power.

It would be a warmer, fuzzier ending if we closed with soft words about global sisterhood and shared meanings. This would not do justice to the pain of the women whose lives have been made public here, nor would it serve our cause, which is to fight to make women, and hence our families, our communities, our nations and our globe, safe from violence and empowered to make the decisions that shape our lives. So we close instead with Glenda Simms's challenge that we keep up the struggle to find common ground and not assume too quickly that we have found it. We may have to create this common ground, in ways that we have not yet thought of.

We have so much more to tell each other. For now, read Glenda Simms, listen to her words, respond to her challenge. We wish you love, strength and courage for the struggle.

Réfléchir au passé et regarder vers l'avenir

Pour terminer, Glenda Simms ose le dire : nous ne parviendrons jamais à une vision universelle tant que nous n'affronterons pas notre réalité locale, nos propres positions raciales et sociales. Tel est d'ailleurs le fil conducteur tout au long du présent ouvrage. Nous avons vu comment quelques-unes d'entre nous sont sorties des siècles de conquête et d'installation privilégiées et apparentées aux puissants, alors qu'un plus grand nombre — les « autres» — en sont sorties déplacées et dépossédées. Sous cet éclairage cru, les affirmations de solidarité féminine semblent vides, vaines, accablantes même, puisqu'elles passent sous silence, voire nient la réalité que les femmes dépossédées vivent quotidiennement. L'un des aspects les plus douloureux de cette réalité tient au fait que les mots que nous employons pour justifier l'exclusion de ces « autres » de notre discours et de notre action, pour toutes conditions autres que les nôtres, sont les mots que les hommes emploient pour exclure les femmes des allées du pouvoir politique, économique et intellectuel.

La conclusion serait plus chaleureuse et plus floue si nous terminions sur des paroles aimables au sujet de la solidarité féminine universelle et de sentiments partagés. Mais ce serait faire fi de la douleur des femmes dont la vie a été rendue publique ici, et cela ne servirait pas notre cause, qui est de lutter pour que les femmes, et donc nos familles, nos collectivités, nos nations et notre planète, soient à l'abri de la violence et puissent prendre les décisions qui influent sur nos vies. Nous concluons donc sur le défi que nous lance Glenda Simms en nous enjoignant de poursuivre le combat pour trouver un terrain d'entente, sans supposer trop vite que nous l'avons trouvé. Peut-être ce terrain d'entente reste-t-il à créer, et ce, de manières auxquelles nous n'avons pas encore réfléchi.

Nous avons tellement plus à nous dire. Pour l'instant, lisez Glenda Simms, imprégnez-vous de ses paroles, relevez son défi. Nous vous souhaitons amour, force et courage dans le combat.

Feminism is Global: Or is it?

Glenda P. Simms

To understand the barriers that separate women and mitigate against global sisterhood in Canada, we must locate contemporary struggles in our colonized past. It is our very different diasporic experiences — the experience of European women with dominance, of African and Asian and Latino women with powerlessness, or of aboriginal women confronted by colonization of their homeland — that lead to the ideological contradictions between privileged and nonprivileged women. As women in Canada, we need not lay claim to each others' experiences and voices through assertion of shared womanhood under patriarchy or through privileged women's appropriation of others' voices through "creative imagination." Rather we must create space for ourselves, a space of constructive, critical dialogue, that will enable different perspectives to come together and to come through.

I would like to share aspects of a conceptual framework in which issues of racism and sexism clash, confront, conflate and contort the avenues of change within our collective search for equity. I have thought long and hard about the topic "Global Vision/Local Action," and I have decided that it is essential for us to take time to reformulate a number of concepts that have characterized feminist thought in Canada before we move, as Canadian women, into the next century.

I will examine the notion of "global vision" within a feminist framework. As I visited and revisited this concept, one of the sources I could not ignore was Robin Morgan's book *Sisterhood is Global*. This book was written in 1984; since then, "global sisterhood" has become a kind of slogan for feminist researchers. I continue to argue that, as feminists, we must move beyond sloganeering. So far, we have given more thought to the word "global" than to the word "sisterhood." We seem to have accepted without question the notion that there is such a thing as "global sisterhood," even before we took time out to investigate all the barriers to sisterhood, those between women of the world in general and, more specifically, those between the women of Canada. In the words of Audre Lorde, "There is a pretence to a homogeneity of experience, covered by the word 'sisterhood,' that does not in fact exist" (quoted in Spelman, 1988:1). My experiences in the Canadian women's movement continue to bring me closer to Lorde's point of view. In light of these experiences, I would say in very strong terms that *we cannot now lay claim to "global sisterhood."* However, we can state definitively that our survival as a social force for change lies in our belief that sisterhood has the potential for becoming a global phenomenon. Rooted in this statement is my personal commitment to positive change and development through the services of the Canadian Advisory Council on the Status of Women, and through my own ideas about the possibility of change within the ever-evolving concepts of feminism.

I will turn to the other half of the model of this conference, "Local Action." Then I will try to connect both ends — the local and the global, the reality and the possibility. Recently, I viewed *Sisters in the Struggle,* a new National Film Board release by Dionne Brand. The group of black women in this film voice one strong message: "There can be no 'global sisterhood' until we, the women of Canada, look at the barriers that still divide the women's movement." These women echoed the sentiments of Gloria Joseph, who wrote, "No colonized people have been so isolated, one from the other, as women" (Joseph, 1981:259). In order fully to understand how formidable are the barriers that separate the women of Canada, we must take a step back in time and locate the contemporary struggles in the framework of our colonized past. We need to examine factors other than gender that have influenced our experiences as women of Canada. We must then take a new look, from a deeper understanding of how to link "local action" to the "global vision." By so doing, ultimately we will develop a realistic idea of the global possibilities for change in women's lives.

I will therefore critique the present state of affairs at the local level, using an analysis of women's histories, and show how our many diasporic experiences have created a multi-faceted dilemma for women, both in North America and throughout the world. Furthermore, I wish to argue that this multi-faceted experience has become a barrier in and of itself, both at the level of the psyche and at the level of objective social, cultural and economic realities. In other words, within the Canadian women's movement, it is unavoidable that we are now forced to confront the ideological clashes that are the natural outgrowth of our differing diasporic experiences. The major challenge for us is to find creative ways not only to understand issues from a new vantage point, but also to find healthy ways in which we can accept that the many streams of our ideas will eventually come together in major rivers of opportunities, change and freedom from all our unique forms of oppression.

I need, therefore, to clarify for you my view of the different diasporic experiences of Canadian women. In light of the fact that 1992 is the five-hundredth anniversary of the landing of Mr. Columbus, I will take the liberty of using this date as the starting point for the diasporic experience of Canadian women of European origin, Canadian women of other origins, and Canadian women of aboriginal roots. I wish to propose that the European men and women who either accompanied or followed Mr. Columbus, under the guise of discovery and in ignorance of geography, experienced a diaspora based on dominance. In fact, the majority of immigrants who settled in Canada — the Irish escaping famine, the Germans escaping war, the British and the French escaping poverty — all have a fundamental linkage, based not only on skin colour, but also on the fact that they moved from these powerless situations to a so-called New World, where they — especially the men — found power, gained assets and, above all, gained control over their destiny. They demonstrated that in a short period of human history, they could transform their powerlessness to power and establish dominance over others. Within this dominance and power mode, material wealth guaranteed that Eurocentric thought and perspective would take precedence over all other streams of thought. In a real way, then, the diasporic experience of the Canadian woman of European ancestry is rooted in the reality of the benefits and privileges that she gleaned from her position as mother, sister, daughter and friend of the patriarchal colonizer.

We now need to look at the diasporic experiences of Canadian women of other origins, such as blacks, Asians and Latinos. Mr. Columbus and his troops, literally and figuratively, ripped these non-European ancestors from their dynasties in Africa, China, Japan, India and South America. These women came from communities in which they had established family structures, customs and cultures. They were captured and herded, as slaves, indentured servants, domestic workers and farm hands, from mountains and valleys where their ancestors had lived and worshipped for thousands of years. Some of them came from civilizations with much deeper roots than those from which the Europeans came. They were set adrift from these moorings and brought into the New World to exist in a situation of powerlessness. In short, within a five-hundred-year period, two distinct groups of Canadians experienced their uprootedness in diametrically opposed ways.

However, displacement is not always rooted in moving from one geographical location to another. Let us examine yet another perspective. For aboriginal peoples, the diasporic experience was one of facing colonizing forces within their own territory, but not on their own terms, an encounter that has textured all aspects of their lives over the past five hundred years. In fact, it can be argued that the aboriginal Canadian has been the recipient of the most destructive aspects of the Canadian diasporic experience.

Within this constellation of diverse experiences of displacement and within the dynamics of our present-day interactions lies the major contradiction within feminism: the basic ideological contradiction of the privileged versus the nonprivileged. It is a dilemma that we must talk about, because we cannot achieve any kind of global vision unless we come to grips with our local reality. As feminists, we have defined ourselves as powerless under patriarchy. However, we now have to seriously ask whether some of us have privilege that is rooted in and related to our unique diasporic experiences. The time has come for those who benefited from the diaspora to attempt to understand the negative experiences of others. Until we develop this understanding, we cannot capture a global vision and we cannot truly say that we have the power to move human development beyond the point to which it has come.

What do I mean by "understanding"? I mean that we must recognize that we are the products of an historical relationship that has significant implications for contemporary feminist discourse. This implication is vividly captured by Buchi Emecheta, an African writer who now lives in England, in her book *The Joys of Motherhood*. Emecheta tells the story of Nnu Ego, the daughter of a tribal chief in the village of Ibuza. Because she is unable to bear a child for her first husband, Nnu Ego is sent back to her father, who promptly forces her to marry a man she despises: a very ugly man. The new husband gives Nnu Ego status by making her pregnant. He renders her a woman and a mother in her culture. But Nnu Ego's respect for her husband soon disappears because of his job as a houseboy. One of his duties is to wash the underwear of the white mistress of the house. In so doing, he loses that which made him a man in his own society: in his tribal community, he would never touch a woman's underwear. Nnu Ego expresses her dilemma: "Was this a man she was living with, she asked herself. Could a situation rob a man of his manhood without him knowing it? I want to live with a man, not a woman-made man" (Emecheta, 1979:47).

The white woman in this story never understands the resentment Nnu Ego feels toward her. The mistress of the house does not comprehend how she has emasculated Nnu Ego's husband. Nnu Ego cannot love her man because he is devalued; therefore, she sees the white woman as an enemy. For the white European woman, this dilemma would not be immediately obvious. She might say to herself,

"I have done nothing wrong. I have in fact given her husband work. I am therefore not her enemy. I am helping her." The white woman has difficulty comprehending her role in the emasculation of that African man and her role in changing the relationship between Nnu Ego and the males of her culture. In this misunderstanding, the dynamics of cultural clash, of privilege versus the lack of privilege, are obscured: the two women have nothing in common except an adversarial relationship.

If we step through time, we can see that here, in contemporary Canadian society, there exists an extension of the same dynamic. White feminists are ignoring the difference between their own diasporic experiences and those of racial minorities. At the same time, racial minority feminists are demanding an understanding and inclusion of their perspectives within all aspects of Canadian life. An example of the modern clash of ideology was exhibited at the PEN (poets, playwrights, essayists, editors and novelists) International Congress in Toronto, in 1989. Black writer Marlene Nourbese-Philip and the protest group Vision 21 challenged the exclusivity of the conference and the Eurocentricity of the publishing industry. They were greeted not with overt racism but with the frustration of mainstream misunderstanding.[1] White feminist writer June Callwood was faced with the demands for inclusion when she entered the conference, but she could not understand what Marlene Nourbese-Philip was talking about, so she reacted in anger and frustration, by telling Ms Nourbese-Philip to "f— off," in front of national television. There is a crucial connection between Marlene Nourbese-Philip and Buchi Emecheta's Nnu Ego. There is an undeniable link between the colonial structures that affected the Third World and the colonial mentality that is an essential feature of Canadian society.

What I have tried to do is give a thumbnail sketch of the problematic relationship of racism and sexism. However, these juxtapositions of our diasporic experiences are only one thread of the complexities of "global sisterhood." To further tease out the contemporary Canadian dilemma within the women's movement, we also have to deal with what is popularly termed the "creative imagination" in feminism. This concept is used by so-called progressive feminists when they are challenged on the continuing exclusion of the voices of minority and aboriginal women and others from the feminist discourse. It is the idea that white feminist "leaders" have validated themselves through their higher education and academic credentials. These feminists argue that because they have gone through the academic process, they possess what is known as a "creative imagination," and this gives them the ability to better understand, empathize with and vocalize the concerns of *all* women, including women of colour and aboriginal women. Some even believe that the "creative imagination" is better equipped to fully conceptualize minority concerns than minority women themselves.

To take this idea further, it means that there is a presumption of the "creative" versus the "primitive" imagination, and that the latter is defined as not being able to reach the highest levels of conceptualization and abstract thinking. College-educated women have always placed themselves in the role of the brokers of knowledge within the women's movement and continue to see themselves as the producers of knowledge. However, the point has to be made that *aboriginal and racial-minority women are not mystified by the idea of the "creative imagination."* They know very well that it has been the "creative imagination" that has, over the past five hundred years, brought them to the point where they have lost their histories, their language and their land. They also know that it was the "creative imagination" that inspired Mr. Columbus to think that he had indeed found a "new land" for the King and Queen of Spain.

By the same token, all women need to know that it was the "creative imagination" of *men* that rendered them "non-persons," so how can feminists, while bemoaning their exclusion from the history of human development, presume to exclude nonwhite or nonprivileged women from the feminist discourse? In a discussion with Mary Childers, black feminist bell hooks asked the question "How can we displace paradigms of domination that in fact establish authority through exclusion by asserting one people — white, educated feminists — as having knowledge, and the other people as not having anything?" (Hirsch and Keller, 1990:67). Let me illustrate the parallel between the male exclusion of women under patriarchy and the white feminist myth of the "creative imagination." In her book *Inessential Woman*, Elizabeth Spelman points out that we condemn men for their repression and oppression, which operate to erase women's concerns and perspectives from all areas of thought and debate. Thus, Western feminists have quite rightly criticized the writings of Nietzsche, Plato, Aristotle and Kant as incomplete examinations of the human condition, because these philosophers wrongly extrapolated and drew their conclusions from their own experience; thus, their conceptualization of the human condition is based on the experience of only one gender: the male. Similarly, white Western feminists who condemn patriarchy believe that their "creative imagination" allows them the privilege of conceptualizing and vocalizing woman's condition, based on the condition of only one cultural group. In so doing, "they conflate the condition of white, middle-class women as the condition of all women" (Spelman, 1988:6). White feminists' inability to see racism and sexism as flip sides of the same coin becomes a systemic barrier to meaningful exchange within Canadian feminism. The resistance to change and the challenge of feminist power have created an uneasy climate within the women's movement, which is best expressed by an aboriginal woman, Lee Maracle (1988:109): "Locked in your white-skinned privilege, and blinded by your arrogance, you call on me to forget the past, and be like you. You know not what you ask. If I forget my past, ignore our ancient ways, only violence will quiet the scream inside me."

While, as feminists, we must postulate a kind of sameness (we are all victims under patriarchy), it is the very notion of cohesion that lays the groundwork for domination based on race. From the very noble goal of speaking with one voice, the voice of "global sisterhood," it is too easy to extrapolate from the experiences of white women, to say that these are the experiences of *all* women. When we reduce ourselves to sameness, then those who question or challenge the cohesion are excluded and their voices are shut out. This is the easy response. It is much more difficult to change the ways in which we have traditionally operated. The concept of sameness is explored in a story used by Spelman in the book that I mentioned, but originating in Iris Murdoch's novel *The Nice and the Good*. She speaks about the character of Uncle Theo, who is sitting on the beach, contemplating the concept of multiplicity. He is terribly uneasy because of the number and variety of pebbles on the beach; there are pebbles of all shapes, sizes and colours. The only way Uncle Theo can feel comfortable with the beach is to reduce the many into one. Thus, rather than pebbles, he begins to think of "pebblehood" (Spelman, 1988:1). Likewise, feminists tend to reduce all women to the notion of "womanhood." It is not only the number of women that is worrisome, but also the many differences between us, which threaten, as Spelman (1988:2) says, the "sweet intelligibility of the tidy and irrefutable fact that women are women." In fact, our differences are just as important as our similarities.

If we continue to deny that Simone de Beauvoir's "other" exists, not only in man's relation to woman, but in woman's relation to woman, then we as feminists face the internal dynamics of not being able to validate all the things we have said about patriarchy. The things we have said about men are the same things others are now saying about us. The fundamental dilemma is that in trying to cast off our oppression, we do not understand others casting off *their* oppression. In a real sense, we refuse to accept our role in the oppression of other women. Women of colour and other minorities have long understood that in a real sense, *we understand the mainstream more than the mainstream understands us*. We went through the colonial experience in a different way. We were forced to understand the colonizer's history, his literature, his culture and his world-view. In a sense, then, we are at an advantage, because we have come from a point of view of being forced to absorb the colonizer's ways, which gives us the possibility, in bell hooks's words, "to operate either in the margin or in the center, but on our own terms" (1984:11).

I see clearly and understand instinctively bell hooks's line of argument. To me, the margin-centre dialectic is captured vividly in the imagery of the biblical Jonah in the belly of the whale. The colonized peoples had to enter into the belly of the whale; by so doing, they moved into a position of strength, *because they understood the whale from the inside, and they also knew what he looked like on the outside.*

If feminism is to be a redemptive and creative force in this society, it must adapt the perspectives of minorities and aboriginal women, in order to gain a deeper insight into the hopes and needs of all women of Canada. Lee Maracle (1988:103–106) articulates the need for the retention of all perspectives in the following passage:

> *You give my children Europe to emulate, respect and learn from, and at the same time, debase native peoples' national roots. Who is going to insist that Europe's descendants in my homeland learn from and emulate the heroes and bright moments in our history? Which European child in your classroom knows of Kitsilano, Coquitlam, Capilano, or our much-lauded statesman and self-taught constitutional lawyer, Andrew Paul? We were almost obliterated by your ancestors. I realize you hold no gun to my head, dear teacher, but it was your culture that spawned physical genocide, and now you ask me to erase the shadow of my grandmother?*

In conclusion, I am saying to you, my sisters, that in order for us to come out of our existential dilemma, as women of Canada, we must look to all our sisters and unite with them on common grounds. As women, all of us must commit ourselves to creating space for ourselves: a space of constructive, critical dialogue, which will enable different perspectives to come together and to come through. We must give voice to all the women of Canada. Giving voice and speaking out are not just simple gestures of freedom, where domination is the norm. Freedom of speech is an illusion for many of our sisters. We fear when we speak, as Audre Lorde writes in her poem "A Litany of Survival" (1984:28):

and when we speak we are afraid
our words will not be heard
nor welcomed
but when we are silent
we are still afraid.
So it is better to speak
remembering
we were never meant to survive.

It is within this committed space that we, as feminists in Canada, are articulating and redefining our realities. It is within this space that we are creating theory that courageously synthesizes into challenge, into change and into new approaches.[2] I wish you well, my sisters.

Notes

1. From a conversation with Jan Bower, executive director of PEN International, Toronto, Ontario, November, 1991. PEN International has since made efforts to include the voices of racial-minority Canadians in the publishing industry.
2. From the words of Janet Yee, Women of Colour Collective, in a speech to the Congress of Black Women of Canada, November, 1991.

References

Emecheta, Buchi. *The Joys of Motherhood*. London: Heinemann Educational Books Ltd., 1979.

Hirsch, Marianne and Evelyn Keller, eds. *Conflicts in Feminism*. New York: Routledge, 1990.

hooks, bell. *Feminist Theory: From Margin to Center*. Boston: South End Press, 1984.

Joseph, Gloria I. *Common Differences: Conflicts in Black and White Feminist Perspectives*. New York: Anchor Press/Doubleday, 1981.

Lorde, Audre. *Sister Outsider*. Trumansburg, NY: Crossing Press, 1984.

Maracle, Lee. *I Am Woman*. Vancouver: Write-On Press Publishers, 1988.

Morgan, Robin, ed. *Sisterhood is Global*. New York: Anchor Press/Doubleday, 1984.

Spelman, Elizabeth. *Inessential Woman: Problems of Exclusion in Feminist Thought*. Boston: Beacon Press, 1988.

Le féminisme est-il ou n'est-il pas universel ?

Glenda P. Simms

Afin de comprendre les obstacles qui séparent les femmes et s'opposent à une solidarité féminine universelle au Canada, nous devons établir le lien entre nos luttes contemporaines et notre passé de colonisées. Ce sont les différences mêmes entre nos déracinements respectifs — celui des Européennes sous la domination, celui des Africaines, des Asiatiques et des Latino-Américaines dans l'impuissance, ou celui des femmes autochtones confrontées à la colonisation de leur terre natale — qui conduisent aux contradictions idéologiques entre femmes privilégiées et celles qui ne le sont pas. En tant que femmes au Canada, nous n'avons pas à revendiquer le vécu et la voix les unes des autres dans l'affirmation d'une féminitude partagée sous le patriarcat, et les femmes privilégiées n'ont pas à s'approprier la voix d'autrui sous prétexte « d'imagination créatrice ». En fait, nous devons créer notre propre espace, un espace propice à un dialogue constructif et critique afin que chacune d'entre nous puisse exprimer son point de vue et que toutes soient entendues.

J'aimerais vous présenter certains aspects d'un cadre conceptuel dans lequel les problèmes de racisme et de sexisme obstruent et déforment les voies du changement dans notre quête collective d'équité. J'ai mûrement réfléchi au thème « Vision universelle, action locale », pour en arriver à la conclusion qu'avant d'entrer, comme Canadiennes, dans le vingt et unième siècle, nous devons à tout prix reformuler un certain nombre de concepts qui caractérisent la pensée féministe au Canada.

Je vais d'abord examiner la notion de « vision universelle » dans un contexte féministe. En réfléchissant encore et encore à la question, le livre de Robin Morgan, *Sisterhood is Global*, m'est apparu comme étant une des sources incontournables en la matière. Il a été écrit en 1984. Depuis lors, la « solidarité féminine universelle » est devenue une sorte de slogan pour les chercheuses qui se penchent sur le féminisme. Je continue d'affirmer qu'en tant que féministes nous devons dépasser le stade des slogans. Jusqu'ici, nous avons réfléchi davantage au terme « universelle » qu'à celui de « solidarité féminine ».

Nous semblons avoir accepté d'emblée l'idée qu'il existe effectivement une « solidarité féminine universelle », avant même d'avoir
examiné tous les obstacles à la solidarité féminine, ceux qui se dressent
entre les femmes dans le monde en général et, plus précisément, ceux
qui séparent les femmes au Canada. Comme le dit Audre Lorde, « On
prétend se trouver devant un vécu homogène, ce que recouvre le
terme "solidarité féminine", or ce vécu-là n'existe pas en réalité » (cité
dans E. Spelman, 1988, p.1). Ce que je vis dans le mouvement des
femmes canadien me rapproche sans cesse du point de vue exprimé
par A. Lorde. Ainsi, je dirais avec assurance que *nous ne saurions nous
réclamer aujourd'hui d'une « solidarité féminine universelle* | ». Cepen-
dant, nous pouvons sans contredit déclarer que notre survie en tant
que force sociale du changement repose sur notre conviction que la
solidarité féminine peut devenir un phénomène universel. D'où mon
engagement à l'égard d'une évolution réelle par l'intermédiaire des
services du Conseil consultatif canadien sur la situation de la femme
et de mes propres idées quant aux possibilités de changement à
l'intérieur des concepts féministes en constante évolution.

Passons maintenant à la seconde moitié du thème de cette
conférence, « l'action locale ». J'essaierai ensuite de réunir les deux
éléments, le local et l'universel, la réalité et la possibilité.
Dernièrement, j'ai assisté à la projection de *Sisters in the Struggle*, une
nouvelle production de l'Office national du film réalisée par Dionne
Brand. Le groupe de femmes noires présentées dans ce film livre un
message très fort; elles disent : « Il ne peut y avoir de "solidarité
féminine universelle" tant que nous, femmes du Canada,
n'étudierons pas les barrières qui divisent toujours le mouvement des
femmes ». Dans leurs propos, elles se font l'écho des sentiments de
Gloria Joseph, qui écrit qu'aucun peuple colonisé n'a été aussi isolé
que les femmes entre elles (G. Joseph, 1981, p.259). Pour saisir toute
l'ampleur des barrières qui séparent les femmes les unes des autres au
Canada, il nous faut prendre du recul et replacer les luttes contemporaines dans le contexte de notre passé de colonisées. Il nous faut
examiner des facteurs autres que le sexe qui influent sur ce que nous
vivons en tant que femmes dans ce pays. Puis il nous faut réexaminer
la question, fortes d'une compréhension plus approfondie des liens à
établir entre « action locale » et « vision universelle ». Ainsi, nous
finirons par nous forger une idée réaliste des possibilités globales de
changement dans la vie des femmes.

Je vais donc examiner d'un oeil critique la situation actuelle sur le
plan local grâce à une analyse de l'histoire des femmes, et montrer
comment nos déracinements respectifs — qui ont donné lieu à nos
diasporas — ont créé un dilemme aux mille facettes pour les femmes,

tant en Amérique du Nord que partout ailleurs dans le monde. J'entends aussi démontrer que ces expériences mêmes sont devenues un obstacle, tant sur le plan psychique que sur celui des réalités sociales, culturelles et économiques objectives. Autrement dit, au sein du mouvement des femmes canadien, il est inévitable que nous soyons aujourd'hui obligées de faire face aux discordances qui sont les excroissances naturelles de nos vécus si différents. Notre principal défi n'est pas que de trouver des façons novatrices de comprendre les problèmes sous une perspective nouvelle, mais aussi d'accepter le fait que de toutes nos idées jailliront des fleuves de possibilités et de changements capables de nous libérer de toutes les formes d'oppression particulières que nous subissons.

Je dois donc préciser ma conception des différentes diasporas des femmes du Canada. L'année 1992 marquant le cinq centième anniversaire de la découverte de l'Amérique par M. Colomb, je me permettrai de prendre cette date comme point de départ de la diaspora des Canadiennes d'origine européenne, de celle des Canadiennes d'autres origines et, depuis lors, de la diaspora des Canadiennes d'ascendance autochtone. J'avancerai que le déracinement des Européens, femmes et hommes, qui ont accompagné ou suivi M. Colomb sous prétexte de découverte et par ignorance géographique, repose sur la domination. En fait, la majorité des immigrants qui se sont installés au Canada — les Irlandais fuyant la famine, les Allemands, la guerre, les Britanniques et les Français, la pauvreté — étaient tous unis par un lien fondamental qui ne tenait pas qu'à la couleur de leur peau, mais aussi au fait qu'ils tournaient le dos à des situations d'impuissance pour un prétendu Nouveau Monde où ils — particulièrement les hommes — allaient trouver le pouvoir, s'enrichir et, surtout, prendre leur destin en main. Ils ont démontré qu'en un court laps de temps dans l'histoire de l'humanité ils pouvaient transformer leur impuissance en pouvoir et établir leur domination sur autrui. Dans ce mode de domination et de pouvoir, la richesse matérielle garantissait la prédominance de la pensée et des points de vue eurocentrés sur tous les autres. Ainsi, la diaspora des Canadiennes de souche européenne est donc enracinée dans la réalité des avantages et privilèges que leur a conférés leur position de mère, de soeur, de fille et d'amie du colonisateur patriarcal.

Voyons à présent la diaspora des Canadiennes d'autres origines, noire, asiatique et latino-américaine, par exemple. Au propre comme au figuré, M. Colomb et ses troupes ont arraché ces aïeules non européennes à leurs dynasties en Afrique, en Chine, au Japon, en Inde et en Amérique latine. Ces femmes venaient de communautés dans lesquelles elles avaient établi des structures familiales, des coutumes et des cultures. Elles ont été capturées et rassemblées en troupeaux, vendues comme esclaves, asservies, placées comme domestiques et ouvrières agricoles, loin des montagnes et des vallées où leurs ancêtres vivaient et adoraient leurs divinités depuis des millénaires. Certaines d'entre elles venaient de civilisations aux racines bien plus profondes que celles des civilisations européennes. On les a arrachées à ces points d'ancrage et emmenées dans ce Nouveau Monde où elles vivraient dans l'impuissance. Bref, en l'espace de cinq cents ans, deux groupes distincts de Canadiennes ont vécu leur déracinement de manières diamétralement opposées.

Cependant, le déplacement n'est pas toujours géographique. Prenons la question d'un autre point de vue encore. Pour les peuples autochtones, le déracinement correspond à la rencontre, sur leurs propres territoires, avec des forces colonisatrices, mais pas selon des conditions qu'ils avaient dictées; or, cette rencontre marque tous les aspects de leur vie depuis cinq cents ans. En fait, on peut affirmer que c'est l'Autochtone canadien qui, au Canada, a subi les aspects les plus destructeurs de l'expérience du déracinement.

C'est dans cette constellation d'expériences diverses et dans la dynamique de nos interactions actuelles que se trouve la principale contradiction du féminisme, la contradiction idéologique fondamentale des privilégiées face aux non-privilégiées. Il faut parler de ce dilemme, car nous ne parviendrons jamais à une vision universelle tant que nous n'affronterons pas notre réalité locale. En tant que féministes, nous nous sommes définies comme étant impuissantes dans un système patriarcal. Mais nous devons à présent nous demander sérieusement si certaines d'entre nous n'ont pas été privilégiées de par leur déracinement même. Le moment est venu pour celles qui en ont tiré avantage d'essayer de comprendre le vécu négatif des autres, sans quoi nous ne pourrons avoir de vision universelle ni réellement dire que nous avons le pouvoir de pousser le développement humain au-delà du point qu'il a atteint.

Qu'est-ce que j'entends par « comprendre » ? Que nous devons reconnaître que nous sommes les produits d'un rapport historique lourd de conséquences pour le discours féministe contemporain. Dans son livre intitulé *The Joys of Motherhood*, Buchi Emecheta, auteure africaine qui vit aujourd'hui en Angleterre, expose de manière colorée ces conséquences. Elle raconte l'histoire de Nnu Ego, fille d'un chef de tribu dans un village appelé Ibuza. Parce qu'elle ne peut donner d'enfant à son premier mari, Nnu Ego est renvoyée chez son père qui, vite, la force à épouser un homme qu'elle méprise. Un homme très laid de qui elle devient cependant enceinte, ce qui lui confère le statut de femme et de mère dans leur culture. Mais le respect qu'elle voue à son mari ne tarde pas à disparaître à cause du métier qu'il exerce, celui de domestique. Il doit, entre autres, laver les sous-vêtements de la maîtresse de maison blanche. Par là-même, il perd ce qui faisait de lui un homme dans sa société. Dans sa communauté tribale, jamais il ne toucherait de sous-vêtements féminins. Nnu Ego est face à un dilemme, se demandant si elle vit avec un homme et si une situation peut enlever sa virilité à un homme à son insu. « Je veux vivre avec un homme, dit-elle, pas avec un homme tourné femme ». (B. Emecheta, 1979, p.47)

Dans cette histoire, à aucun moment la femme blanche ne comprend l'animosité de Nnu Ego à son égard, et elle ne voit pas comment elle a émasculé son mari. Nnu Ego ne peut aimer son homme parce qu'il est dévalorisé et, partant, considère la femme blanche comme une ennemie. Ce dilemme n'est pas évident à prime abord aux yeux de la femme blanche européenne. Elle se dira sans doute qu'elle n'a rien fait de mal puisqu'elle a donné du travail au mari, qu'elle n'est donc pas l'ennemie de Nnu Ego et qu'au contraire elle lui rend service. La femme blanche a du mal à comprendre son rôle dans l'émasculation de cet Africain, tout comme dans l'évolution des rapports entre Nnu Ego et les hommes de sa culture. Dans cette méprise, la dynamique du choc des cultures, des privilèges face à l'absence de privilèges est masquée. Les deux femmes n'ont rien en commun excepté leur antagonisme.

Si nous faisons un bond dans le temps, nous pouvons voir qu'il existe une extension de la même dynamique ici, dans la société canadienne contemporaine. Les féministes blanches ignorent la différence entre leur vécu et celui des minorités raciales. Parallèlement, les féministes des minorités raciales demandent avec insistance que l'on comprenne leurs points de vue et qu'on les intègre dans tous les aspects de la vie canadienne. Le Congrès international de PEN (association des poètes, dramaturges, essayistes, auteurs et romanciers), qui s'est déroulé à Toronto en 1989, a donné un exemple de la confrontation idéologique moderne. L'auteure noire Marlene Nourbese Philip et le groupe contestataire Vision 21 ont remis en question le caractère exclusif du congrès et l'eurocentrisme du monde de l'édition. Ils furent accueillis non pas par un racisme déclaré, mais par de l'agacement né d'une incompréhension de la part du courant dominant[1]. À son arrivée au congrès, l'auteure féministe blanche June Callwood a été abordée par les contestataires qui revendiquaient l'inclusion. Incapable de comprendre ce dont Marlene Nourbese Philip parlait, elle a réagi avec colère et frustration, l'envoyant très crûment promener, et ce, devant les caméras des chaînes de télévision nationales. Il existe un lien essentiel entre Nnu Ego, le personnage de

Buchi Emecheta, et Marlene Nourbese Philip. Il existe un lien indéniable entre les structures coloniales qui pesaient sur le tiers monde et la mentalité coloniale qui est un trait fondamental de la société canadienne.

J'ai essayé de vous tracer un croquis sur le vif de la relation problématique entre racisme et sexisme. Toutefois, ces juxtapositions de nos passés ne constituent qu'un fil de l'écheveau complexe de la « solidarité féminine universelle ». Pour démêler plus encore le dilemme contemporain que connaît le mouvement des femmes au Canada, nous devons aussi nous pencher sur ce que les féministes appellent communément « imagination créatrice ». Les féministes soi-disant progressistes utilisent ce concept lorsque les minorités, les Autochtones et d'autres contestent leur exclusion continue du discours féministe. En fait, les « leaders » féministes blanches croient avoir fait leurs preuves par leurs diplômes d'études supérieures et leur intellectualisme. Ces féministes prétendent, sous prétexte qu'elles sont passées sur les bancs de l'université, posséder ce que l'on appelle une « imagination créatrice », qui leur donne la capacité de mieux comprendre et de mieux exprimer les préoccupations de *toutes* les femmes, y compris des femmes de couleur et des femmes autochtones. Certaines croient même que « l'imagination créatrice » leur permet de conceptualiser les préoccupations des minorités mieux que les femmes de ces minorités elles-mêmes.

Si l'on va plus loin, cela signifie qu'il existerait une imagination « créatrice » opposée à une imagination « primitive », cette dernière ne permettant pas d'atteindre les plus hauts sommets de la conceptualisation et de la pensée abstraite. Les femmes qui ont poursuivi des études supérieures se sont toujours placées dans le rôle d'agents de la connaissance au sein du mouvement féministe, et elles continuent de se voir comme celles qui créent le savoir. Cependant, il faut bien dire que *les femmes autochtones et les femmes appartenant à des minorités raciales ne se laissent pas prendre au piège de « l'imagination créatrice »*. Elles savent pertinemment que c'est « l'imagination créatrice » qui, au fil des cinq cents dernières années, les a conduites au point où elles ont perdu leur histoire, leur langue et leur terre. Elles savent aussi que c'est « l'imagination créatrice » qui a incité M. Colomb à penser qu'il avait effectivement « découvert de nouvelles terres » pour le roi et la reine d'Espagne.

De même, il faut que toutes les femmes sachent que c'est « l'imagination créatrice » des *hommes* qui a fait d'elles des « non-personnes ». Par conséquent, comment des féministes, tout en déplorant leur exclusion de l'histoire du développement humain, peuvent-elles se permettre d'exclure du discours féministe des femmes qui ne sont pas blanches ou privilégiées ? Au cours d'un débat avec Mary Childers, la féministe noire bell hooks posa la question suivante : « Comment pouvons-nous déplacer des paradigmes de la domination qui, en fait, font autorité par l'exclusion en affirmant que certaines personnes — les féministes blanches instruites — possèdent le savoir et les autres, rien » ? (M. Hirsch et E. Keller, 1990, p.67)

Permettez-moi d'illustrer le parallèle entre l'exclusion des femmes par les hommes dans le patriarcat et le mythe de « l'imagination créatrice » entretenu par les féministes blanches. Dans son livre intitulé *Inessential Woman*, Elizabeth Spelman souligne que nous condamnons les hommes pour la répression et l'oppression auxquelles ils se livrent et qui ont pour effet de gommer les préoccupations et les perspectives des femmes de tous les domaines de réflexion et de débat. Ainsi, c'est avec raison que les féministes occidentales ont reproché aux écrits de Nietzsche, Platon, Aristote et Kant de n'être que des études incomplètes de la condition humaine, ces philosophes ayant à tort extrapolé et tiré leurs conclusions de leur propre expérience, la conséquence en étant que leur conceptualisation de la condition humaine repose sur la réalité d'un seul sexe, le sexe masculin. De même, les féministes occidentales blanches qui condamnent le patriarcat croient que leur « imagination créatrice » leur confère le privilège de conceptualiser et d'exprimer la condition féminine en se fondant sur celle d'un seul groupe culturel. Ce faisant, « elles font de la condition des femmes blanches des classes moyennes celle de toutes les femmes » (E. Spelman, 1988, p.6). L'incapacité des féministes blanches à voir que racisme et sexisme sont les deux côtés de la même médaille devient un obstacle systémique à des échanges positifs au sein du féminisme canadien. La résistance au changement et la mise en question du pouvoir féministe ont suscité dans le mouvement des femmes un malaise qu'exprime fort bien une Autochtone, Lee Maracle (1988, p.109) : « Enfermées dans vos privilèges de Blanches et aveuglées par votre arrogance, vous me demandez d'oublier le passé et d'être comme vous. Vous ne savez pas ce que vous demandez. Si j'oublie mon passé, rejette nos coutumes, seule la violence apaisera le cri qui monte en moi ».

En tant que féministes, nous devons certes poser le postulat de l'identité commune (nous sommes toutes victimes du patriarcat), mais c'est la notion même de cohésion qui jette les bases d'une domination fondée sur la race. À vouloir parler d'une seule voix, la voix de la « solidarité féminine universelle », objectif très noble en soi, il est trop facile d'extrapoler et de dire que le vécu des femmes blanches est celui de *toutes* les femmes. Lorsque nous nous réduisons à une seule identité, celles qui mettent en doute ou en question la cohésion sont exclues et leurs voix, étouffées. C'est une réaction de facilité. Il est beaucoup plus difficile de changer nos modes de fonctionnement traditionnels. L'idée d'identité commune est explorée dans une histoire qu'Elizabeth Spelman utilise dans le livre que j'ai mentionné, mais qui est tirée d'un roman d'Iris Murdoch, *The Nice and the Good*. Elle parle du personnage de l'oncle Théo qui, assis sur la plage, réfléchit au concept de la multiplicité. Le nombre et la variété des galets sur le rivage — il y en a de toutes les formes, de toutes les tailles et de toutes les couleurs — le déconcertent profondément. La seule façon pour lui de se rassurer consiste à réduire la multitude en un. Donc, au lieu de galets, il se met à penser à une « galétude » (E. Spelman, 1988, p.1). À l'instar de l'oncle Théo, les féministes ont tendance à réduire toutes les femmes à la notion de « féminitude ». Ce n'est pas seulement le nombre de femmes qui est inquiétant, mais aussi les nombreuses différences entre elles qui menacent, comme le dit E. Spelman (1988, p.2), la « douce intelligibilité du fait net et irréfutable que les femmes sont des femmes ». En réalité, nos différences importent tout autant que nos similitudes.

Si nous continuons, en tant que féministes, de nier que « l'autre » de Simone de Beauvoir existe non seulement dans la relation de l'homme avec la femme, mais dans les relations entre femmes, nous serons confrontées à la dynamique interne suivante : l'incapacité de corroborer tout ce que nous avons dit au sujet du patriarcat. On est en train de dire de nous ce que nous disions des hommes. Le dilemme fondamental est celui-ci : en essayant de nous libérer de l'oppression, nous ne comprenons pas celles qui font de même avec leurs propres oppressions. En vérité, nous refusons d'accepter notre rôle dans l'oppression d'autres femmes. Les femmes de couleur et les autres minorités savent depuis longtemps qu'en vérité, *nous comprenons le courant dominant plus qu'il ne nous comprend*. Nous avons vécu le colonialisme différemment. On nous a forcées à comprendre l'histoire du colonisateur, sa littérature, sa culture et sa vision du monde. En un sens, nous sommes avantagées puisque, partant du point de vue de celles qui ont été contraintes d'absorber les méthodes du colonisateur, nous pouvons, pour reprendre les termes de *bell hooks*, « nous placer en marge ou au centre, mais de notre propre chef » (1984, p.11). Je vois bien l'argument de bell hooks et je le comprends instinctivement. Pour moi, la dialectique marge-centre est très manifeste dans l'imagerie biblique de Jonas dans le ventre de la baleine. Les peuples colonisés ont dû entrer dans le ventre de la baleine; ce faisant, ils sont passés à une position de force *parce qu'ils comprenaient la baleine de l'intérieur, tout en sachant ce à quoi elle ressemblait de l'extérieur*.

Si le féminisme doit être une force rédemptrice et créatrice dans cette société, il lui faut adapter les perspectives des minorités et des femmes autochtones afin de mieux comprendre les espoirs et les besoins de toutes les femmes du Canada. Dans le passage suivant, Lee Maracle (1988, p.103-106) dit qu'il est nécessaire de conserver toutes les perspectives :

> *Vous donnez l'Europe en exemple à mes enfants pour qu'ils la respectent, apprennent d'elle et l'imitent et, en même temps, vous avilissez les racines nationales des peuples autochtones. Qui osera m'affirmer que les descendants d'Européens sur ma terre apprennent à connaître les grands moments de notre histoire et imitent nos héros ? Quel enfant européen dans votre classe a entendu parler de Kitsilano, de Coquitlam, de Capilano ou d'Andrew Paul, homme d'État et spécialiste du droit constitutionnel autodidacte tant admiré ? Vos ancêtres nous ont pratiquement anéantis. Je sais que vous n'appuyez pas de revolver sur ma tempe, cher professeur, mais c'est votre culture qui a engendré un génocide et, maintenant, vous me demandez d'effacer l'ombre de ma grand-mère?*

En conclusion, je vous dis, mes soeurs, que pour nous sortir de notre dilemme existentiel, en tant que femmes du Canada, nous devons regarder toutes nos soeurs et nous rassembler toutes sur des bases communes. En tant que femmes, nous devons toutes nous engager à créer un espace pour nous-mêmes, un espace propice à un dialogue constructif et critique, afin que chacune d'entre nous puisse exprimer son point de vue et que toutes soient entendues. Nous devons donner la parole à toutes les femmes du Canada. Donner la parole et parler ne sont pas de simples expressions de la liberté là où la domination est la norme. La liberté de parole est une illusion pour beaucoup de nos soeurs. Nous avons peur lorsque nous parlons, comme Audre Lorde l'écrit dans son poème intitulé « Litanie de la survie » (1984, p.28) [traduction] :

> *et lorsque nous parlons, nous avons peur*
> *que nos paroles ne soient pas entendues*
> *ni bienvenues*
> *mais lorsque nous nous taisons*
> *nous avons encore peur.*
> *Mieux vaut donc parler*
> *en n'oubliant jamais*
> *que nous n'étions pas supposées survivre.*

C'est dans cet espace réservé que nous, féministes du Canada, exprimons et redéfinissons nos réalités. C'est dans cet espace que nous créons une théorie qui se synthétise courageusement en défi, en changement et en nouvelles démarches[2]. Bonne chance, mes soeurs.

Notes

1. Extrait d'une conversation avec Jan Bower, directrice générale de PEN International, à Toronto (Ontario), en novembre 1991. PEN International a depuis lors fait des efforts pour que le monde de l'édition exprime les voix des Canadiens et Canadiennes appartenant à des minorités raciales.

2. D'après Janet Yee, du collectif des femmes de couleur, dans un discours prononcé pendant le Congrès des femmes noires du Canada, en novembre 1991.

Références

Emecheta, Buchi. *The Joys of Motherhood*. Heinemann Educational Books Ltd., Londres, 1979.

Hirsch, Marianne et Evelyn Keller, sous la dir. de. *Conflicts in Feminism*. Routledge, New York, 1990.

hooks, bell. *Feminist Theory : From Margin to Center*. South End Press, Boston, 1984.

Joseph, Gloria I. *Common Differences : Conflicts in Black and White Feminist Perspectives*. Anchor Press/Doubleday, New York, 1981.

Lorde, Audre. *Sister Outsider*. Crossing Press, Trumansburg, (N.Y.), 1984.

Maracle, Lee. *I Am Woman*. Write-on Press Publishers, Vancouver, 1988.

Morgan, Robin, sous la dir. de. *Sisterhood is Global*. Anchor Press/Doubleday, New York, 1984.

Spelman, Elizabeth. *Inessential Woman : Problems of Exclusion in Feminist Thought*. Beacon Press, Boston, 1988.

The Contributors

Marilyn Assheton-Smith is an associate professor of educational foundations and currently the associate chair of the department at the University of Alberta. She has a strong background in sociology of education, intercultural education, education and minorities and women and education.

Karen Blackford is an advocate for sole-support mothers, low-income tenants and persons with disabilities. Currently completing her doctoral research in sociology at York University, she is on leave from the School of Nursing, Laurentian University, Sudbury, Ontario.

Claire Bonenfant is a member of the Political Action Committee of the Québec Federation of Women and a recipient of the Order of Quebec.

Lynn Bueckert is a project coordinator at the Women and Work Research and Education Society in Burnaby, British Columbia. Women and Work is a feminist, community-based organization that focusses on women's occupational health. Lynn is also a master's student in the Women's Studies Department at Simon Fraser University.

Jaya Chauhan and Anne-Louise Brookes. Jaya taught sociology at St. Francis Xavier University in Nova Scotia for one year. Anne-Louise is an assistant professor in the Department of Sociology and Anthropology at St. Francis Xavier University. She has a Ph.D. in sociology of education from the Ontario Institute for Studies in Education, University of Toronto. Her book Feminist Pedagogy: An Autobiographical Approach was published by Fernwood Publishing, Halifax (1992). She is currently working on a second text within which she explicates her critique and application of Sylvia Ashton-Warner's Creative Teaching Scheme.

Denyse Côté, originally from Ottawa, became a community worker for the Company of Young Canadians in Hull, Quebec, after completing her studies (M.A. in political science from University of Ottawa) and her thesis on community groups in the Outaouais region. She also has been a community worker in a rural region of Mexico and a teacher in Colombia. When she returned to Canada, she taught in a low-income neighbourhood in Montreal. She then became a lecturer at the Université de Montréal and the Université du Québec à Montréal. She is presently a professor of social work at the Université du Québec à Hull.

Elizabeth R. Epperly was head of the Department of English Language and Literature at Memorial University of Newfoundland and is currently a member of the English Department at the University of Prince Edward Island. She has written articles, a monograph and a book on Anthony Trollope. Her most recent book, *The Fragrance of Sweet-grass: L.M. Montgomery's Heroines and the Pursuit of Romance* (University of Toronto Press, 1992), explores her interest in feminist criticism and the power of romance.

Pauline Fahmy is a professor in the Department of Educational Psychology of the Faculty of Education, Université Laval, and has a Ph.D. in psychology from the University of Paris. She is also a member of GREMF (Interdiscplinary Feminist Research Group) at Laval.

Danielle Forth recently completed her degree in women's studies at the University of Alberta. She is currently working as an editorial assistant with the University of Alberta and hopes to explore further the relationship between young women and feminism as a graduate student.

Renate Krause was born in World War Two Germany and immigrated to Canada with her parents in the mid-fifties. An associate professor of English at Canadian Union College, a small liberal-arts college in central Alberta, Krause defended her doctoral thesis, "From 'Hard Fragments' to Fuel for Flight: The Role of Image in the Writings of Virginia Woolf," at the University of Alberta in 1991.

Diana M.A. Relke is coordinator of women's and gender studies at the University of Saskatchewan. She has published numerous articles on writing by women. Currently, she is working on a series of biographies of Canadian feminist scholars and activists.

Colette St-Hilaire teaches sociology at Collège Édouard-Montpetit in Longueuil, Quebec. During 1989–90, she conducted research on women and development in the Philippines with the assistance of a grant from the International Development Research Centre in Ottawa. She is presently completing a doctoral thesis entitled "The Integration of Women in Development in the Philippines: A New Social Management of Women," under the direction of Micheline de Sève and Chantal Rondeau of the Department of Political Science at the Université du Quebec à Montréal. In 1990–91, she was a member of the Canadian Committee of the Philippines Canadian Human Resources Development program, funded by CIDA.

Glenda P. Simms moved to Canada from her native Jamaica in 1966, continuing her teaching career in northern Alberta. She is an acknowledged advocate of women and minority groups, and she has a unique vision of an inclusive feminism. In 1989, she was appointed president of the Canadian Advisory Council on the Status of Women. She is currently working on a book that examines racism and sexism in Canadian society.

Barbara Spronk received her Ph.D. in anthropology from the University of Alberta in 1982. She is presently associate professor of anthropology at Athabasca University and manager of a CIDA-supported institutional-linkage project in Thailand. In addition, she is seconded part-time to the Division of International Development at the University of Calgary, where she works on the Canada-Asia Partnership project.

Susan Stone-Blackburn is a professor of English at the University of Calgary. She has published articles on drama in a variety of journals, and a book, *Robertson Davies, Playwright* (University of British Columbia Press, 1985).

Evangelia Tastsoglou was born in Greece, where she enrolled in law before moving to the United States to study sociology. She presently resides in Toronto and teaches in the Faculty of Arts at Ryerson Polytechnic Institute.

Sylvia Vance is a free-lance writer and editor who lives in Edmonton. She has two small sons, Sam and Harry.

Sharda Vaidyanath, a first-generation Canadian, lives in Gloucester, in the Ottawa/Carleton area. She holds an M.A. in Canadian studies from Carleton University, where she studied under the supervision of Dr. Jill Vickers and Dr. Nalini Devdas.

Les auteures

Marilyn Assheton-Smith est une professeure associée aux *Educational Foundations* et est présentement vice-présidente de cette école de l'Université de l'Alberta. Elle a une grande expérience en sociologie de l'éducation, en éducation interculturelle, en éducation et les minorités ainsi qu'en les femmes et l'éducation.

Karen Blackford milite en faveur des mères qui sont l'unique soutien de leur famille, des locataires à faible revenu et des personnes handicapées. Elle termine actuellement des travaux de recherche ouvrant droit à un doctorat en sociologie à l'Université York, étant en congé de l'école des sciences infirmières de l'Université Laurentienne à Sudbury (Ontario).

Claire Bonenfant est membre du Comité d'action politique de la Fédération des femmes du Québec et elle est récipiendaire de l'Ordre national du Québec à titre de Chevalier.

Lynn Bueckert est coordonnatrice de projet à la Women and Work Research and Education Society à Burnaby en Colombie-Britannique, qui est une organisation féministe communautaire axée sur la santé professionnelle des femmes. Lynn est également étudiante de deuxième cycle (M.A.) au Département des Études féminines à l'Université Simon Fraser.

Jaya Chauhan et Anne-Louise Brookes. Jaya enseignait la sociologie pendant une année à l'Université St-François Xavier en Nouvelle-Écosse. Anne-Louise est assistante-professeure au Département de sociologie et d'anthropologie de l'Université St-François Xavier. Elle détient un doctorat en sociologie de l'éducation de l'Ontario Institute for Studies in Education de l'Université de Toronto. Elle a un premier livre de parue depuis 1992 chez Fernwood Publishing d'Halifax intitulé *Feminist Pedagogy : An Autobiographical Approach*. Elle est actuellement à travailler à son deuxième livre qui constituera une vision critique et présentera son interpretation personnelle du « Creative Teaching Scheme» de Sylvia Ashton-Warner.

Denyse Côté est originaire d'Ottawa. En terminant ses études universitaires (M.A. en science politique, Université d'Ottawa) et sa thèse sur les groupes populaires de l'Outaouais québécois, elle a été organisatrice communautaire avec la Compagnie des jeunes canadiens à Hull (Québec). Par la suite, elle a été organisatrice communautaire en région rurale au Mexique et enseignante en Colombie. De retour au pays elle a enseigné trois ans en milieu défavorisé à Montréal. Puis elle a enseigné l'organisation communautaire comme chargée de cours à l'Université de Montréal et à l'Université du Québec à Montréal. à l'heure actuelle, elle est professeure au programme de travail social de l'Université du Québec à Hull.

Elizabeth R. Epperly était chef du Département de langue et de littérature anglaises à l'Université Memorial de Terre-Neuve ; elle est maintenant professeure d'Anglais à l'Université de l'Ile du Prince Édouard. Elle est auteure d'articles, d'une monographie et d'un livre sur Anthony Trollope. Son ouvrage le plus récent, *The Fragrance of Sweetgrass : L.M. Montgomery's Heroines and the Pursuit of Romance* (Presses de l'Université de Toronto, 1992), fait état de son intérêt pour la critique féministe et le pouvoir du roman.

Pauline Fahmy est professeure titulaire au département de counseling et orientation de la faculté des sciences de l'éducation de l'Université Laval, et titulaire d'un Ph.D. (psychologie) de l'Université de Paris. Elle est aussi membre du GREMF

(Groupe de recherche multidisciplinaire féministe) de l'Université Laval.

Danielle Forth a récemment obtenu son diplôme en études féminines à l'Université de l'Alberta où elle est actuellement secrétaire de rédaction. Elle espère étudier plus à fond les rapports qui existent entre les jeunes femmes et le féminisme au cours de ses études deuxième cycle.

Renate Krause est née en Allemagne pendant la Seconde guerre mondiale et a immigré au Canada avec ses parents vers le milieu des années 50. Professeure adjointe d'anglais au Canadian Union College, un petit collège libéral pour l'enseignement des arts situé au centre de l'Alberta, Mme Krause a défendu sa thèse de doctorat intitulée « From Hard Fragments to Fuel for Flight : The Role of Image in the Writings of Virginia Woolf » à l'Université de l'Alberta en 1991.

Diana M.A. Relke est coordonnatrice des Études féminines et des sexes à l'Université de la Saskatchewan. Elle a publié de nombreux articles sur des textes de femmes. Elle travaille actuellement à une série de biographies d'universitaires et de militantes féministes canadiennes.

Colette St-Hilaire est professeure de sociologie au Collège Édouard-Montpetit, Longueuil. Elle a effectué une recherche sur les femmes et le développement aux Philippines en 1989-90, avec l'aide financière du Centre de recherches pour le développement international à Ottawa. Elle prépare actuellement une thèse de doctorat sous la direction de Micheline de Sève et Chantal Rondeau, du département de science politique de l'Université du Québec à Montréal. En 1990-91, elle a été membre du comité canadien du programme Philippines Canadian Human Resources Development, financé par l'ACDI.

Glenda Simms est arrivée au Canada de sa Jamaïque natale en 1966 et a continué sa carrière d'enseignante dans le nord de l'Alberta. Elle est la championne reconnue des groupes de femmes et des minorités et a une vision unique du féminisme inclusif. En 1989, elle a été nommée présidente du Conseil consultatif canadien sur la situation de la femme. Elle travaille actuellement à la rédaction d'un livre qui examine le racisme et le sexisme dans la société canadienne.

Barbara Spronk a reçu son doctorat en anthropologie de l'Université de l'Alberta en 1982. Elle est présentement professeure associée en anthropologie à l'Université Athabasca en Alberta et gestionnaire d'un projet d'échange avec la Thaïlande financé par l'ACDI. De plus, ses services sont prêtés sur une base partiel par l'Université Athabasca au Division of International Development de l'Université de Calgary pour un projet de partenariat entre le Canada et l'Asie.

Susan Stone-Blackburn est professeure d'anglais à l'Université de Calgary. Elle a publié des articles sur l'art dramatique dans une variété de revues et un livre intitulé *Robertson Davies, Playwright* (Presses de l'Université de la Colombie-Britannique, 1985).

Evangelia Tastsoglou est née en Grèce où elle s'est inscrite à la faculté de droit avant de venir aux États-Unis pour étudier la sociologie. Elle habite actuellement à Toronto où elle enseigne à la faculté des arts de l'Institut polytechnique Ryerson.

Sylvia Vance est écrivaine pigiste et éditrice à Toronto. Elle a deux jeunes fils, Sam et Harry.

Sharda Vaidyanath, une Canadienne de « première génération » demeure dans la région de Ottawa/Carleton. Elle est titulaire d'une maîtrise ès artes en études canadiennes de l'Université Carleton, où elle a étudié sous la supervision des professeures Jill Vickers et Nalina Devdas.

Conference Presenters

Abu-Laban, Sharon
Artiss, Phyllis
Badir, Doris
Baudoux, Claudine
Begum, Shahinoor
Bell, Noreen
Bella, Leslie
Bensalah, K.M.
Blackford, Karen
Boisvert, Micheline
Bonenfant, Claire
Bray, Catherine
Brookes, Anne-Louise
Buchanan, Roberta
Bueckert, Lynn
Buss, Helen
Campbell, Marjory
Cardinal, Linda
Carlson, M.
Chauhan, Jaya
Cheverie, Anne
Chisaakay, Molly
Choldin, Sudha
Chown, Diana
Christiansen-Ruffman, Linda
Cooke, Katie
Côté, Denyse
Couillard, Marie-Andrée
Creasy, Lavera
Dallaire, Hélène
Das, Shima
Deringer, Ingrid
Deunida, Carmen
Dhruvarajan, Vanaja
Drain, Susan
Drolet, Dominique
Dumont, Marilyn
Dunphy, Sheila
Epperly, Elizabeth
Evans, Barbara
Fahmy, Pauline

Fleming, Deborah J.
Forth, Danielle
Foster, Deborah
Fulton, Keith Louise
Gendron, Colette
Gouëffic, Louise
Grier, Sandra
Gronnerud, Paul
Hamre, Kathy
Haslett, Jane
Hofmann-Nemiroff, Greta
Hubert, Evelyne St-Amand
Husaini, Zohra
Iordanova, Kostadina
Jackel, Susan
Janz, Heidi
Judd, Ellen
Kareja, Rosedell Mathoni
Kirby, Sandi
Krause, Renate
Krishnan, Vijaya
Krull, C.
Kunin, Roslyn
Laidlaw, Toni
Langford, Nanci
Lee, Alice
Lee, Annette
Lévesque, Suzie
Liburd, Rosemary
Lloyd, Karen
Luxton, Meg
MacAulay, Rosemary
Malmo, Cheryl
Manneschmidt, Sybille
Martin, Lise
McGrath, Anne
McIrvin, Sharon
McLean, Marilyn
McMahon, Kathy
Mitchell, Claudia
Moore, Melanie

Morouney, Kim
Mundle, Carol
Nelson-McDermott, Catherine
Ng, Roxana
Noble, Jean
Oakes, Jill
Oglov, Valerie
Orser, Barbara
Parmar, Aradhana
Parsons, Marianne
Payeur, Gaétane
Pennell, Joan
Penrod, Lynn Kettler
Peredo, Petite
Peters, M.
Pettifor, Jean
Poff, Deborah
Pypops, Annette
Rankin, Pauline
Raoul, Valerie
Rasmussen, Pa
Read, Daphne
Relke, Diana
Robinson, Ann
Rodney, Anesta
Rosentreter, Donna
Ryan, Lyndall
Safwat, Khadiga
Saint-Pierre, Chantal
Schulz, Linda Zelda

Selman, Jan
Sethna, Christabelle
Séguin, Michelle
Shogan, Debra
Simpson, Evanna
Simms, Glenda
Smith, Bobbi
Smith, Malinda
Sow, Ndeye
Spénard-Godbout, Christiane
St-Hilaire, Colette
St. Peter, Christine
Stewart, Houston
Stone-Blackburn, Susan
Strobel, Christina
Sylvestre, Melody
Tastsoglou, Evangelia
Thurston, Wilfreda
Tremblay, Diane-Gabrielle
Tremblay, Marie Lyne
Udegbe, Bola
Vaidyanath, Sharda
Valentine, Patricia
Vance, Sylvia
Vickers, Jill
Von Roosmalen, E.
Watkins, Barbara
Williams, Barbara
Wine, Jeri
Zuk, Rhoda

A Note on the Cover Art

The stained glass artwork on the cover is called "Daughters, Dream, and in Dreaming, Take Back the Night." The panel is ninth in a set of thirteen called *The Illuminated Series*, created by Deborah J. Fleming between 1986 and 1990.

The sequence of the series is based on some of the categories and page formats of the medieval illuminated (meaning adorned or decorated) manuscripts. The series is a feminist revisioning of the christian holy books and the sacrilege that has occurred as a result of their teachings.

Currently, women are creating the means to overcome the desperate and vicious patriarchal systems that are breaking down and threaten us all in the process. *The Illuminated Series* is an artwork that affirms the past achievments of women, agitates for changes to what exists, and dreams of what will be.

The series has been shown in many different cities and settings. The panels continue to tour, primarily to various women's gatherings, but have also been shown in art galleries. This travel would not be possible without the support of the women who have purchased individual pieces, but who are committed to the display of the series as a whole.

Groups interested in talking to the artist about displaying the series may contact her through the publisher.

The Artist

Deborah J. Fleming is a stained glass artist living in Black Point, Nova Scotia. She is also an art educator, and taught art/art education for several years in Alberta.

355116

Printed by
Ateliers Graphiques Marc Veilleux Inc.
Cap-Saint-Ignace (Québec)
in October 1993